TRAIL TO HEAVEN

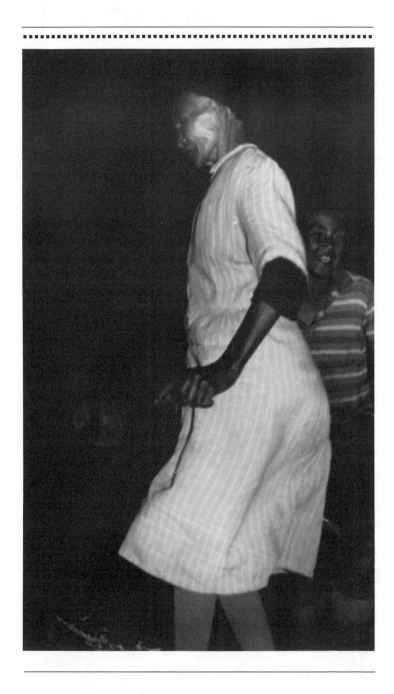

TRAIL TO HEAVEN

KNOWLEDGE AND NARRATIVE IN A NORTHERN NATIVE COMMUNITY

ROBIN RIDINGTON

UNIVERSITY OF IOWA PRESS   IOWA CITY

University of Iowa Press, Iowa City 52242
Copyright © 1988 by the University of Iowa
All rights reserved
Printed in the United States of America
First edition, 1988

Book and jacket design by Sandra Strother Hudson
Typesetting by G & S Typesetters, Austin, Texas
Printing and binding by Edwards Brothers, Ann Arbor, Michigan

Frontispiece: Dedama (Anno Davis) dancing, 1966

Library of Congress Cataloging-in-Publication Data

Ridington, Robin.
Trail to heaven: knowledge and narrative in a northern Native
community/by Robin Ridington.—1st ed.
p.   cm.
Bibliography: p.
Includes index.
ISBN 0-87745-212-1
1. Tsattine Indians—Philosophy. 2. Tsattine Indians—Social life
and customs. 3. Indians of North America—British Columbia—
Philosophy. 4. Indians of North America—British Columbia—Social
life and customs. I. Title.
E99.T77R53   1988   88-17098
971.1'00497—dc19   CIP

To the memory of Howard Broomfield

CONTENTS

INTRODUCTION

Trail to Heaven describes moments in the life of a northern Indian community. It describes these moments from the point of view of my own involvement with the community and its people. It begins with the story of my first encounter with "real live Indians." It is about the thoughtworld of Beaver Indian people and about the world of ideas and assumptions I brought to my encounters with them. As such, it is also a commentary on the ideas and assumptions of the thoughtworld we call anthropology.

In 1964, I began anthropological fieldwork in a Beaver Indian community in northeastern British Columbia. I soon learned that the Beavers call themselves Dunne-za, "Real People," in their northern Athapaskan language. I had not encountered this name in the standard academic reference work, Murdock's *Ethnographic Bibliography of North America*, which lists them as Beaver or "Tsattine," the Athapaskan word meaning "Beaver People." None of the academic sources I consulted referred to them by their own name, Dunne-za. In the same way that I had accepted the authenticity of the name "Beaver Indian" as it appeared in the academic literature, I also assumed that the methods, purposes, and metaphors governing that literature ruled supreme. I had been socialized to think about people, particularly Indian people, as the proper and inevitable subjects of an objective and imperial social science. More significantly, I did not question the style of that science. I assumed that the people I had come to study were, if not my personal subjects, surely subjects of the kingdom of science whose unquestioned objectivity ruled both their experience and mine. Objectivity required that what I did as a person and what I reported as a social scientist were related only in that one was instrumental to the other. I expected the experience of fieldwork to be entirely different and separate from its results.

Gradually, sometimes painfully, often comically, it dawned on me that this instrumental separation of experience from accomplishment made no sense at all to the people with whom I was living. Knowledge, for them, was something a person integrated immediately into a shared thoughtworld through the authority of his or her own experience. Knowledge, I came to learn, was a primary form of individual empowerment. I realized that, if for no other reason than my presence among them, Dunne-za of all ages were trying to teach me something. To my astonishment, I found myself learning from my subjects as well as about them. Part of that learning was the realization that an anthropologist's own experience is a proper, even essential, subject of inquiry. Part of that learning was the search for an appropriate language of interpretation, one that would do justice both to the Indian reality and to my experience of it.

Over the years, the Dunne-za have studied me and my world. Our relationship has been mutualistic. Recently, Dunne-za chiefs, councillors, and elders have visited Vancouver to testify in a lawsuit they are bringing against the government of Canada for breach of trust. The suit relates to their loss, in 1945, of the summer gathering place that they call Where Happiness Dwells. At the time they lost the land, the Dunne-za and Cree of the Fort St. John band were unable to protect their resource because they lacked knowledge of the new white culture that was bringing industrial expansion and white settlement to their country. Without knowing a language of discourse that would give them entry to the white man's world of law and politics, they lacked the power to defend themselves against the vested interests of outsiders who wanted their land.

During the years I have known the Dunne-za, many of them have studied and come to understand the mentality and institutions of the people who wronged them. They have also found friends and allies among the whitepeople. They have been practicing anthropology as much as I have. Both they and I hope to benefit from what we learn of the other's world. Both they and I also hold fast to a common core of identity that defines us as human beings. We can communicate because we share that human center. We can communicate because we listen to one another's stories. We can communicate because we are characters in one another's stories.

As I came to understand bits and pieces of the Indian reality, I realized that I would have to discover a language of interpretation and description to communicate between Dunne-za knowledge and the knowledge of academic anthropology. Both forms of knowledge use metaphors based on unstated assumptions about the fundamental nature of reality. The metaphors of Western culture have exerted a strong influence on how anthropologists explain such fundamentals as time, causality, subjectivity, objectivity, myth, and history. The metaphors developed by northern hunting people over thousands of years have been just as important in organizing Dunne-za ideas about these same realities.

People in Western culture, for instance, assume that we can know and experience events only after they have begun to take place in a physical world accessible to our senses. The Dunne-za assume, I came to learn, that events can take place only after people have known and experienced them in myths, dreams, and visions. Even their concept of person is different from ours. In Dunne-za reality, animals, winds, rocks, and natural forces are "people." Human people are continually in contact with these nonhuman persons. All persons continually bring the world into being through the myths, dreams, and visions they share with one another. Western culture views "myths" and "dreams" as false and illusory. The Dunne-za experience myths and dreams as fundamental sources of knowledge. My academic training taught me that knowledge would come down to me from duly established books and authorities. The Indians taught me that knowledge would reveal itself to me from within personal experience. It might even come to me through myths and dreams.

Trail to Heaven is, to the best of my ability, a true story and a very personal one. It reflects intimate, unguarded, and special moments in the lives of people I have known for a long time. It reflects and honors both the knowledge I have obtained from my own culture's intellectual traditions and Indian knowledge that has evolved over thousands of years of life on this continent. *Trail to Heaven* is personal and particularistic, but it uses specific events and experiences to explain a discourse between the two different systems of knowledge. *Trail to Heaven* describes how my own thoughtworld was changed by that of the Dunne-za. It describes how together, and in collaboration with my friends and family, we brought an anthropology of the two systems of knowledge into existence.

Recently, anthropologists have begun to question the validity of an "ethnographic authority" they once assumed was theirs exclusively. They have come to recognize that writing ethnography is a collaborative effort, a shared discourse. *Trail to Heaven* describes how I became involved in just such a discourse. I have sought to describe northern Indian reality in a language that reflects both Indian experience and my own experience. I have combined their stories with my story. I have nested their texts within an overall text of my own construction. I have used a narrative style to develop some sense of the mutual understanding, based on shared experience, that underlies Dunne-za discourse. I have written with a combination of retrospection and introspection to describe the dynamics of change and stability in a northern hunting culture I have known for more than a quarter century. I have attempted to show how Dunne-za mythic reality lies within the reality of everyday experience.

Anthropologists are beginning to think about the importance of their own ethnographic language and the unspoken assumptions its metaphors take for granted. In his introduction to a collection of essays titled *Writing Culture: The Poetics and Politics of Ethnography*, James Clifford points out that "academic and literary genres interpenetrate," and that "the writing of cultural descriptions is properly experimental and ethical" (Clifford and Marcus 1986: 2). His point is that style cannot be separated from substance. The way we write about culture is itself highly cultural. I have chosen a narrative style to write about the Dunne-za world because it allows me to present their metaphors and their ideas about the authority of individual experience in the context within which I learned them. The Dunne-za experience one another's lives as stories. The narrative form may be experimental in social science, but it is normative and well established within the Dunne-za tradition of teaching. Narrative ethnography is radical only in its questioning of the social science assumption that experience should be instrumental rather than integral to ethnographic description. The narrative style of

Trail to Heaven is intended to support rather than reject previous ethnographic writing about the Subarctic. Narrative gives voice to the people and events on which any generalizations and abstractions must be grounded. Narrative presents rich detail. It refers to actualities. It is a discourse in which ethnographic authority is shared.

Ethnographic writing has typically been organized around a paradigm or theoretical model such as functionalism, structuralism, or an "interpretative" point of view. Such paradigmatic writing has been firmly grounded in Western intellectual history. It seeks to explain or interpret other cultures in the language of one or another of the competing paradigms that rise and fall like empires within Western intellectual history. In *Anthropology as Cultural Critique*, George Marcus and Michael Fischer identify a contemporary trend toward writing "experimental" ethnographies that are not bound to one or another of the competing paradigms. These works, they say, represent an "exhaustion with a paradigmatic style of discourse altogether." They describe a "crisis of representation . . . when theoretical concerns shift to problems of the interpretation of the details of a reality that eludes the ability of the dominant paradigms to describe it, let alone explain it." Ethnography, they say, has become both a genre of writing and "a very personal and imaginative vehicle by which anthropologists are expected to make contributions to theoretical and intellectual discussions, both within their discipline and beyond" (Marcus and Fischer 1986: x, 12, 21).

Narrative ethnographic writing provides a genre in which to communicate another culture's metaphors, philosophy, and style of discourse to a Western audience. *Trail to Heaven* is a narrative ethnography that attempts to use not only Indian texts but also the stylistic conventions and teaching methods through which knowledge is conveyed in a northern hunting culture. Its paradigm, if any, is that of Dunne-za culture itself. It assumes that myth and dream are interior to events in the world of sensation. It assumes that knowledge is a form of power. It assumes that discourse is meaningful in the context of shared experience. It assumes an Indian philosophy of time and causality.

A moment in Indian time includes every other moment shared

in the individual and collective memories of individuals, community, and culture. A single moment is meaningful in relation to every other moment that is part of shared experience. Communication within a small native community relies extensively on a background of shared experience and unstated mutual understandings. Every moment is meaningful in relation to all moments that have gone before. Every event makes sense in relation to shared knowledge and experience. Communication within a particular moment refers back to the unstated understandings that connect people's lives together. The moments described in *Trail to Heaven* include and refer to all the moments I have shared with the Dunne-za over nearly thirty years.

Trail to Heaven describes some hard times in the lives of people I know and respect. It describes their strengths in relation to moments of anguish. It describes their triumphs and their adherence to the spiritual values that have always given them strength. These values are reflected in the traditions and teachings of their Dreamers, as well as in their integration of these teachings into Christianity. I hope the reader will take what I have written as a teaching rather than as a curiosity. I hope the people who revealed their lives to me will recognize that I have also revealed myself in what I have written about them. I hope they will be tolerant of the inevitable misunderstandings or inaccuracies in what I have written. I have done the best I can to put together what I have experienced into a meaningful pattern, but I am still learning and still discovering that the trail sometimes turns in unexpected directions.

A person sometimes learns by making mistakes but never by denying that mistakes have been made. I have tried to tell the story in an Indian way, relying ultimately on the authority of my own intelligence and my experience of Dunne-za traditions within the context of real events. I have integrated Dunne-za stories into my own story about how I came to understand the Dunne-za world. The Dunne-za told me most of their stories in *Dunne-za zage*, their Athapaskan language. Young people fluent in both languages put them into English for me. Some of these young people also told me stories directly in English. I have indicated which passages are translations and which are verbatim transcriptions of audio documents recorded in English. The texts I have included are only a small portion of the total body of stories and oratory archived as tape actualities or in written form.

My Dunne-za teachers have been extraordinarily patient and kind. Some of my first teachers were elders: Sam St. Pierre, Jean St. Pierre, Japasa, Johnny Chipesia, Sitama, Augustine Jumbie, Charlie Yahey, Anachuan, Amma, Albert Askoty, Jack Acko, Eskama, Aku, Nachin, Thomas Hunter. Some of my early teachers were children, who are now themselves older than I was when I first knew them. Some were people my own age. Most of the elders I knew in those days have now followed Yagatunne, the "Trail to Heaven." Some of my contemporaries have also gone in that direction. I owe a special debt to the memories of Sally St. Pierre, Billy St. Pierre, Willy Olla, and Mackenzie Ben. I have also learned more than I can say from Tommy Attachie, Peter Chipesia, Gerry Attachie, Billy Attachie, Margaret Davis, Jack Askoty, Leo Acko, Sammy Acko, Eddie Apsassin, Ricky Apsassin, and Katie St. Pierre. I am particularly grateful for the remarkable presence of Johnny Chipesia, who died about the time *Trail to Heaven* was accepted for publication.

Trail to Heaven reflects both my anthropological understanding of Dunne-za culture and my personal understanding of moments I shared with these people and many others. I would like also to thank Antonia (Ridington) Mills for her contribution to the texts that appear in the book. My special thanks go to Jillian Ridington for her continuing partnership in the process of learning, both from the Dunne-za and from the legacy of our friend and teacher, Howard Broomfield. She shared in the process of discovery and provided a critique of the manuscript as it emerged. I am especially grateful for the continuing support of my parents, Bill and Edie Ridington, and for their confidence in the sometimes unorthodox directions I took in search of an education.

Finally, I would like to thank the Canadian Ethnology Service for their support of our work through a series of Ethnographic Field Research Contracts. Howard, Jillian, and I used to begin our "talking fieldnotes" tapes with a greeting to the chief ethnologist, Annette McFadyen Clark. I will close this introduction with the same greeting, "Thanks, Annette."

NEW MOCCASINS

Overleaf: Japasa (George Chipesia), 1964

1. A BEGINNING

I made my first contact with the world of people native to this continent in 1959. Like Columbus, I had not intended to discover a new world. It simply happened. I entered a country where the Indian presence remains strong. I entered with preconceptions and found them wanting. I began a trail of learning that is still ongoing. Part One of *Trail to Heaven* is the story of my first contact with the Indian world. There is a bit of the Columbus in all of us whose traditions came from outside North America. Columbus was not alone in mistaking the native people of this continent for people he was expecting to find elsewhere. Columbus found Indians on an island in the Caribbean. I found Italian boy scout vandals in the forests of northeastern British Columbia. We were both wrong in interpreting what we saw in terms of what we were expecting. We were both taken by surprise.

Part One of this book describes an attempt to learn from my mistakes, to redirect the energy of my surprise. "New moccasins" suggests a new path, a new way of thinking about the world. The thoughtworld of North American Indians may be new and different to non-native readers. I hope they will find it rewarding. I hope native people who read my story will find it interesting and perhaps amusing.

2. ITALIAN BOY SCOUT VANDALS

In the twilight of a northern night near the summer solstice of 1959 I found myself at Mile 210 on the Alaska Highway, setting out along a trail into the bush of northeastern British Columbia. The trail led seven miles down to where my friends from Swarthmore College, Eric Freedman and Jimmi Mead, were planning to homestead on a flat in the Prophet River Valley. The trail led into a landscape of spruce and poplar, jack pine and muskeg. The trail led into a world I had not anticipated or even imagined. Although I did not know it at the time, the trail led into the country of the Dunne-za. The trail also led into the Dunne-za thoughtworld. I am still following the trail I began on that evening in 1959. Until that summer I had never met a "real live Indian" or even thought very much about the Indian world except as something that belonged to a distant and fabulous past, irretrievably distanced from the places I knew in Maryland, Pennsylvania, and New Jersey.

The following pages describe my first contact with the Dunne-za world and my subsequent attempt to understand that world as an anthropologist. In both cases, I first experienced and interpreted the lives of northern hunting people through the categories of my own experience and education. In both cases, I found these categories misleading. In both cases, I sought to find a language of translation between the two worlds.

I saw my first Indian on a family trip west in 1957. He was a poor, paunchy man in tattered Plains regalia, dancing for tourists outside a gift shop in the shadow of Mount Rushmore's stony American presidents. The sight of this disheartened captive dancing in place, forever out of place, like a tired old bear in chains, moved me to sorrow, confusion, and embarrassment. His dance must have been meaningful in some other context, the world of "real live Indians," but it was a humiliation to us both outside the Mount Rushmore gift shop. Is this, I thought, all there is left of a great Indian nation? Are there any real Indians left? Later in the trip we did glimpse Navajos in satin, velvet, and a hint of turquoise and silver, flashing by the window of our Buick Special station wagon as it rolled on its "dyna-flo" fluid drive through the brilliant and shimmering dry lands of New Mexico and Arizona. But I did not make contact with them. They remained merely moving pictures brought "back east" from my first "trip west."

Until that trip in 1957, the year I graduated from Westminster High School in Carroll County, Maryland, I had never experienced a natural landform or a climax community of plants and animals. Throughout all the country I knew, from the rolling farmlands of Carroll County to the hardwood forests that surround our summer home in Sussex County, New Jersey, the land and its life had been transformed by farming and industry. The woods through which I hiked, following the Appalachian Trail, were cleared, regrown, logged, transformed into charcoal, and then abandoned, years before, to grow again into forests. The history of that land seemed dead and gone from the breath of experience. The history I studied in college was about a past that would not return to life. Beyond history lay myth and legend. Beyond history lay the land as it was before being shaped to the purposes of our civilization. Beyond history lay the world of Indians, to me as yet a dreamworld.

I knew the history of forest lands in Sussex County as it was written in the language of glacial boulders that early settlers sweated and skidded from the forest floor and heaped at the boundaries of now forgotten property lines. Occasionally, I came across stone-lined springs, tumble-down lime kilns, or nearly buried foundations of buildings in my walks through these woods. A long ridge called Kittatinny Mountain lies across the lake from our cottage. Local tradition has it that the name is Indian. It may be, but I remember once thinking the name of a boy scout camp near our lake was Indian too, until I learned that Nobebosco is an acronym for North Bergen Boy Scout Council.

A spring of cool water flows from the mountain just below the crest of the ridge. In centuries past, it is said, Lenapes, Iroquois, or Susquehannocks refreshed themselves from its waters during the restless, enigmatic journeys these legendary people of the forest were reputed to have been constantly undertaking. Perhaps they visited it when they were "on the warpath." There are no traditions that Indians lived permanently in any of the country I knew. I never found arrowheads or saw the remains of villages. Even the shoreline of our lake was manmade. The lake was created from a pond when its owners built a dam to increase the volume of ice they could cut from its surface for the New York market. Indians could not have lived there or known its shoals, lily pads, and enormous croaking bullfrogs as I have known them.

The winter of 1959 was a time of discovery and change in my life. I was nineteen years old and had been in school since I was five. I needed to experience another form of education to complement what I was being taught in school. I decided to take that semester off from college to build a small shack in the New Jersey woods. I wanted, like Thoreau, to look back on the academic world from a quiet place. I wanted to play house, bake bread, cut firewood, listen to the eerie booming of ice on the lake, and write about the immense silence of that winter world. My parents supported the plan, and the college was willing to give me a leave of absence.

Miraculously, the nearest neighbor with whom I had contact was a ninety-year-old Swedenborgian mystic. Mrs. Tinsley was also a southern gentlewoman. When I trudged through the snow to visit her, she would make me southern spoon bread and talk about the philosophy of her spiritual mentor, Emanuel Swedenborg, whose books filled her little house. It was my first experience of really listening to the story of an old person's life. Although I did not realize it at the time, listening to Mrs. Tinsley was my first ethnographic experience. A few times during that winter I walked and hitchhiked from the New Jersey woods to a fifth-floor walk-up railroad flat on West 45th Street in Manhattan, where my friends Eric and Jimmi were getting together information and tools for their move to the Peace River country in far-off northeastern British Columbia. They left for the north that spring. I planned to meet them there in June.

As I drove north into the late evening twilight that suffused the bush that stretched, apparently without end, on either side of the Alaska Highway, the hardwood forests surrounding Kittatinny Mountain seemed a world away. The trees here were poplar, willow, jack pine, and spruce. The muskeg was something I had never seen before. The trail I took from Mile 210 on the Alaska Highway led away from a familiar past and into the world of an unknown future. My friends Eric and Jimmi had left Swarthmore College to test their skills and energy against the demands of life in a real wilderness. Less adventurous than they, I planned to join them for the summer and then return to college in September.

Eric and Jimmi had written me with meager instructions for finding them in the bush. "Drive to Mile 210 on the Alaska Highway, hide your car in the bush out of sight from the road, and follow a trail that leads about seven miles to where you will find us on a flat near where the Minnaker Creek joins the Prophet River." With two college friends, I had driven from Pennsylvania to San Francisco. My friend Bob Gelardin and I then headed north up the coast, through the Fraser Canyon and caribou country, north on the Hart Highway, then onto a gravel road, and then northeast to the Alaska Highway, also gravel.

Late in the evening we found Mile 210 and maneuvered my little blue Renault 4CV off the highway. We discovered a clearing in the bush and the remains of a campfire. Someone had left cans and bottles strewn about. Embedded in a nearby tree we discovered a rusty axe. From the same tree hung a pair of snowshoes, rusty traps, and coils of thin blue electrical wire. Some poles were lashed together enigmatically with twists of the same wire. Many of the spruce trees had been blazed with an axe. On some of them we discovered names, dates, and short messages written in pencil. A trail led away from the highway. It was similarly blazed and marked with penciled messages. We managed to decipher some of the writing. One of the names was Johnny Chipesia.

In the woods of Sussex County I had also seen trees blazed with an axe. I was familiar with graffiti scribbled on blazes. This was usually the work of wayward boy scouts from Nobebosco or one of the other camps. Kids from Newark, Passaic, and Montclair sometimes went crazy when they were turned loose in the woods. Some of them, I knew, were Italians. The name Chipesia sounded Italian to me. "Oh, no," I lamented. "Even here in the wilds of northern

British Columbia the Italian boy scout vandals from Passaic have been here before me." I had always held vandals from the city in utter contempt. I respected the forest. I followed only the white blazes neatly painted by volunteers of the Appalachian Mountain Club. I did not leave cans or bottles in the woods. I kept my axe bright and shiny. I did not litter the forest with junk. I respected nature. I was organized and civilized.

Even though it was late, we decided to set out and camp when it got dark. In addition to our heavy packs, I carried an ancient single-barreled Stevens 12-gauge shotgun and a pocket full of rifled slugs. If there were bears or wolves, we would be able to defend ourselves. I had never shot anything larger than a groundhog, but I felt prepared. We walked until it began to get hot rather than dark. It had not occurred to us that we were far enough north that it would never get dark at this time of the year. The trail was easy to follow. We knew we were on the trail because the blazes left by the Italian boy scout vandals continued.

Somehow we did not notice that we were walking along a well-travelled horse trail and that the Italian boy scout vandals had been riding horses. Sometimes the trail crossed great straight swaths cut across the bush by some kind of machine. We later learned these were seismic lines cut by giant D-6 Cats to test this vast wilderness for deposits of oil. Sometimes the trail followed one of these lines for a time before resuming its way among the jack pine, spruce, and poplar. The blackflies and mosquitoes were ferocious, but we slathered ourselves in bug dope and carried on. Eventually, we lay down on a grassy slope on one of the seismic lines and slept.

Although the bugs were fierce, the bears and wolves were content to leave us in a state of ignorant grace. The ancient Stevens remained silent. Indians were the last thing on our minds. Eventually, providence brought us to the end of the trail. There on the flats Eric and Jimmi had begun to build a wilderness cabin from the design in a book by Horace Kephart and to put in a brave little garden. They assured me that we were several thousand miles from the nearest Italian boy scout vandals from Passaic. They told me that Johnny Chipesia was a Beaver Indian. He had already been down to check them out, and they had been to his home on the Prophet River Reserve at Mile 232 on the highway. The flat where they were building the cabin was in his hunting and trapping territory.

Within a few weeks, a party of men and boys on horseback arrived at our little camp on the flat. The adults among them were Johnny Chipesia, Sam St. Pierre, Augustine Jumbie, and Shorty Wolf. They asked what we had been eating. We showed them our sacks of whole grains, tubs of peanut butter, tins of Empress jam, and our hand-carved wooden bowls. As we talked, some of the boys rode their horses across the river and disappeared. Soon we heard the ping of a .22-caliber rifle shot. In less than an hour, the boys returned with a deer, neatly skinned and quartered. They built up the fire and impaled a rack of ribs on a green poplar pole pushed into the ground at an angle. After a largely vegetarian diet, we tore into the meat like hungry wolves. It was my first taste of deer meat. We were amazed. This was not New Jersey. These people were Indians, "real live Indians," not Italian boy scout vandals from Passaic.

Until Johnny and the others rode into my life on that June day in 1959, I had not really thought of native Americans as people living in a world that could connect to my own. Since that day, I have not been able to think about life in North America without reference to their existence. The contrast between their way of being in the northern forest and our own was immediately obvious. What had been difficult or impossible for us seemed effortless to them. Once or twice, Eric had risen before dawn and stealthily crept with his army surplus British Enfield .303 rifle to a place downriver where we had often seen deer tracks. Each time, he returned in the heat of the day to a meal of rolled oats and boiled wheat with honey. Now, at midday, in the midst of considerable nonchalant commotion, the Chipesia boys had splashed their way across the river on horseback and brought down a deer with a rifle considered inadequate even for shooting squirrels and groundhogs in Pennsylvania and New Jersey.

According to hunting books I had read, the deer hunter must carry a small block and tackle with which to hang the carcass in order to drain the blood and remove the intestines. The deer should be taken home whole and given to a professional game butcher for processing. Then the meat should be hung for a few days before it is fit to eat. I remember seeing cars going by in hunting season with whole gutted deer lashed to their fenders. Suddenly, I realized that this technique had been for display rather than any practical purpose. These boys had done none of the "right things" according to the hunting books, yet here was the meat in convenient pieces, each cut looking as though it had been disarticulated from the whole with surgical precision. Here we were eating the meat of a deer that had been walking within earshot of our camp not more than an hour before.

Johnny seemed to take these events as being completely ordinary. He did not remark upon the boys' accomplishment any more than my father would have remarked on my return from the store with a loaf of bread. Meat, in fact, seemed to be like bread for these forest people, although they also brought with them a kind of biscuit called bannock which, I learned, is made in a tin skillet over an open fire. As we ate, the boys eyed us shyly and giggled behind their hands when they thought we were not looking. Our blundering presence must have been as outlandish to them as their finesse was miraculous to us. Their visit was partly motivated by curiosity and the entertainment value we surely provided, but it was also a subtle assertion of their rights to the land on which we were squatting. They had come to show us what it means to be on Indian land.

Through this encounter, I first came into contact with the delicate discourse of a communication system that depends on establishing and maintaining mutual understandings. In this case, Johnny wanted us to know that this valley, although perhaps formally listed as Crown land in a land office registry somewhere, was theirs because of the intimate knowledge they have of it. The ease they displayed in this place where we were as yet clumsy and ill at ease gave us their message in a language more powerful than words. The effortless way the boys made contact with the deer suggested a power and knowledge we could only imagine. We began to understand that the land is theirs because of the way they know it. The rights they demonstrated by feeding us that day carried more authority than stacks of dusty documents in distant offices. Johnny's way of telling us we were on his land was to feed us from it.

Thus, in the cups of tea and freshly roasted meat we shared that afternoon, a mutual understanding was established. I am sure the executives and engineers who decreed that seismic lines should be cut through these Crown lands never took tea with Johnny Chipesia. I doubt they entertained the possibility of any relationship to the land other than the documentary one of the land office registry and corporate balance sheet. Unlike a registered landowner who might very well have thrown us off his land at gunpoint, Johnny saw the needs that arose out of our ignorance and offered us the benefit of his knowledge. The deer meat we shared was sacramental.

To Johnny, we were funny, interesting, harmless, and in need of all the help we could get. He undertook to teach us what he could by example, in the Indian way. We had little with which to reciprocate then, but we decided that when the cabin was completed we would hold a housewarming party and invite our newfound friends and neighbors. Other visits followed the first one. From time to time I was able to give people rides along the highway on our weekly mail and ice cream runs to the little store and café at Trutch, Mile 200 on the Alaska Highway. Later, when I knew Johnny's people better, I learned that they referred to us by the name of a band in the Beaver language, Tlukawutdunne, "people who live on the flat." Some of the older people still know me by this name. Years later, when I taught a course on native people of Canada at the University of British Columbia, I discovered the irony that Trutch is named for Joseph Trutch, a racist nineteenth-century developer responsible for systematically depriving Indians of their lands throughout the province.

While we were finishing the cabin's hand-carved door latch and furnishings made from split spruce smoothed with a drawknife, we sent out word to the people at Prophet River that we were ready to host the housewarming party we had promised. For the occasion we filled a washtub with hop-flavored malt extract, sugar, and water. We added yeast and waited for the miracle of life to manifest itself. We baked bread and cookies. By the time a string of saddle horses came into sight down the trail toward our establishment, the little yeasts had gone forth and multiplied wonderfully, suffusing the frothy mud-colored tub of liquid with the alcoholic byproduct of their metabolism. The next three days remain a blur in my biography, but from time to time I surfaced sufficiently to register a few clear impressions.

Only men and boys had made the trek to our miraculous roadhouse. Presumably, the women had better things to do with their time and remained in their camps or at the Prophet River Reserve at Mile 232 on the highway. There were about half a dozen guests in all. We discovered during the course of those merged days an apparently immutable principle of nature: drinking in the bush continues until there is nothing left to drink. The brew was young and yeasty and without pretense. We soon discovered that we had inadvertently reinvented the brew party, a venerable institution of northern forest life. In 1959, people with the legal status of Indians were prohibited from buying alcohol from the government liquor stores of British Columbia, although they had recently been given the right to drink beer in the hotel beer parlors. Consequently, a tub of brew sequestered furtively in the bush was a common form of entertainment.

The program began after a period of shy silence, polite conversation, offerings of drinks in white enamel cups, and curious inspection of the odd dwelling we had brought into being. Gradually, the reserve of the formal guest-host relationship began to dissolve as the brew dissolved the myelin sheathing of our respective neurons. The volume of talk in Beaver and English began to increase. Eventually, the talk reformed itself into the more liquid tongue of song. Eric and Jimmi and I broke into "Salty Dog," "Boil that Cabbage Down," and a generous sample of songs learned from folk records.

Then some of the older Indians began to sing in a form of expression that I knew was literally out of a world other than the one I was familiar with. Their songs were without words. In my altered state of consciousness the melodic line seemed to rise and fall like the wind. It was a wind that dissolved history. When I closed my eyes, the cabin, my little blue Renault, the Alaska Highway, my image of Italian boy scout vandals from Passaic all disappeared. Only the tall, singing spruces remained and the soaring sound of wind, the flow of river water, distant voices calling out of a dim past, distant memories calling like dreams to the fleeting, waking mind. The singers were intoxicated Indians. I was an intoxicated white boy. Our differences seemed temporarily obliterated by the alcohol and by the situation. Hidden correspondences were highlighted by the psychic shadows they generated. I felt as if the spruce trees themselves were singing like some long lost ancestor come back to earth in the roots of this northern forest.

I remember once being put on a horse. It waited patiently for some forthcoming intelligence on my part. Then, with resignation, the thoroughly disgusted animal made its way slowly along the riverbank. My greatest accomplishment was in persuading the beast to reverse its direction and plod back to where its Indian masters were splitting their sides with laughter. At times, the party maintained a manic mood late into the misty border-light between dusk and dawn. At times, it slept in sodden repose through the daylight hours. As we slowly measured the foamy liquid down our throats, the atmosphere clouded to rain and the river began to rise with alarming alacrity. On the last morning, some of us rose into consciousness. We gathered together to take stock of the situation. The brew tub was empty, the skies drenched the forest, and the river had risen above the first terrace of its bank. One of the guests, Shorty Wolf, was not to be found among us. Someone thought he had last been seen sleeping by the bank of the river. Now, the water had risen to cover part of the bank. There was a flurry of bleary consternation. At last he was discovered, sleeping peacefully just above the rush of the river's muddy water.

Our housewarming was accomplished. No doubt the tales we told of those days were outdone by the embellishments offered by our guests as they told the story to the people back in their own camps and on the reserve. In some obscure way we had become real to the people of Prophet River as they had become real to us. After the headache was gone and we returned to our labors, the sound of their singing blew through my dreams like wind through the spruce trees. It is with me even now as I close my eyes and conjure the sweet scent of willows, the cold silence of midnight twilight, and the warm enclosure made by a circle of fire.

3. WHERE HAPPINESS DWELLS

In days gone by, Dunne-za from various scattered bands used to come together in the Montney Prairie country north of Fort St. John. The place was named for Johnny Chipesia's grandfather, Chief Montagin or Montney. In the Beaver language it is known as Where Happiness Dwells. Between 1918 and 1945, it was Indian reserve land held in common by members of the Fort St. John band, of which Johnny was a member. People would hunt, pick saskatoon berries, sing, dance, and "play gamble," the Indian hand game. After the reserve was taken from them in 1945 and sold to veterans returning from World War II, people continued to come together during the annual Fort St. John Stampede.

By midsummer of 1959, I had come to know Johnny well enough to appreciate that his curiosity about the world was matched only by the hyperbole of his descriptions. His nickname, I learned later, is Wuscide, "storyteller," or, in colloquial English, Johnny Bullshit. Thus, it was not difficult for Johnny to convince me that my education would not be complete without attending the stampede at Fort St. John. There I would meet Indian people from the other Dunne-za reserves at Halfway River, Doig River, and Blueberry. Since I would, of course, be driving down to the stampede, it would be no trouble to take along Johnny, his wife, Julie, and their two youngest children, Thomas and Kathryn.

Once we had set out, Johnny began telling me of the wonderful Halfway River Reserve "just a little bit off the highway," west of Mile 95. Under the influence of his genial persuasion, I found myself heading west on a gravel road "to see a different country." The country was indeed different and breathtaking, as the road wound toward the loom of distant mountains. After driving about twenty-five miles, we finally descended a steep hill and turned off across a large open valley bottom toward an irregular cluster of plywood houses, cabins, and wall tents with tepees attached to one end. We stopped, and a round of gentle greetings began, men and women coming up in ones and twos to exchange softly touching handshakes with Johnny and Julie.

One of the men was named Aballi Field. He moved with the grace of a hunter, and I saw in him a kind of beauty that reflected the beauty of this place. Johnny introduced him as a relative of his wife's. He said Julie had come from the "same people" as Aballi and "sure she happy" to be back at Halfway visiting with her people. Seeing Julie and Aballi together, I noticed a strong physical resemblance. Watching the stream of people who came by to shake hands and talk, I understood that a strong emotional and social bond went along with the physical relationship. Now Johnny revealed, with consummate finesse, the second part of a plan he must have had in mind all along. Aballi and his family would "sure like to go to the stampede" too. Maybe I could drive them into town, eighty miles away, and then come back for Johnny and Julie. That way, the Chipesias would have time for a longer visit at Halfway. Slowly, it dawned on me that Johnny was a master hunter and I was his willing game.

I gave my assent to the proposition and soon was heading toward town with the tiny car full of people and the smell of wood smoke, spruce boughs, and snoose. At the end of the long day of driving, I found myself camped in a patch of bush near the stampede grounds, which, in 1959, were just at the edge of the developed part of town. For whitepeople of the Peace River area, the Fort St. John stampede is a civic celebration and an opportunity to demonstrate riding skills. The cowboy image it fosters is proud, aggressive, competitive, vain, maudlin, controlled, and violent. Riders apply their skills in the control of brute force. Calves are roped from horseback, thrown violently to the ground, and bound, bawling, with tight ropes. Young men are tossed from the lurching backs of horses and bulls and trampled underfoot. Flags are flown, hats are held over hearts. The cowboy's prayer is read over the public address system. At night, around campfires and in tents, trailers, and

makeshift campers, whiskey seizes throats in spasms. In the morning, indications of fornications lie flaccid in the moiling mud outside these accommodations.

In 1959, very few Dunne-za were part of this strutting and stud-
ding. It did not occur to them that their masterful skills as horsemen
and hunters should have to be proved in the public arena of the
white men. Instead, they came to Fort St. John as they had come
together in a summer gathering for centuries. Because they no
longer owned the land at Montney Prairie, the closest replacement
available to them was the stampede ground at Fort St. John. Here,
people came together to meet one another, to sing, to dance, and
to listen to the words of their "prophet," someone the white men
called "Old Charlie." They came to resolve differences or create
them, to flirt, to visit relatives, and to pass from the pace of ordinary
existence into a ceremonial space. The stampede was, in fact, an
excuse for a pow-wow. The major difference between this pow-
wow and those held away from the white men was that, during
stampede time, they were beset by bootleggers and drinking.

I do not remember much about the stampede itself. I experienced
it through the world of the Dunne-za. They were my sole contacts
and companions. The whitepeople seemed foreign and unapproach-
able. Their world was only the background for the Indian world
that had brought me there. I remember hearing the wailing lament
of the rodeo announcer working his audience as the riders worked
their animals and themselves, but I never made direct contact with
their world. I must have been equally invisible to them, staying as
I did within the Indian camps. I experienced the whitepeople as
aliens. The Indians, strange and enigmatic as they still were to me,
were real people whom I knew and trusted. The cowboys appeared
tight, difficult, and closed into their own system of mutual postur-
ing, while the Indians seemed to acknowledge some form of relationship I did not as yet understand. I did not know, then, that I
was Tlukawutdunne, but I did know that I was not a cowboy.

Some of the Indians had come to town in wagons. They were
from the Doig River Reserve, a small community of log cabins
about forty-five miles northeast of town. Until 1945, they had gathered each summer with other members of the Fort St. John band
at Where Happiness Dwells. Now, their summer gathering took

place at the Fort St. John stampede grounds. Other people from Halfway joined our camp. They had hitched rides to town in cars or trucks. None of the Indians had vehicles of their own. None of them had driver's licenses. They set up their camps at the edge of town in the same way they set up hunting camps in the bush.

The space they created within the very shadow of town renewed and continued a tradition that was theirs from before living memory. They set up tents, built fires, cooked meat from recent hunts, ate drymeat and bannock, and passed food around from camp to camp as a natural and familiar form of communication. People who had not seen one another since the previous summer told the stories of their respective experiences. Groups of men sang and played single-headed hand drums. Men, women, and children alike shuffled easily around the fire, merging the signature of many footprints into a single trail.

People also drank. Although I had already been through the transformative experience of our housewarming party, I was not really prepared for the fierce and massive intoxication of the stampede. Unlike our party in the bush, where drinking was paced by the trickle of mild brew from its tub in our cabin's loft, in town it had no regulation beyond the cash available to pay ready bootleggers and the body's capacity to metabolize the gallon jugs of sweet red fortified Slinger's Grape Wine that passed in a circle, pulling and sucking at thickening lips. I remember jugs of wine going around in a similar circle, and the rodeo announcer's voice becoming the echo of some unimaginably distant future, and the poplars and their sweetly scented smoke asserting a sensual priority, and a woman from Prophet River pursuing me through the trees shouting, "Come here, Robinson, you handsome son of a bitch," and the roots of trees clutching at my legs, and a mickey of rye pulling me down. I remember breaking away from the bush and into the maze of streets in town, studded with little frame houses with picket-fenced yards, and one of them enclosing me and drawing me down into a thick, hot oblivion.

When I returned to the bright and thirsty sun, a kindly house-holder was assuring me that I was alive and that it was stampede time. Like others who were there in the summer of 1959, cowboy and Indian alike, I recovered. I filed the experience away in an archive of memory. For the Indians, the 1959 Fort St. John Stampede reflected and repeated a form of expression going back to a time before there was a town in their Peace River country. The old people still remembered trails beneath the streets of town. For me, the experience was new and exotic.

Looking back over the events of that summer, I can see a pattern very different from my initial expectations. I had been prepared to experience book knowledge being applied to taming the wilderness. We built our cabin by the book. We painstakingly notched each log to fit the rounded course below it rather than cutting notches from the course already in place. In theory, ours would last longer, but in practice it was far more time-consuming to build. The Indian trapping cabins were all made the easy way. Ours took months to build. An Indian cabin could be put up in a few days. My friends and I used the only formula for which our education had prepared us. It worked against us as much as for us.

We struggled where the Indians were at ease, but in town the roles were reversed. They struggled and we were at least relatively at ease. Their relations with government were controlled by a little white man named Joe Gallibois, the Indian agent. They called him "small Indian boss" because he attempted to tell them what they had to do in relation to the white man's government. I had expected to find an empty and pristine wilderness in a country named for peace. Instead, the wilderness was both occupied by people indigenous to it and savaged by massive industrial intrusion. On the very first day, I had seen an Indian pack trail intertwined with seismic lines. I have followed the braided path of white and Indian trails ever since that time.

I interpreted what I saw through the structure of my past experience. Italian boy scout vandals from Passaic were a category I knew from experience. Indians were as yet outside anything I knew. The Indians I met that summer belonged to the northern forest country. Their thoughts, their songs, their ease of living in the bush took me back to a mythic time before the advent of history as I knew it. Their evident struggle to maintain themselves in a world of highways, seismic lines, towns, stampedes, alcohol, and government officials forced me to confront the forces of history I had taken for granted. As yet, I had little concrete knowledge of these forest people, but I could intuit from what I had experienced at least what kind of knowledge might be available to me upon further study.

Here in the forest north of the Peace River, I found a country still occupied by people whose right to the land was demonstrated, at least in their own thinking, by their knowledge of it. They had not paid for the land or possessed it by changing it. Their right was the right of belonging. It was the right of knowing. Their relationship to the land was more complex, more deeply rooted, more spiritual than simple material possession. The Indians acted as if they and their ancestors had been on the land as long as the animals themselves. Although they used such modern technology as horses and guns and even the little blue Renault of a young white man who appeared on the scene in the summer of 1959, their ways of thinking about themselves and their country remained inseparable. In spirit, they were autochthonous, born of the land. I felt in them a sense of place I had never before experienced. Every person I had met before could say what place his or her ancestors had come from. The Dunne-za did not seem to be *from* anywhere. Although they could recall a complex pattern of movements within the Peace River country, it made no sense for them to think of being from any other place. As the summer drew to a close, I resolved to learn more of what it means to be truly native to a place.

4. SAM AND JUMBIE

When I returned to Swarthmore in the fall of 1959, I decided to study anthropology, even though at the time the college did not offer any courses in it. I majored in history but managed to take an introductory anthropology course at the University of Pennsylvania. Later, I took Carleton Coon's upper level course on the cultures of hunting and gathering people. Coon suggested that I apply to Harvard for graduate school. Thus, early in 1962, I began my initiation into the mysteries of professional anthropology at Harvard's Peabody Museum. Most of the other graduate students had come to Harvard with undergraduate majors in anthropology. Most of them came to study with a particular faculty member, often as part of a large ongoing team project. I was an oddity. I did not know enough about the politics of professional anthropology even to think about becoming someone's disciple. I did know that I wanted to return to the Peace River country and learn more about the Beaver Indians. I did understand that an opportunity to know about the hunting way of life was a rare and special gift. I hoped to integrate what the Dunne-za could teach me with what I could learn from anthropology.

By the summer of 1964, I was ready to begin the anthropological "rite of passage" known as fieldwork. I had been granted a small sum of money by the National Institute of Mental Health to study the cultural psychology of people who live by hunting. I wanted to look at the personality structure of people living in a low accumulation economy to see if they were high in a personality trait known as "need for achievement." I planned to measure this trait by giving people projective tests in which they would be asked to tell a story about an ambiguous picture I would show them. A content analysis of imagery in their responses would later reveal their level of "N

Ach," as it was known in the argot of psychologese. But first, I would have to make contact with the Indians, my subjects.

My fieldwork began on June 13, 1964, when I and my former wife, Tonia, pulled our VW camper into an Indian camp near the familiar little café and gas station called Trutch at Mile 200 on the Alaska Highway. Evening had descended into the half-light I remembered from 1959. This time, I knew it would soon be the dawn of a new day without ever being fully dark. The sky was clear. Only the brightest stars and planets pierced the half-light of that evening sky so close to the summer solstice. Under these conditions the major constellations stood out more prominently than they would have in the searing cold and velvet dark of a winter solstice sky. Among them was Cygnus, the starswan who flies like a Dreamer between heaven and earth. Frost etched grasses in crystalline designs. Mosquitoes swarmed in loud black hordes against a blue-black horizon. Smoke rose from a fire and encircled dim figures, sheathed like sheikhs against the piercing penetration of these large, stupid, bloodthirsty insects.

I opened the car door against the swarm. I spoke toward the fire's figures, invoking the ancient Italian name of Chipesia, but this was a Frenchman, not an Italian. His name was Sam St. Pierre. I had met him in 1959, but because he was as quiet as Johnny was talkative, I had not known him well. Later, I learned that Sam's name derived from the kind of multicultural muddle that so often happens when immigrants or Indians have to validate their existence on official lists. Sam's father was a man called Bob Bighead in English, according to the recollection of Johnny Beatton, son of Frank Beatton, who was Hudson's Bay factor at Fort St. John in the first two decades of this century. Bob Bighead died when Sam was very young. Sam was raised near Moberly Lake by a French Cree half-breed named Baptiste Lalonde. Baptiste had Sam christened with the name Sam Pierre Lalonde. One year, when the Indian agent was paying treaty money of five dollars a head, he realized that Sam was an Indian but not on the treaty list for the Fort St. John band. He asked Sam his name. Sam replied, "Sam Pierre." The agent wrote down, "St. Pierre." Next, he asked Sam his first name. Sam, who does not care to repeat himself unnecessarily, replied tersely, "Sam," meaning to say, "I already told you my name is Sam." The agent dutifully wrote down "Sam" in front of St. Pierre. To the Indians, he is known as Sam Pierre (pronounced Sam-Pier), but on the band list he is the founding father of a new patronymic family line surnamed St. Pierre.

Sam indicated that his daughter Sally was pregnant and near full term. Her first child, Katie, was four years old. Sam's wife, Jean, kept to the back of the tent, while mosquitoes hurled themselves against the protective netting that enclosed a double bedroll. We left in wonder and went to sleep in our van where a side road met the same small river that flowed past the place of Tlukawutdunne. In the morning, we drove Sally and Katie up to the reserve at Prophet River. We were shy and quiet on the thirty-two-mile drive. Once there, we parked the van midway between the two rows of new but already deteriorating pastel plywood government issue Indian houses. Sally and Katie disappeared and we were left to ourselves on display for a circle of curious eyes.

It was lunchtime. We began to make bologna sandwiches. A round old man, his black hair streaked with white like the back of a wolverine, came up to our van. He appeared to be in his seventies. I was not sure if I had met him five years before or not. He was round in the belly. His face was round. His cheekbones were high. His eyes were piercing. His teeth were perfectly formed and came together in a gracefully occluded arc. He accepted the bologna sandwich I offered. He began to speak, choosing his subject from some inner world apparently removed from what I understood to be the social situation. Ever since that first encounter, Jumbie has always spoken to me from this world rather than from the world of appearances. Sometimes, younger people have been impatient with him and called him a crazy old man, but his communication to me has always been clear. I care for the world of his dreams and memories.

Jumbie spoke this day as if he had always known me. He spoke to me of a world he had known when he was the age I was then. He spoke as a Dreamer who sees into the past in the same way that the Prophet, for whom Prophet River is named, could see into the future. Jumbie named the animals of this country. Sheep, goat, grizzly bear, caribou, whistler (Rocky Mountain marmot), chicken (grouse) lived in the mountains to the west. At Fish Lake to the east there were whitefish and jackfish. He named moose, beaver, deer, lynx, wolverine as animals of the muskeg country. Then, Jumbie named the people who once lived in the country he knew. The country of his recollection was fabulous with their names: De-cutla, Hoho, Makenacha (Bigfoot), Zoda, Notseta, and many others. Jumbie named the people of the country in the same way he named its animals. Listening to Jumbie, I realized that most of the people whose stories form the story of his own life were no longer alive. Jumbie remembered back to a time long before the Alaska Highway. He remembered to the time when he was one of many people who knew this Prophet River country. The people he named and the animals of this land were still alive in Jumbie's mind. They lived in his evocation of their names.

Jumbie's people used to hunt up the Muskwa River and the Prophet River toward where these waters gathered themselves up out of the mountains. At that time, Jumbie said, the tracks of people were as thick as the tracks of rabbits. People went to the mountains for sheep and goats. They hunted whistlers for their meat and their fat. They made sleeping robes and winter jackets out of sheepskins. There were lots of elk in the mountains. Elkhide was good for summertime clothing because it was waterproof. They made shirts and pants and moccasins out of it. They tanned hides to sell to the Hudson's Bay Company post at Fort Nelson. Then, they made canoes covered with spruce bark, loaded them with people and hides and clothing and drymeat and guns and tools, and ran down the Prophet River's impetuous course from rapid to rapid like leaves in a torrent. This was before there were horses in the Prophet River country. People travelled on foot, on snowshoes, and by canoe. They used their dogs to pack their belongings in the summer. In winter, they used them to pull toboggans.

Jumbie's people moved in a circle from mountain to muskeg. Some of them wintered at Fish Lake. Others, the Tuchodi people, stayed closer to the mountains. They hunted south as far as the Sikanni Chief River, named for the Prophet Makenunatane, who first dreamed of the white men coming into the Peace River country at the end of the eighteenth century. Sometimes, the Prophet River people met their relatives for summer singing and dancing at Where Happiness Dwells. For generations, Beaver Indian people, the

Dunne-za, girded the trees around Montney for firewood and kept the prairie country open by selective burning. They called the place Where Happiness Dwells because it was where they went to meet their relatives. They thought of this place as an earthly reminder of the land at the end of Yagatunne, the Trail to Heaven. Sometimes, Jumbie said, the circle of people gathered at Montney Prairie was as large as the space between two of these houses on the reserve. People danced tightly packed into circles around their fires. They danced and play gambled. They had lots of fun. They courted and told stories. They honored those who had died recently. They celebrated the birth of new people into their world.

Most of the old people Jumbie remembered were no longer alive. Their descendants were the people now living in an abandoned army camp on the Alaska Highway. Much of the bush they knew was now empty of people. Only their names and the animals remained—only the memories of a few old people. Those were the good times for Jumbie. Those were the times when people danced in a circle like the sun's circle from horizon to horizon. Jumbie remembered the terrible winter of 1918–19 when his world died in a scourge of flu that swept across his people's lakes and rivers from the country of the whitepeople and then carried its devastation on to Fort Nelson, Fort Simpson, Great Slave Lake, and the Mackenzie River.

Jumbie's way of speaking English depended as much on gesture, phrasing, and coloring of sound as it did on vocabulary. I did not attempt to write it down verbatim on this first occasion, but I remember him saying something like this:

> Flu clean 'em up, Indians. Just about everybody die. No eat, maybe twelve days. All Indians pretty soon die. Clean 'em up, just like flu. That's good, should be all die. No have to work, no more hungry, no more have no money, no more have to hunt all the time. They all go to a place [pointing to the sky] where they don't have to work. That is good. Good they all die. No more next time hungry.

There must have been more, but I was unable to remember it all or Jumbie's exact words. I did come away with a vivid image of this old man as he had been at my age, crying for a world that became memory in the space of a few terrible days. My recollection may also be colored by what he told me about the same events on subsequent occasions. Jumbie's story accumulates in my memory, as his own memories accumulated to produce the story he told me.

Jumbie said that he remembers stories about the sickness travelling toward them. Some of the old people dreamed about it. He said that Old Man Bigfoot had good Indian medicine. For a while, he pushed the sickness away from them. Still, it came on like a giant animal to consume them. Most people were taken sick suddenly. They were dead in just a few days. Bigfoot was taken even faster. He had been planning to travel to Fort Nelson. He had everything he needed for the trip in his pack. People told him, "Don't go now. It is too late. Wait until morning." Soon he began to feel ill. Blood came from his mouth. He tried to get up. In two hours, he was dead. His pack was still ready for the trip he would never take. People died quickly.

Jumbie said that nearly a hundred people had lived at Fish Lake. Only eleven of them survived. Jumbie and his wife and Joe Bigfoot were among the survivors. It took them nine days to bury the dead. It was winter, and the ground was frozen. They built big fires to thaw the ground. They dug graves. They split logs for coffins but there were too many bodies to bury them all beneath the ground. They left some of the bodies in little wooden houses above ground. Then, they burned all the cabins and left for Fort Nelson. When they got to the trading post, the Hudson's Bay man was in tears. "Everyone is dead here," he told Jumbie. Jumbie replied, "You will die too, sometime, and so will I." He told the Hudson's Bay man not to cry.

After the flu, this beautiful country lay almost empty of people. A few remained. Others came north, from where the whitepeople were beginning to settle the country closer to the Peace River. Some brought horses with them. They filled in the spaces, made new contact with the land, and avoided the ghosts of the past. Jumbie avoided his ghosts for a time by leaving his country altogether. He headed north up the Liard River. He worked for whitepeople on scows that carried supplies north to the "Eskimo country." He worked on the scows with his brother Joe Bigfoot.

Jumbie's story made me sad, and I said I hoped that Indians

would not die like that anymore. Jumbie pointed again to the sky and said it was a good place up there. Then I knew that the death he referred to was the death of a way of life. It was no longer possible for Indians to live throughout the vast Prophet River and Sikanni Chief River country. The flu had reduced their numbers and the Alaska Highway had concentrated the few that remained. Now, people spent their winters in square plywood government-issue houses beside the dusty highway. Children went to school on the reserve. The land was empty of people living as they had when Jumbie was young. People no longer lived by moving in circles like the sun's circle to where the animals could be found. For Jumbie, only the sun's sky circle remained. Only the songs of his people continued to come to him in dreams. Although the Prophet River people continued to obtain much of their food and livelihood from the bush and its animals, their movements were now determined by the highway that army engineers had cut across their country in 1942.

For Jumbie, real Indians were the people who ran the Prophet River rapids in fragile spruce bark canoes, laden with the hides of elk and sheep and goats. Real Indians were at home throughout the lands drained by these waters. Most of the people who were real to Jumbie had died in the winter of his twenty-fourth year. Throughout the rest of his life, Jumbie has kept them alive in his memory. In his mind, the rivers are still alive with people and animals. He calls to their spirits in the sky. Even in the Peace Lutheran Care Home where he has spent his final days, Jumbie's dream life takes him into a past that will never return and will never go away. He is one of the old people with animal friends. Jumbie is someone who "little bit know something."

During June, we provided the service of driving people from Prophet River out to their summer hunting camps. Without ever conducting any formal negotiations, we came to spend much of our time with Sam and Jumbie. Jean St. Pierre fed us. By the beginning of July we had become part of her camp. Sam and Jumbie had been hunting intensively in the area within a day's ride from Trutch. By the beginning of July, they decided it was time to move camp to fresh hunting grounds near the Buckinghorse River at Mile 176 of the Alaska Highway. On a rainy Thursday, July 9, 1964, we quickly packed up the entire camp at Mile 202 and moved to Buckinghorse. The move was accomplished in two stages. The most difficult stage involved rounding up Sam's three saddle horses and four packhorses and loading them with box panniers and raw moosehide panniers full of hunting gear and camping equipment. Just before noon, Peter Chipesia, Billy St. Pierre, and Freddie Jumbie started out down the highway on horseback, followed by two camp dogs. We set out later in the van. With us were the old people and kids as well as the remaining tents, tarps, and camping gear. I wrote in my field notes that the St. Pierre camping equipment and supplies included the following items:

1 10 × 12 white canvas wall tent
1 hand sewn tepee about 12′ in diameter (made by Anachuan, wife of the Dreamer, Charlie Yahey)
3 pots (with lids) of different sizes—one for tea, one for soup, one for boiling meat
1 washtub and detergent
2 washbasins—one for face washing, one for mixing bannock and washing dishes
3 bedrolls of three blankets each
2 mosquito nets
– groceries—tea, flour, catsup, salt, sugar, mayonnaise, white bread, sweet pickles, butter, lard, margarine, baking powder, jam, cigarettes, drymeat
1 pair binoculars
3 plastic one gallon water buckets
1 large axe
1 small axe
1 metal hook for hanging kettles
2 sheet metal frying pans—one big, one small
2 heavy canvas tarps 8 × 10 for covering a conical shelter
4 rawhide bags which can be carried either on the back or used as horse panniers—one contained clothes, one drymeat, and two could be used for bringing in fresh meat
5 long pieces of babiche [rawhide thong]

1 sewing kit—beads, thread, one pair pinking scissors, two pairs ordinary scissors, awl, needles, tanned smoked moosehide, red and blue felt cloth (HBC stroud)
- personal clothing—long stockings, head and neck scarves, long skirts, blouses for the older women—pants and shirts for the younger women—jeans, western shirts and western hats or bill caps for the younger men—western shirts, work pants, suit coats and wool jackets for the older men—moccasins with moccasin rubbers for older men and women—moccasins and rubbers also for the younger men and women—leather riding boots, gum boots
- dish towels, face towels, wash cloths
- hide-working tools—2 scrapers made of truck springs bent into an S shape and filed to a curved edge—flesher made of moose or bear femur—triangular leather-working needle used for frequent touch-up sharpening of scraper
1 Winchester model 94 lever action .30–30 rifle—one British Enfield 303 bolt action rifle with clip—several boxes of shells for each rifle
- assorted bags containing silverware, cosmetics, medicines
5 knives suitable for cutting meat
2 saddle pack tarps 4 × 6 and assorted tarps of various sizes, suitable for covering meat racks and making lean-tos
8 saddle blankets for sitting on as well as for use on horses
4 pack saddles and ropes
6 plywood box panniers
3 riding saddles—assorted bridles, hackamores, and latigo
1 small bundle wrapped in moosehide and hung from a leather thong above where Sam and Jean slept

When we arrived at the place where a seismic road led steeply down from the highway's muddy shoulder, we found Jumbie, Granny, and their stepdaughter Rosie with her family already camped on a steep slope overlooking the Buckinghorse River. They had ridden down with Daryll Street, a white man who lived with Jumbie's stepdaughter Junie Bigfoot. Jumbie had not bothered even to set up a wall tent but had pitched two lean-tos facing one another with a long fire in-between. The lean-tos were made by placing tarps over a frame of poles. The backs and sides were closed in with branches from spruce trees and the floor was covered with fresh, sweet-smelling spruce boughs.

Jumbie and Granny were already warm and comfortable in their bush camp despite the continuing rain. Rosie had made her camp by pitching a conventional wall tent nearby. Within a few hours of our arrival, Sam and Jean and Sally, with our help, had set up Sam's large wall tent and the beautiful tepee that had been made by the oldest living Dunne-za, Anachuan, the wife of the Prophet Charlie Yahey. Sally set up her own smaller wall tent. We continued to use our van as both sleeping place and office. Later, Daryll Street arrived with Junie and her aunt Bella Bigfoot. They set up another tent. By the end of the day, the boys had arrived with their pack train and set up another tent for themselves. Altogether, our little settlement consisted of seven canvas enclosures, several frames used for drying meat, and one VW van. There were about twenty people in our entire camp. The two main centers of the settlement were the camps of Sam and Jean and of Jumbie and Granny. Each of these older couples was joined by their children or stepchildren. The ages represented by this population ranged from less than one to over seventy.

Although the weather continued cold and damp, our fires were well tended, our shelters were secure, and our gear was arranged to provide furnishings against which to recline. Pack boxes, saddles, and saddle blankets were stored at the back and sides of the tepee or in Jumbie's lean-to near the back of the covered area. The fresh spruce boughs and a warm fire made the St. Pierre tepee a comfortable living space in which family members spent most of their time during the day. To an outsider, we might have appeared to be roughing it, but in practice, life in camp settled quickly into an easy combination of order and casual comfort. It was hard to realize that these marvels of comfort and practicality were being set up in the rain-soaked northern forest by people who would have been forced to retire because of their age had they lived in the white man's world.

The decision to move to Buckinghorse had been made for several reasons. First of all, it was known to be an excellent place for moose and caribou. Sam and Jumbie were confident that a steady supply of meat could be obtained from an area no more than a day's horseback ride from camp. Second, Wes Brown, a white man who hired Indians to guide for big game hunters, lived nearby. Sam knew him from having guided for him in the past. Third, there was a large oil rig construction camp, run by the Majestic Construction Company, only a mile or two down the highway. Johnny Chipesia and others had worked there previously. The Majestic camp could provide a supply of cash as well as the occasional case of beer or jug of wine brought in by construction workers looking for a good time. People hoped that by camping at Buckinghorse the families might obtain both sufficient game to lay in supplies of drymeat and hides for the winter and some cash from employment as slashers for Majestic or as guides or wranglers for the outfitter Wes Brown.

Our camps were set on either side of the seismic line that ran from the highway, down across the swift river, and then up and across the top of a hill on the other side. The artificial clearing it made brought light into the space between the St. Pierre and Jumbie camps. The blue plastic detonation wire that could be found along the seismic lines inevitably found its way into camp. People used it as a substitute for *babiche*, or rawhide thong, to tie the frames of lean-tos and meat racks together. This was the real world of 1964. Behind it lay the real world of dreams.

Camp was the center to which we all returned. Camp was the place of our fires. Camp was where women made drymeat. Camp was human and social and comfortable. The people of camp were related to one another. Camp was surrounded by the bush and its animals. On the very day of our arrival, Sam set out on foot to examine the bush around our camp for tracks. He came back late without having seen any animals in the flesh, but he was confident they were there in good numbers. His knowledge came from the signs he read in a language for which I had received no education. Sam's only concern was that the rainy weather would raise the level of water in the river enough to prevent getting packhorses across to bring back the meat.

Sam and Jumbie had both known the open grasslands, spruce forests, muskeg, hills, and cutbanks of the river long before there had been any highway or seismic lines. Their trails still took them to where animals could be found. Unlike the seismic lines, these

Indian trails followed the logic of the local terrain. They were made for local human intelligence, not for that of an engineer or petroleum geologist in Fort St. John, Calgary, or Dallas. Unlike the engineers and geologists, Sam and Jumbie knew this country from their dreams. Behind where each of these hunters slept hung a small bundle wrapped in moosehide. Each bundle compressed inside it the signs of its owner's knowledge and power. I did not know what these bundles meant, but it was obvious they should be respected. I did know enough to refrain from asking questions about them. I did know enough to watch and listen carefully to what people said and did. Their teachings were in their words and actions, not in responses to direct questions.

The camp assembled itself that day as other camps had taken form for thousands of years. Although the axes and guns and canvas and blue dynamite wire were new, the principle of bringing together whatever materials were available represented an ancient intelligence. Our camp was convenient to firewood, water, animals, cash, the highway, and the things that could be gained from the white men. It was convenient to the medicine bundles that hung to the east of where Sam and Jumbie slept.

Our camp was obviously convenient to the bush and to the trails of animals. It was also, but less obviously, convenient to the dreams through which hunters and animals come into contact with one another. During the time I was camped at Buckinghorse, I began to understand that these hunters could project themselves onto the trails that lay ahead of their bodies with as much ease as they could recall this country before the existence of Majestic Construction and its seismic lines. I began to understand their use of dreams in hunting. I was beginning to learn in the Indian way. I was beginning to learn that people would only give me answers to questions they knew I understood. Although I was not obtaining data on N Ach, I was learning to learn in a system of education based on an exchange of mutual understandings. I was learning that in Dunne-za thinking, *how* a person knows something defines his or her humanity more than *what* he or she knows.

The bond between people and animals took these hunters back thousands of years. It took them back to mythic times. The bond between people and animals also took the hunters ahead to the place where they would make physical contact with the animals. In their dreams, hunters experienced the place where their trails came together with those of the animals. The physical touching of the hunt completed a contact that was already held firmly in mind. I understood that the small brown bundles hanging by each hunter's head were somehow connected to this dreaming power.

Jean St. Pierre and Japasa (George Chipesia), 1964

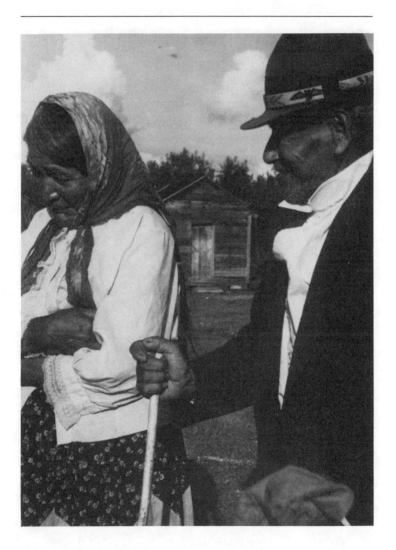

Johnny Chipesia, 1965

Sam St. Pierre, 1966

Sally St. Pierre and her children (from left), Katie, Bobby, and Sandra, 1966

Pow-wow singers (from left) Albert Askoty, David Davis,
Johnny Chipesia, and Jack Acko at Doig, 1966

Sitama (Julie Chipesia), Danny Chipesia, and Johnny Chipesia, 1966

Saweh (Granny Jumbie), on left, and Jean St. Pierre, 1964

Saweh (Granny Jumbie) and Jumbie, 1966

5. NEED FOR ACHIEVEMENT

By August 1964, I had been doing fieldwork as a professional anthropologist for about six weeks. I was learning a good deal about the tricks Indian horses use to squeeze riders against muskeg jack pines, but I was not obtaining much in the way of hard data about need for achievement. I struggled with a conflict I could not even identify or express at the time, even though it affected me deeply. My conflict was the inevitable consequence of trying to learn within two different systems of knowledge. Within the thought-world or "reality set" of academic culture, I had given myself the task of gathering information that would make sense only on later analysis. Within the Dunne-za thoughtworld, information had to make sense to a person's intelligence immediately.

Anthropology conventionally assumes that the language of social science is objective and absolute. The Dunne-za conventionally assume the same about the language of myth. Sam and Jumbie and the people my own age took me out with them in the bush. These situations compelled me to make sense of my experiences. They also compelled me to respect the obvious competence and authority these people displayed. People also began to tell me about the stories to which they reference their lives. I was learning about the achievement motivation of hunting people, but not within the reality set of my academic objectives. My conflict, typical of fieldwork in general, was particularly pronounced in this northern hunting culture.

Work done by the Indians was clearly divided by sex. Men rode into the bush on horseback to hunt or bring back meat. Women regulated the distribution and processing of meat in camp. My own work was ambiguous both to the Indians and in my own mind. I felt I was supposed to be administering thematic apperception tests

(TATs), but what I was coming to enjoy most was riding out into the bush with the men and boys. I had finally learned to ride a horse. The trick was not so much to stay aboard the beast as it was to keep from losing a limb. The wily creature took every opportunity to walk so close to a tree that there was no room for both its body and my leg. I learned to push the entire equestrian assemblage of self and horse to one side, as one tree after another marched up to assault me. Riding through muskeg was even more bizarre, because the weight of the horse bearing down on the ground next to a jack pine would cause the tree to lurch crazily toward me as if in league with the horse. I learned to fend off this standing army of trees by watching the rider in front of me, but I also marvelled that riders like Jumbie and Sam somehow managed to direct their steeds along happier paths than mine by force of mind alone. From time to time, Jumbie would look back at me and burst out laughing.

My greatest equestrian performance came in mountain country far from the highway. We were picking our way through a jumble of blown down and burned out jack pines that came up nearly to the bellies of our steeds. Just as I was congratulating myself and my horse on the delicacy of our maneuvering through this overgrown game of pick-up-sticks, we were suddenly assaulted by a maddened swarm of hornets from a nest in a rotten log that the horse's hoof had inadvertently disturbed. Suddenly, it was rodeo time on that tangled hillside. Horse and I reached for the sky. We touched down only often enough to make another take-off attempt. In the end, we stayed together, horse and I. Throughout our flight, Jumbie was beaming from ear to ear. When we finally settled down to earth, quite a miraculous distance from the scene of our first rise to glory, Jumbie was still convulsing his big belly with laughter. Our performance had been a huge success.

My attempts to administer projective tests were considerably less successful than my performance in the saddle. The tests we gave the kids in school back at the reserve had yielded interesting, sometimes revealing glimpses into the concerns of Dunne-za growing up on a reserve beside the Alaska Highway, but I had little success giving tests to the adults in our camp. Because the kids' tests were given during school hours, the children wrote out their stories for us as a diversion from their usual routine. Their written stories were interesting, but they also revealed a dark side of life on the reserve. The following stories give a flavor of what they wrote:

Boy—age 14

There was lots of grave. one man was bad. he died not long ago. he came out of his box. and walk around the grave yard. later the gose got in his box and he was never seen again. Once there were lots of lazy mens they just lay around outside. they just chew snuff. when they get hungry they just eat with some body. but one day no body feed them. and they start working when they get paid they buy groceries. from there they were not lazy.

Once there was people fighting. with everythink what they get hold of. they were hitting each other and throwing stones at each other. they hit a man with stones. the man got mad and said I will shoot you but his wife hold him and said dont shoot that man. next day thay man thanked his wife. he said if i shot that man i will be in jail right now. the end.

Girl—age 11

the three Man is died in the grass and one boy saw them died he got so scared and he is so sorry for them

the girl want to Merried that Man and but the Man don't want to Merried that girl and the Man look so sad.

grandmother look out of the window that Man look so sad and he hold his had.

the Man is died in his house and he is died in his bed.

the two Man look so poor and so sad the first Man look so sad and poor

that girl is died on the bed the Man saw his wife died on the bed and the Man turn around and he start to cry

Girl—age 13

> that man cried because his wife die they stayed in the dark
> place and the house is dirty theres is a table and one chair
> beside the bed were the girl is laying and the Man put his arms
> across his eyes and he is standing beside his wife the man is
> feeling bad
>
> the boy is feeling bad because he have heard what that old man
> tell him about the long ago and that man feel sad for the long
> ago who are starving and sick.
>
> once there's is an old man praying to the grave yard he was
> bad and stealing and he have lots of sin so he want to be kind
> to the others he pray to all the cross he standing there holding
> his hand together.

Even taking into account the ambiguous and somewhat sinister
nature of the pictures to which the children were asked to respond,
the tests still seemed to reflect the deaths and killings and sadness
and loss that these children knew from their own experiences. Several of the children we tested died violent deaths before they had
finished their teens. In the relatively familiar atmosphere of the
schoolroom, they made up stories that reflected their own experiences of violence and sadness. Perhaps their stories were also prescient of the desperate conditions they would know on an impov-
erished northern Indian reserve in the late 1960s and 1970s. In a
strange way, their stories of death and loss and sadness recapitu-
lated Jumbie's story about the flu of 1918. The difference was that
their stories also reflected fighting and violence, a problem Jumbie
had rarely experienced in his own bush childhood.

Unlike the stories written down for us by the kids in school, the
ones we managed to extort from adults camped out in the bush
were strained and seemed to reveal severely withdrawn, if not virtually autistic, personalities. This did not make any sense at all,
since we knew from our own experience that they were competent,
expressive, and communicative people. Whenever I would bring up
the subject of doing one of the tests, my potential subject would
agree in principle but discover some urgent task that prevented him

or her from complying just at that very moment. Occasionally, someone would respond to my evident anxiety and near obsession with this exercise. They would take pity on me and sit down forlornly to do what had to be done.

Some of my potential victims tried to get out of it by offering to tell me "Indian stories" or suggesting that I ask Jumbie or Johnny Chipesia or John Andree to tell some of the stories they knew. These diversionary tactics did not put me off from my determination to obtain a significant sample of protocols. I did not take them up on their offers. As a result, the sessions that I did bring about revealed far more about my own performance anxiety than about their need for achievement or lack thereof as I desperately tried to elicit responses of more than a few words. The following is an example of what I got from eighteen-year-old Peter Chipesia when I finally managed to hound him into going through the motions as I wished:

Card No.

1. This boy want to play his violin. He can't play it. He don't know how to play it. He looks kinda worried. Can't play his violin. [Why is he sitting there? Why does he have to play it?] He is learning some lesson. Try to learn it, learn how to play it. [What do you think he is feeling?] Feel sad, kinda sad. Yes, kinda sad. [What do you think's going to happen? . . .]

3BM. I think she's crying. [Why? What happened before? What's going to happen?]

4. no response

6BM. no response

10A. A man is trying to jump over that, that pole. Don't know if he gonna jump over or not. [What's going to happen? Does he feel he's going to make it over?] No. [He doesn't think he's going to make it?] No. [Why do you think he was trying to jump over, then?] To show all the people. He's going to show all the people.

16A. Man is fishing. Looks like he got fish. Hard to get

him out of there, you know. [What's going to happen? Is he going to get it out?] He going to get it out somehow but, don't got enough room to stand, you know. Looks like he's going to get the fish out too.

8BM.   Looks like boy is dreaming. He going to kill someone.

17BM.   [Looks like he's climbing on a rope. Is he trying to go up or down?] He's trying to go up. [Does he have far to go?] He got far to go.

Looking back on the results of this exercise, I realize it revealed the unnatural and uncomfortable test situation and elements of my own biography as much as it did Dunne-za personality. Clearly, the people I tested were not fundamentally withdrawn. Rather, they chose to withdraw themselves from an uncomfortable and meaningless situation that they endured only for the sake of maintaining a good relationship with me. My own belief in the authority of an instrument of social science blinded me to the fundamental cultural reality that asking direct probing questions is both meaningless and insulting to the Dunne-za intelligence.

My attempts to administer the tests revealed that the Dunne-za regard storytelling as an important form of communication. Their responses also suggested that a storyteller can act only upon the basis of personal knowledge and understanding. The cards I presented were doubly difficult for people because they showed foreign images that were intentionally ambiguous. They were almost impossible for people to use as the basis of a narrative because they were purposefully removed from any meaningful context. To the Dunne-za way of thinking, you can only tell a story about something you have experienced personally and understand fully. They experience direct questions as insulting intrusions. The only honest response is to remain silent or to walk away from the entire situation. Because some of the cards suggested absolutely nothing, Peter had nothing to say about them. If they did not relate to anything he knew from personal experience, he could not speak about them in any meaningful way.

Peter's lack of response to the test situation contrasted dramatically with the animated and detailed stories of hunting that Jumbie had been telling me and Peter and Billy by the dancing light and shadow of his fire when the day's work was done. Jumbie knew what he was talking about because he had experienced it directly. He knew the animals from his dreamsight, and he knew them from the sight of his eyes. He also knew them in the precise moment of contact framed in his gun sight. Jumbie understood his environment. He understood the animals with whom he shared it. He understood himself. Jumbie was known by all to be a master storyteller, although his style was less flamboyant than the style that earned Johnny Chipesia the name of Wuscide, Johnny Bullshit.

As I continued to go through the motions of collecting stories in the test situation, I was also becoming aware that other stories were part of the ongoing lives of these hunting people. Some of the stories were about recent hunts. Some were about people who lived only in the memory of old people like Jumbie and Sam. Some were about people who had died recently. Some were about the Cree and Dunne-za fighting long ago. Others were about trips to town, being drunk, being in jail, dreams, hard times, good times, old times. The field notes that Tonia and I kept that summer now provide a narrative account of a way of life that has since become memory. Some of the stories we heard were items of news about events in the Chipesia camp and back on the reserve. In particular, we listened for stories about the health of Johnny's father, Old Man Chipesia.

I had first seen Johnny's father in the Fort Nelson hospital on our third day of doing fieldwork at Prophet River. When Johnny arrived at the reserve, he asked if we would drive him up to see his father. At Harvard, I had found a physical anthropology study containing photographs taken of Beaver Indians at Fort St. John in 1929. One of the people in these posed anthropometric photographs was Johnny's father, George Chipesia. His Beaver name was Japasa. Johnny told me the name means "Chickadee," but the word in Beaver commonly refers to a small spruce tree. I am not sure if he was bullshitting, or if the tree stands for the bird in a metaphor that is lost to younger people who did not know the old man. Whatever Japasa means in Beaver, it is clear that the family name, Chipesia, came from the Beaver name of Johnny's father. Most people at

Prophet River referred to him simply as Asah, "grandpa." According to the official government band list, Japasa was born on October 1, 1884. In Frank Beatton's Hudson's Bay Company journal, Japasa is listed as the head of a family during the teens and early twenties. In the picture from 1929, Japasa looked alert and intelligent. He was a small man, dressed in a dark suit coat and a pleated cotton shirt, buttoned at the collar. I could see the stem of a pipe sticking out from his breast pocket. He wore a thick scarf, tied at the back, as a headband. His hair was tousled above the scarf's confinement. He looked to me like a pirate or gypsy.

When I first met Japasa in 1964, he was perched cross-legged on a narrow white hospital bed in the old army hospital at the Fort Nelson airport. He seemed to accept as a matter of course that these strangers should appear there, miraculously bearing an image of his past life and images of people he had known long ago. Because he was old, and sick, and Indian, and non-English-speaking, the hospital staff treated him as if he were a child. Ultimately, they knew he was beyond their help. When the crisis passed, they sent Japasa back to Prophet River. Back at the reserve, he stayed in the bachelor house with Alex Moose. His young wife, Annie, had begun a new family with a much younger man.

Japasa was now a tiny old man who seemed to have shrunk inside clothes that were too big for him. I remember watching as he sat on an old cot in bright sunlight. I could hear bird songs blended with the drone of diesel trucks gearing up and down on the Alaska Highway. He sat there with his work pants rolled up at the bottoms, wearing an old but fancily embroidered cowboy shirt with pearl snaps, a shiny nylon shell jacket that seemed to engulf his frail body, and a broad-brimmed Mountie hat trimmed with a plastic imitation beadwork band. When the sun was hot in the mid-afternoon, he would sleep on the bare bed frame under a mosquito bar and arbor of poplar boughs Johnny had fixed for him. One of his grandchildren would help him into this enclosure. The kids played around where he was sleeping. At night, his youngest daughter, a nine-year-old girl, would sleep with him to keep him company.

Around his neck, Japasa wore a leather thong to which was attached an amulet of some sort. It was wrapped in a small leather pouch. On June 30, when we were back at Prophet River, people had said, "Asah not feeling good." That afternoon, as I was asking Jumbie about the different bands he remembered, Asah came up to us and talked to Jumbie. He did not look well. Jumbie told me, "Yesterday, his heart pretty near stop." Around nine in the evening, the old man had another attack. He was unconscious for about four hours. Johnny put the mosquito bar over his cot, but otherwise people left him alone. Finally, his breathing changed into the gentle rhythm of peaceful sleep.

Now at Buckinghorse, we continued to keep the old man in our minds as we went about our activities in camp and in the bush. On Friday, July 31, I spent a long day on horseback in pouring rain, going out with Sam, Charlie Bigfoot, Billy St. Pierre, and Fred Jumbie to pick up a caribou Charlie had shot the day before. The boys joked about the rain. Billy made up names for the three of us boys. He was Brother Grey Fox, Fred was Brother White Fox, and I was Brother White Man. At the kill site, we found the caribou neatly butchered and lying on boughs in the mossy muskeg. We made a huge fire, dried ourselves somewhat, roasted the succulent kidneys, and cracked the leg bones for marrow, which we poked out with long sticks.

When we finally returned to camp and began to unpack the horses, I heard Rosie's daughter Linda, looking very sad, say something about Asah to Fred Jumbie in Beaver. During the day, the schoolteacher had phoned Wes Brown to tell people in camp that Asah was dying. Jumbie had already left to go back to the reserve. Billy told me sadly, "Well, he's gone to a good place now. No suffering in heaven." Tonia wrote in her notes for that day that Sally cried when she heard about the phone call. Sally said that when Asah came back from the hospital the last time, he told her he had come to say good-bye. "He's dreamed," she told Tonia, "about what's going to happen. Not everybody believe that. That's the Indian way." Bella told Tonia that since Jumbie had not returned, Asah must have passed away. Around midnight, Daryll Street brought everyone back from Prophet River. Tonia asked Rosie if Asah had died. Rosie said to ask Junie. Tonia then asked Junie and Junie told her, "He's OK."

The next day, Bella told Tonia that Asah had been praying for rain at Prophet River. That seemed strange, because during the rains we were having Jumbie had been singing for the weather to improve. Bella said simply that Asah sang for the rain to make him well. The rainy weather continued. On Sunday morning, Jumbie rose at five and began singing and drumming on a two-headed drum he held by a thong in his right hand. He sang steadily until early afternoon, took a two-hour break, and then continued until sundown. He sang steadily and with concentration. He sat in his open lean-to shelter of poles and brush covered with tarps with his knees resting on a fragrant fresh bed of spruce boughs. Between songs, he spoke. People came and went. Jumbie continued to communicate with a presence that was beyond our immediate time and place. He gestured with his hands and directed his voice toward a spot in the air above the fire. His voice seemed to rise with the smoke.

As Jumbie sang into the afternoon, the cloud over our camp thinned. Blue patches of sky began to appear. By mid-afternoon the sky was beginning to clear. In the evening, we enjoyed a fine sunset. Later, we saw stars for the first time in several weeks. Although I did not yet understand just what Jumbie had been doing, I was impressed at the way it all worked out. Everyone in camp was pleased. We all felt strengthened as throughout the day his strong voice and drum kept pace with the change in the weather. While Jumbie was singing, the schoolteacher and Alex Chipesia came down to report that Asah had suffered three more attacks. He wanted to see Sam and Jean. They left with the teacher to see him at Prophet River.

6. THE BOY WHO KNEW FOXES

On Tuesday, August 4, Sam and Jean returned to Buckinghorse with Johnny Chipesia and most of the people who had been staying with Asah at Prophet River. With them, to my surprise, was Asah himself, led by his grandson, Willy Olla. Asah had suffered another attack the night before. The schoolteacher made arrangements to fly him back to the hospital in Fort Nelson, but at the last minute the old man said he wanted to go to Buckinghorse with everyone else. He needed moose meat, wind, stars, his language, and his relatives rather than the narrow white bed on which I had seen him perched cross-legged like a tiny bird. As he had told Sally the week before, Japasa wanted to say good-bye in his own way. He stayed in Jumbie's camp while Willy set up a small wall tent for him. Sam and I hauled a load of wood from behind our camp and I bucked it up for the old man with Billy's power saw. I could hear the gentle rise and fall of Jumbie's voice in song throughout the rainy afternoon.

About 9:30 that evening Dolf Andree came into the tepee and whispered something to Sam and Jean. They left hurriedly. Sally told us that Asah was having another attack. In the silence of that gentle northern evening, we could hear the old man's cries coming from the tent Willy had set up for him. Jean told Sally to stay in the tepee. I asked Sally if she thought people would mind if we went to the old man. She said, "No." At Asah's camp, we found a circle of people gathered around the entrance to his tent. Jumbie, Sam, Bella, Willy, and Asah's young daughter Janice were inside. They held the old man. They rubbed his arms and chest as he struggled and moaned. Among those who watched in silence, women were on the right and men on the left. Bella called for "holy water,"

water gathered as rain ran down the trunk of a spruce tree, to sprinkle on the old man. Later, Sam threw some of it on the fire. Gradually, Asah became quiet and fell into the gentle breathing of sleep. A group of people stayed in a circle around the mouth of the tent, watching silently while men and boys brought in wood for the fire. Sam and Jean and Willy settled in to keep watch over Asah during the night and to keep the fire burning. Charlie Bigfoot returned late from hunting and brought a small bottle of holy water in a paper bag to put under the old man's pillow. Johnny arrived around midnight and joined the vigil. I wrote in my notes that this evening had brought people together in a way I had not seen before. Asah had become the center of our camp and the center of our concerns. Our thoughts and dreams circled around his tent as we slept that night.

The schoolteacher arrived in camp the next morning. I wrote in my notes that she "talked our ears off about how she knew better what to do for Asah than the Indians—how he should be in hospital—general implication that it wasn't proper to camp at all. Why should people camp with their nice houses up there?" She was particularly critical of the people who had held the old man down as he struggled, and she told them so directly. A woman from Prophet River attempted to make peace by explaining that she was afraid he would get so strong no one could hold him down. The teacher did not understand this concern or even listen to it as anything beyond superstition. She obviously thought it ludicrous that anyone should be afraid that a tiny, sick old man could become "too strong." Bella told the teacher directly that it was none of her business if they wanted to hold him down. She said, "It's the Indian way."

Much later, I learned that in Dunne-za understanding, a person who "knows something" would become "too strong" if his power came too close to the surface of everyday reality. That could happen if the events of a person's life became too much like those of the mythic animal or power he or she had encountered in the searing transformation of a childhood vision quest. It could happen when a person's power began to take control of him. Holding Asah down during his attack was a necessary precaution. Hence, Bella insisted that what she did was the "Indian way." A person was particularly in danger of becoming "too strong" if someone else intentionally confronted him with a food or activity that he must avoid because of its central place in the mythic story of his empowering animal or natural force. I also learned that the person who becomes "too strong" is called Wechuge.

Wechuge (pronounced way-chu-gay) is a cannibal monster who hunts and eats members of his own community. His power derives from the power of giant animals that existed in mythic time, before the vision quest of the culture hero Saya. A person experiencing an attack like those Asah was having would have been seen as becoming too strong. I also learned later that Asah had actually become "too strong" on several previous occasions. Once, some people had given him meat with fly eggs in it. The old man had not protested, but not long after he began to sing his song and then to hop up and down, like a human frog on the old bed frame, on which I had seen him perched so quietly earlier that summer. People knew then that he was becoming "too strong." They knew he was becoming Wechuge. Unless another person's power was applied to bring him back to the world of ordinary reality, he would begin to eat his own lips. The flesh would turn to ice within him, and he would become a superhuman cannibal monster, capable of hunting people in the way that people hunt animals. In this case, I was told that people called Johnny, who sang over his father, placed his coat over him, and brought him back into the circle of human relationships. His actions were the same ones that elders take when children return to camp from the isolation of their vision quest experiences.

Despite the schoolteacher's complaints, Asah stayed in camp. He continued to be well and in good spirits. He seemed more at home in the little wall tent Willy had set up for him than he was sitting on the old bed frame at Prophet River. He was at home with his people around him. He was at home near the trails of animals. He was happy to hear the words of his own language, to smell wood smoke, to eat moose meat, and to sit on a bed of fresh spruce boughs. He was happy to know the wind was at his call. At 10:30 in the morning something remarkable happened. I heard excited voices and saw people looking down the seismic line to where it passed over the crest of a hill beyond the river. To my astonishment, a bull moose was walking slowly in plain view across the open space. Never before or since have I seen a moose within sight of a hunting camp. We all stared in disbelief. Charlie Bigfoot started out toward where we had seen the moose. He returned in the evening without having made contact. Later, Bella said that the moose had come to say good-bye to Asah. This moose, she meant to say, would nourish us more as a living presence than with its meat.

As the sun circled down toward the place where it goes beneath the earth, people began to drift toward Asah's camp. During the dark of night, some of them had been dreaming for him. Now the sun had returned full circle, to set "one chicken step" from where it was on the horizon a day before. A bull moose had come within sight of camp. People had watched over the old man throughout the day. The time had come to bring a circle of relatives close around the old man the young people called Asah. Willy went into his grandfather's tent. The rest of us gathered around outside.

Johnny began to tell about how he and his father had survived the terrible flu of 1918–19. Japasa listened quietly to his son's words. Sometimes Johnny spoke in Beaver, sometimes in English for my benefit. Johnny had just turned six in September 1918. His story reminded us of Japasa's importance as a link to the past. He was one of the old-timers who survived. Johnny spoke the names of others who survived. He spoke the names of some who died. His story also reminded us that Japasa was a man who knows something. The Indians, he said, knew about the sickness coming from their Dreamers. This is what Johnny said as I have reconstructed it from notes I made later that evening. I have taken the liberty of integrating my notes of what he said then with a verbatim transcription of another occasion when I wrote down his account of the same events in full. Together, they give Johnny's story of the winter that followed his sixth birthday.

People stay at Cecil Lake.
Then go to Muskeg where Fort St. John is now.
That Prophet, Kayan, came over there.
Jebis [Old Man Davis] too—Asah Montney—
all those big old-timers.
In the morning, that Prophet, medicine man, make new song.
People dance three days. That song, talking song.

"People move to heaven," that song.
After that, start cold.
Everybody went to store at St. John
and took stuff—blankets, everything.
Old Montney went three camps away.
Big Charlie was at Charlie Lake.
My dad, Asah Billike, Jebis, Jari, took me to Spirit River.
We stay winter at prairie this side Hines Creek.
Nobody know flu.
One morning, Old Jebis—funny song he sing.
Charlie Wolf, Dan Wolf, Tanesun, Aske Kwolan, Wolf's sons,
stay with my dad.
Jebis sing in the morning.
What kind of song?
He say,
"Nobody live. Pretty soon, you hear bad story."
He say,
"Every day, you shoot down the road to chase away the flu."
Old Aku knew old people story.
He told my dad, "We got lots ammunition. We go try."
Five nights they do that.
Old Jebis stood outside tepee and talked—
"You lucky, you shoot him."
Pretty soon, Jim Jedeya, Yeklezi boy, and Jack Appaw come.
Lamas, whitepeople from Spirit River, had store. Aku went to
    store with team. I got one weasel.
"What you want?"
"Brown sugar."
Three night he came back with one big sack brown sugar.
Fur good price then.
"You get my sugar, Huana [older brother]? You carry my
    sugar?"
Sundown—we heard people cry—coming from St. John.
Something happen. Jim, everybody coming. "What happen?"
"You see, nobody left."
I cry and dance when I hear that.
Then Fairview people came too.
Nobody left there too—Alex Moose people.

Most people die around Christmas.
One camp, someone shot a skunk in the summer.
They hung it up to protect them.
The white man's cure was rum.
Other camps—Indians try bear paw, other magic,
but it didn't help. Men said their power wasn't enough.
Some camps, everyone but a few kids died.
Old Man Jebis alive.
One camp, he found just two kids in camp, just around stove.
Everyone else dead. Indians and whites too.
He took those kids on sleigh with him.
My dad went to St. John to make grave for Asah Montney.
Six days we travel. I go too. I walk—little snowshoes.
My dad, Charlie Wolf, me, Aske Huane, went.
Some relatives left.
We make grave for Attachie, Big Charlie, Montney.
We got to St. John. Montney's wife, Katige, we met her.
Those people stay there too long.
Harvey's sister, Jack Appaw's wife, other woman, Asah.
We went up to Montney. Put good clothes on him.
He was still in tree. About ten people dead there [they first
placed his body in a tree].
My dad made big spruce box.
Montney had big bag full of silver
and my dad put it in box with him.
Prospectors give him silver. He don't use money at St. John.
He just save it. Atluke and Wolf there too. They helped.
From Charlie Lake, just Charlie Yahey and wife,
Yeklezi daughter, Peter Attachie, Anachuan, and Sitama
[Johnny's wife, Julie].
When we got to Charlie Lake graveyard, they just half
finished.
Some people, ears, nose gone.
Mice put house in lungs.
You take blankets off old people—mice all run.
After we finish, we go back again. We no get flu.
Must be we shoot—that make it OK. We go Spirit River.
Old Jari and seven old people playing cards all dead.

Money all around. My dad take Jari money.
Jari old lady die making wood.
My dad, Thomas Pouce-Coupe work making lots of graves.

Johnny finished telling the story. For a few moments nobody
spoke. We could hear the large fire crackle, feel its heat on our
faces. Firelight had replaced the sun's light as Johnny spoke. Then,
Japasa himself began to speak quietly in his own language. He
spoke as if he were reaching back into a dream to find the words.
The circle of people moved in closer to listen. Johnny came over to
where we were sitting at the edge of the circle. He whispered a
translation of his father's story for our benefit. Although Johnny
must have known that I would not understand the meaning of what
he told me at the time, he also trusted that I would remember and
learn from what he said as I developed a deeper understanding of
the Indian world. It must have been important for him that I share
this event. He wanted me to understand enough of what was going
on to discover its meaning later in my life. This is the essence of
what Japasa told as I wrote it down from notes I made later in the
evening:

My dad said that when he was a boy, about nine years old,
he went into the bush alone.
He was lost from his people. In the night it rained.
He was cold and wet from the rain,
but in the morning he found himself warm and dry.
A pair of silver foxes had come and protected him.
After that, the foxes kept him and looked after him.
He stayed with them and they protected him.
Those foxes had three pups.
The male and female foxes brought food for the pups.
They brought food for my dad too.
They looked after him as if they were all the same.
Those foxes wore clothes like people.
My dad said he could understand their language.
He said they taught him a song.

Japasa began to sing. The song seemed to be part of his story. It
must have been the song the foxes gave him. It must have been one

of his medicine songs. I believe he sang the song to give it away. He did not want to become "too strong." He was prepared to follow his dreams toward Yagatunne, the Trail to Heaven. I did not know, then, that a person could sing his medicine song only when death was near to him or to the listener. I did not know that the song had power to restore life or to take it away. I did not know he was giving up power the foxes gave to him in a time out of time, alone in the bush in the 1890s. The song fell away and Japasa resumed his narrative. Johnny continued to whisper a translation:

My dad said he stayed out in the bush for twenty days.
Ever since that time, foxes have been his friends.
Anytime he wanted to, he could set a trap and get foxes.
When he lived with the foxes that time, he saw rabbits too.
The rabbits were wearing clothes like people.
They were packing things on their backs.
The first night out in the bush
he was cold and wet from the rain.
In the morning he woke up warm and dry.
The wind came to him too.
The wind came to him in the form of a person.
That person said,
"See, you're dry now. I'm your friend."
The wind has been his friend ever since.
He can call the wind. He can call the rain.
He can also make them go away.
One time when I was twelve
I was with my dad and some other people
when we got trapped by a forest fire.
One of our horses got burned and we put the others in a
    creek.
My dad told all the people to look for clouds
even though it hadn't rained for a long time.
They found a little black cloud and my dad called it to help
    us.
In just about ten minutes, there was thunder and lightning
and heavy rain that put out the fire.

We were really wet but we were glad to be saved from that
　　fire.
My dad sang for rain to come a couple of days ago.
He sang for it to come and make him well.
That rain came right away.
This morning he called the wind and rain.
They came to him right away.
Then he told them to go away.
He told them he was too old and didn't need them.
He said it was time to die.
He told the wind and rain they could leave him now.
After he had been in the bush twenty days,
he almost forgot about his people.
Then he remembered them.
The old people must have been dreaming about him.
He heard a song.
He went toward the song.
Every time he got to where the song had been,
it moved farther away.
Every time he followed it, he moved a little farther.
Finally, by following that song
he found his way back to his people.
Sometimes the old people used to take a boy
and put him in a box under the ice.
He would stay there for ten days, maybe even a month.
If he had been a bad boy,
the ice would freeze over and trap him there.
The ice would melt for a good boy.
The old people would put holes in the box.
Fish could swim in and out of the holes.
People could get songs from the fish.
One time they left a boy in the box too long, maybe a month.
When they pulled the box out of the water
there was a big fish inside it.
"Maybe," he said, "that boy turned into a fish."
My dad asked me this morning,
"Why did you sit up all night?

If anything happened to me in the night,
you would know it in the morning.
Then you could put me in a box and throw it in the mud."

Talking about the stories of his father's vision quest experiences
must have made Johnny think about those of his own childhood.
But unlike Asah, who was letting his powers go, Johnny was not
free to tell me about his own empowering experiences directly. He
did tell me, though, that when he was a boy he went out for ten
days in the bush alone. He was tracking a moose to get a song. He
might have caught up with it, he said, but Old Man Davis came out
and found him. That is why he didn't get a song from the moose
then. I think Johnny was telling me that some other time he did get
a song from the moose. A person's animal friend may go away or
even cause harm if he or she talks too openly about the vision quest
experience. Even Johnny Bullshit is bound by this reality. Stories
of the vision quest are secrets that must be told indirectly.

Johnny's thoughts then returned to Asah and to the day's events.
He said that the moose we had seen that morning was trying to
come to Asah. That is why Charlie could not shoot it. Johnny told
me that the moose wanted to come to his dad but there were too
many people around. It came as close as it could for a moment. In
that moment, we were able to see it. In that moment, we were able
to understand its being there as a sign. Then the moose returned to
its trails in the bush. Johnny told me about one of the old-time
Indians who had died in the flu. That man had been friends with
the moose. After he died, moose always came around his grave in
the same way moose came around salt licks in the bush. Their
tracks circled around the grave. They circled around it, making a
single trail like the one that circles a moose lick. They circled
around making the old man's grave into a place like the one from
which he had gotten power many years ago. Still today, there are
always moose around that grave, even though the white men have
made their farms there.

As Japasa finished speaking, I became aware again of the contrast
between cold air at my back and a flush of the fire's radiance on my
face. The air was calm and bright with patches of stars shining
down between the scattered clouds. It was good to be here in Ja-

pasa's world. It was good to be among his relatives. His words were a gift to treasure all my days. Although I had never heard the story of a vision quest before, I knew already that the old man had certain powers. His teaching served to integrate separate bits and pieces of information I was already holding in my mind. His stories made sense in relation to my growing familiarity with the trails and ways of the hunters. They made sense of what I had seen of the animals. They made sense of the bull moose I had seen from camp in the morning. They made sense of the special relationship I knew Japasa had with the wind and rain. That night our camp slept in peace. Japasa remained well. I am sure the dreams that came to people that night gave them strength. In the morning, people told me they had seen the tracks of foxes all around Japasa's camp. The foxes, too, had come to say good-bye.

7. NEW MOCCASINS

The next morning was beautiful. Scattered to broken high cumulus clouds drifted shadows back and forth across the landscape. Whenever the sun shone directly on my face, its heat reminded me of the evening's fire. It reminded me of the old man's stories, already dreamlike and multifaceted in my memory. Most of the men went hunting, each in a different direction. About 5:30, Johnny Chipesia came back. He had shot an old bull moose across from Mason Creek. Charlie Bigfoot came back around 7:30. He'd seen a bull moose and shot twice but missed. Shortly after that, Jumbie came back reporting having shot a yearling and a two-year-old bull. One of his moose had stuck in the mud and he was unable to skin it without help. He went off immediately with three of the boys to help him pull it out and skin it. Shortly after they left, Sam returned, his skin panniers bulging with meat from a moose he had killed. Granny Jumbie came over to Jean's camp and picked up a rib piece. Jean took some of the backstrap over to Liza and Rosie. By the end of the day, our camp was full of meat. It was the best day the hunters had enjoyed since coming to Buckinghorse. The old man's stories must have given direction to their dreaming the night before.

Johnny came over to Sam and Jean's camp while I was watching the distribution of meat. Sam and Johnny have always maintained a friendly rivalry. I could tell they loved one another for their differences. Their different ways of living were one another's stories. Sam prided himself on being silent rather than speaking about something he did not know from his own experience. Johnny continually polished his reputation as a talented bullshitter. This evening he could not resist putting it on in his best style for my benefit. "Indians," Johnny said, "can read tracks in the bush just like white men can read the words of a newspaper." What he said was true, of course, and Johnny was recognized as a talented hunter. As Johnny went on and on elaborating the story, Sam remained completely silent. I thought back to another of Johnny's stories, this one about his wager with a white hunter who offered to pay him five dollars to demonstrate the Indian moose-calling technique. According to Johnny, he walked across to the other side of the Alaska Highway, took a few steps into the bush, and called out loudly in English, "Here moose, moose, moose!" Then he walked back and collected his five dollars. My mind returned to the present story about reading tracks. Johnny finally came to what he considered a good stopping place. Then Sam spoke. He said simply, "Why didn't your paper tell you that moose too old?" Johnny beat a hasty retreat and Sam got in a few more digs. "Don't believe him. He bullshit. Maybe not kill moose. He always say how many moose, beaver, he shoot. Always bullshit." Thus the day ended as beautifully as it had begun.

The life of a hunting camp continued. Everyone was busy during the next few days bringing in the meat, making drymeat, and fleshing the hides. Whitepeople went by on the Alaska Highway in a constant stream of vehicles, plumed in dust or caked in mud, depending on the weather. As Peter told me later, Japasa said that the ghosts of Indian people who die in car accidents mistake the highway for Yagatunne, the Trail to Heaven. He said that people who step into vehicles of the white men step out of their tracks. They step out of the trails that root them in the country to which they belong. It is hard for someone who dies on the highway to find the place where he or she could begin to walk back along the trail of a life on earth. "Even them turnout roads," Japasa told Peter. "They travel on that and when they get to the end, they turn back and go on this highway all the time. They think it's the road to heaven."

Army engineers had pushed the highway through Dunne-za territory about twenty years before. The event was still fresh in people's memories. Indian families camped in the bush, hundreds of miles from the nearest road, had suddenly found themselves confronted by huge snarling D-6 Cats pushing down the trees. Someone told me a story about a woman who encountered one of the clattering monsters when she was out in the bush by herself. She ran back to her people yelling, "Usa ka kwudge!" ("There's a kettle walking this way!"). Bulldozers were "kettles walking" to her in the same way that Indian blazes had been the work of Italian boy scout vandals to me. The metaphor of her language suggested the clank and clamor of kettles, propelling themselves on self-made trails through the bush.

By Sunday, August 9, Sam was ready to hunt again. The drymeat racks were full and the meat was nearly dried. The weather remained clear and sunny. Asah was healthy and he was also very happy. He was with his people and his people were doing well in their hunting. Sam returned about 5 : 30 with fresh meat in his saddlebags. He had shot a cow that had recently lost its calf. The next day, Monday, August 10, he planned to get up early and take three or four packhorses out to pick up the meat. I wrote a long description of the trip in my field notes for that day:

—August 10, 1964—

Sam got the horses about 8 : 30 am and began to get ready to go out and pick up the kill of yesterday. He was quiet but angry again at the boys who were asleep. He whipped the horses for no good reason and generally acted bad tempered. When he'd put pack saddles on three horses he went over to the boys' tent where Peter and Billy and Michael were sleeping and violently shouted at them to get up, threw things around the tent, obviously mad and disgusted at them.

Jumbie saddled up Red, and Peter got up and went to breakfast at Julie's. Later, Billy finally got up after a proper amount of passive resistance and went into the tepee for breakfast. Toni said they were discussing whether I was going, in the tepee, so I finally asked Sam if I could go. He said, "Saddle up Pat." I had never been taught how to tie a saddle cinch so I had to ask Sam to do it. He did it and answered angrily that he only has to see something once to get it and expected me to pick up by watching. I guess my going meant that Billy wouldn't, so Sam, Peter, Jumbie, and I and three packhorses set out at a very fast clip at 9 : 30.

We went up Grassy Creek toward the first ridge you can see from the road. Sam really set a fast pace, galloping on the flats, trotting on open trail, and walking fast on brushy trail. On the way, they spotted a moose, which they pointed out to me but I never saw it. Up the creek the trail cuts up high on a side hill and the country opens up into very wide meadows and willow swamp for several miles. It's lovely country and also perfect moose range. After two and a half hours we came to Wes Brown's 10 Mile cabin. I guess the trail goes on up to Redfern Lake. The kill was just behind the cabin. Sam said he'd tracked it quite a long way. On the way back last night he'd made it in two hours flat, impressively fast.

The kill was gutted and skinned and quartered as usual. A carcass is never left intact. The skin is usually laid out flat with the hair up. The head is removed and moss is stuffed in the mouth. The kit a hunter takes with him consists of a knife and file wrapped in a cloth, a can with a wire bail for tea, and a cup, tea, bannock, drymeat, sometimes a meat axe. All this is put in a shoulder bag of canvas about the size of a shopping bag and tied behind the saddle. It's carried on the shoulder, hunting.

I guess Sam hadn't taken an axe yesterday since the ribs and backbone were intact. First thing we did was make three fires to drive the flies away. Then we unpacked the horses and finished butchering. The ribs were cut off with the axe, and the backbone cut into three pieces. The legs were broken off and later cracked, and Sam and Jumbie ate the marrow raw for lunch. Sam told Peter and me to cook something and we spitted the kidneys, cutting them in half. Jumbie spitted a piece of tripe and esophagus. He also got water for tea. Sam seemed impatient about Peter and me not getting the meat ready soon enough for lunch but when we finally settled down to eat he got in a much better mood, made jokes, and talked. There had been very little talking before. We ate bannock, kidneys, marrow, tripe, and a piece of cooked drymeat Sam had brought, drank lots of tea, and had a pleasant and leisurely meal.

Butchering took about a half hour, and lunch took an hour. Then we put the meat in the skin panniers and packed the horses. Once, Peter tied a pannier rope too long and Sam told him so and tied it for him. We set off at 2 : 30 but Jumbie went out on the flat to hunt. Although we stopped once to repack one horse, we were back by 4 : 30. Billy and Sally helped unload the panniers and put the meat on a bed of spruce boughs. Before leaving the kill, Sam completely covered the remains with boughs, and Jumbie got water to douse the fire. I asked why the remains are always covered but Sam gave a noncommittal answer about how it has to be like that.

Back in camp, Jean distributed the meat. She first carefully looked over what there was, made passes over it with her knife, and then divided the ribs into several pieces and cut off pieces of meat from the pelvis and back. Women wandered down and were given meat by Jean. Julie got a haunch, the heart, and the udder. When Sam came back the night before, he sent the tenderloin to Asah. Julie also took three ribs and some "steak." Granny got three ribs, a haunch. Rosie got ribs and a haunch. Liza took ribs and miscellaneous meat.

As far as I could tell today, Jean didn't tell anyone to come for meat, but all the adult women walked by and were given some. Julie, Rosie, Liza, Granny, Dolf, and even Bella came. Although we don't know what was said as Jean divided the meat, it looked as though she thought it out beforehand and then asked the women if that was all right. Everyone sort of picked over the meat and recut some. Sam sat back and drank tea as he watched the distribution. It was a moment of peace, pleasure, and relaxation.

Around 5:30 there was a disturbance around Asah's tent. It felt as if a strong wind were sweeping across the entire camp. It was a wind of alarm, of emotion, of change. I saw people flying toward Asah's fire like wind-blown leaves. Their words seemed to be swept away like cries in a storm. In a moment, most of the people in camp were heaped and drifted against the entrance to the old man's tent. My fatigue and saddle sores from the day's ride vanished as I joined the wave of people. When I fetched up alongside the tent, Bella and Jean were already inside rubbing the old man's arms and chest. Asah was limp and unconscious. A thin line of saliva fell from his mouth. This attack was not like the struggle we had seen before. Someone ran to get Sam, who had just left to see Wes Brown. Peter came over, and Billy and Liza. Breath from deep inside the old man's body forced its way up past slackened throat muscles in a hollow rattle I shall never forget. By the time Sam came there was no sign of breath at all, but he and Bella kept massaging him. After a few minutes Sam got up and said, "He's finished." There was no pulse. His face had relaxed into the unmistakable mask of death.

A stillness came over us, then a gentle rain of tears. For a few minutes we sat and watched in silence. I thought to myself how near and how far a moment's edge divides one time of life from another. In this case, the moments on either side of Japasa's last breath divided different eras in the life of an entire culture. I could hear Bella, Rosie, and Julie Chipesia crying. For a few minutes more, the rest of us sat and watched. In those few moments of repose, each of us turned toward the inner spark of self that lives and dies. When our minds finally accepted that this would be the last attack, Bella and Billy pulled back the tent so that Japasa lay out in the open. It seemed important that Asah should be where the winds could touch his body from heaven. Then Bella and Billy, with help from Rosie and Julie and Liza, picked him up on the mattress and turned him around 180 degrees. They pulled the tent back farther to make a sort of backdrop. Jean got a mosquito bar and covered him with it.

The women brought out the clean set of clothes he had been keeping to be buried in. Bella and Rosie washed their hands. Then Bella washed the old man's face. Liza told me to help Billy change his underclothes. Bella cut off his shirt with scissors. We put on new long underwear after taking off his pants and underwear under the blankets. Someone brought the bottle of holy water, yellow liquid in a square plain glass bottle wrapped in a paper bag. Liza threw it into the bush. Some of his personal effects, a cup and a spoon, were also thrown away.

Julie took his old clothes away after we got them off. She was crying hardest, partly because he had asked to see Mary Jean, who was at the reserve. She took ten dollars from his wallet and gave it to Daryll to go get Johnny. Alex Moose arrived and helped Billy wash his feet and put on a pair of Sam's new socks. Finally, we placed a new pair of moccasins on his feet. Asah had been saving them to be buried in. He wanted to look his best as he began to travel Yagatunne, the Trail to Heaven. These moccasins, which he had brought with him, were special. They had been made by Mary

Tachie, a young woman who had died in an accident the year before. They were beaded with an unusual design of triangles that circled around the upper panel and pointed inward toward a common center. New western-style pants and an old-fashioned white shirt without a collar completed his dress. His mattress was moved back against the end of the tent, a clean sheet laid on it, and the mosquito bar replaced. Liza brought a rosary and they put it on his wrist. They put on his belt. Sam, who'd been away during the dressing, asked what they'd put on him. When they told him what they had done, he was satisfied.

In an hour all these arrangements were completed. The activity had given us something to do while the fact of Japasa's death became real to us. When the laying out was completed, people sat down and watched over him, women on the right and men on the left, after the fashion of their seating during Mass in the little mission church at the edge of the reserve. Johnny Chipesia, George, and Willy arrived unexpectedly shortly after he'd been laid out. Johnny had come down to visit after work and didn't know Asah was dead. He was told, looked under the mosquito bar at his father, and began to cry, stroking the old man's hair. Then he walked away to cry by himself. We went with Sam and Jean to the tepee for supper. Then Sam said he'd go over and keep Johnny company. Later we went over and joined the watch, which lasted all night. People spoke softly. There were also long moments when the only sound was the fire, the river, a gentle breeze, and the distant rumble of trucks on the highway.

As our night vigil moved to the dawn of another day, I thought about the moccasins the boy who knew foxes would be wearing on the Trail to Heaven. They were among the last works of Mary Tachie, who had died at an age Japasa would have been during the flu that killed so many of his people. She would be there to meet him. After her death, Japasa dreamed of the song she followed to heaven. Now she would be sending a song down for him to follow. I remembered the story of Japasa's return to camp from his vision quest:

He almost forgot about his people.
Then he remembered them.

The old people must have been dreaming about him.
He heard a song.
He went toward the song.
Every time he got to where the song had been,
it moved farther away.
Every time he followed it, he moved a little farther.
Finally, by following that song,
he found his way back to his people.

Japasa would be following Yagatunne, a trail of song linking heaven and earth. He would be wearing Mary Tachie's beautiful beaded moccasins. He would be following her song and the songs of all the people who used to come together in the place the old people call Where Happiness Dwells.

8. MYTH AND HISTORY

After Japasa died, the tests seemed less important to me. I cared less about data relevant to the language of personality theory and more about data relevant to understanding the stories the old man had made known to me before I heard the rattle of breath leave his body forever. In the years that have passed since I heard Japasa give away his songs, I have never again been so close to a death as to hear medicine songs or to see a person's animal friends close about camp. I have, however, listened to a wealth of Indian stories. I have heard stories of other vision quests. I have continued to follow the stories of Indian lives. I have listened to the songs and oratory of the Dreamer Charlie Yahey. I have even come to be regarded as an old-timer by young people for whom the elders I knew live only in their names and in the stories of their lives. I have studied Indian stories, dreamed them, told them, taught them, and made them my own.

Stories are windows into the thoughtworld of Indian people. Their time is different from ours. The old man and the boy circle around to touch one another, just as the hunter circles around to touch his game. They circle one another as the sun circles around to touch a different place on the horizon with each passing day. During the year, it circles from northern to southern points of rising and setting. It circles like the grouse in their mating dance. It circles like the swans who fly south to a land of flowing water when winter takes the northern forest in its teeth of ice. The sun circles like the mind of a Dreamer whose body lies pressed to earth, head to the east, in anticipation of another day's return. The sun and the Dreamer's mind shine on one another.

On the evening when Japasa's animal friends circled around his fire, he gave the circle of his relatives two stories. One story was about how Indian people from far and wide used to gather on their lands at Montney Prairie. They came to that place to dry saskatoon berries. They sang and danced and gambled the nights away playing the hand game. They talked and listened and integrated the stories of their separate lives into a connected pattern of meaningful trails. Japasa's other story was about animals with whom he had lived as if they were people. Foxes wore clothes and brought him food. He could understand their language. They taught him a song. He knew fish. The rain was also his friend. Later, Johnny and Peter told me Japasa knew frogs who play gamble just like people. He lived with them on the bottom of a lake.

The old man's stories recalled times we would think of as being very different from one another. One we would call history, the other myth. Written documents going back as far as the late eighteenth century describe Beaver Indians coming together in the Peace River prairie country to sing, dance, and gamble. We can use the traditions of historical scholarship to substantiate that what Japasa described really happened. We know that Indians continued to meet every summer at Where Happiness Dwells until they lost their land in the years following World War II. Even after that loss they continued to meet during stampede time.

There is no documentary or scientific evidence to indicate that frogs really sing and dance and gamble beneath the waters of a pond, but the old man said he experienced this, too. There is no documentary evidence of foxes who live like people. Because we lack documentary evidence, we are compelled to class his second story as myth. In our thoughtworld, myth and reality are opposites. Unless we can find some way to understand the reality of mythic thinking, we remain prisoners of our own language, our own thoughtworld. We will be forever mistaking Indians for Italian boy scout vandals from Passaic. The language of Western social science assumes an object world independent of individual experience. The language of Indian stories assumes that objectivity can *only* be approached through experience. A hunter encounters his game first in a dream, then in physical reality. In the Indian thoughtworld, stories about talking animals and stories about the summer gathering are equally true because both describe personal experience. Their truths are complementary.

Both of Japasa's stories were true to his experience. When he was a boy, Japasa knew frogs and foxes and wind. He knew their songs. He entered the myths that are told about them. He made elements of these stories talismans of his own life's story. He obtained power by joining his life force to theirs. He knew them in the bush away from the society of other humans. He knew them in the searing transformation of his vision quest. He became their child, one of their kind. He saw them clothed in a culture like his own. He carried them through to the end of his life, and then he let them go. Their tracks circled around his fire in the summer of 1964. They circled around him in a time that our history can identify, but their real time was a circle back to the mythic time when he first experienced them as a child alone in the bush. Japasa knew the social power created by his people when they came together in good times. He knew the power of animal friends. At the time of his death, both forms of power were strong all around him. Hunters were making contact with their game. Women passed the meat from camp to camp, making the people strong together. The rain had come and then gone away.

Historical events happen once and are gone forever. Mythic events return like the swans each spring. The events of history are particular to their time and place. They cannot be experienced directly by people of different times and places. Mythic events are different. They are true in a way that is essential and eternal. In mythic time a person can be a frog or a fox and still be a person. In mythic time a person can follow a trail of song to another country. In mythic time a child can be led toward the place where knowledge and power will come to him or her naturally. The foxes that came to Japasa before he died were the same as the foxes he knew as a boy. The wind came to him as a person. The foxes wore clothes and spoke in a language he could understand. The frogs gathered to sing and dance and play gamble. They gave this boy their songs as guides to the powers he would have as a man. Throughout his life he returned in his dreams to that visionary "time out of time." His powers were forces within him as well as forces of nature. His experience was always within nature. Even in times of hardship he did not move against it. At the end of his life, people and animals came together around him. When he died he returned to mythic time like the swans who fly south in the fall. As long as mythic time remains, we can expect his return.

For northern hunting people, knowledge and power are one. To be in possession of knowledge is more important than to be in possession of an artifact. Their technology depends upon artifice rather than artifact. As Sam told me in his gruff way, "If I see something once, I know it." Northern hunters live by knowing how to integrate their own activities with those of the sentient beings around them. The most effective technology for them is one that can be carried around in their minds. The Indian stories they wanted to tell me were elements of their technology, not merely fanciful tales. Hunting people are able to create a way of life by applying knowledge to local resources. Their stories and their dreaming provide access to a wealth of information. Their vision quests integrate the qualities of autonomy and community that are necessary for successful adaptation to the northern forest environment.

I first came to Dunne-za country thinking that blazes on trees were the work of Italian boy scout vandals. Later I returned, having been told to impose the ideas and instruments of academic social science on the Dunne-za thoughtworld. During the course of living with Sam and Jumbie in the summer of 1964, I struggled against the Indian teaching with which they surrounded me. Then Japasa opened his world to me. He opened it to me and then he let it go. I could not help but fall into the language of that world. I had no choice but to accept the validity of dreams and talking animals as part of the world's fundamental core of meaning. Although I retain, and continue to honor, methods of scientific inquiry and the traditions by which scholars validate their sources of information, I have used these methods and traditions to inform a different anthropological language from the one I was taught in graduate school. I know as a responsible academic that I cannot dream *up* another culture that does not exist, but I also know that in order to understand the Dunne-za thoughtworld I must be willing to dream *into* it. Japasa taught by telling me stories. Sam taught by showing me silently what he knew. Johnny fed me, both from his country and from his creative imagination.

Our own traditions strongly stress obedience to duly constituted authority. This authority may be intellectual as well as social and political. Anthropology must be careful that its own traditions and assumptions are not merely Italian boy scout vandals in disguise. Japasa's traditions stress the empowering authority of individual knowledge and experience. His northern forest world gave him experiences that nurtured his knowledge and gave him power. When I heard Japasa speak in 1964 about his medicine animals, I knew with absolute certainty that he was neither lying nor deluding himself. It was I who indulged in self-delusion when I persisted in asking for data in a form that could not accommodate Dunne-za reality. I hope that the trust he placed in me has been justified in some small measure by the work I have chosen to do in my life. *Trail to Heaven* is an attempt to find words that do justice to Dunne-za reality as I have come to know it.

PART TWO

SWAN PEOPLE

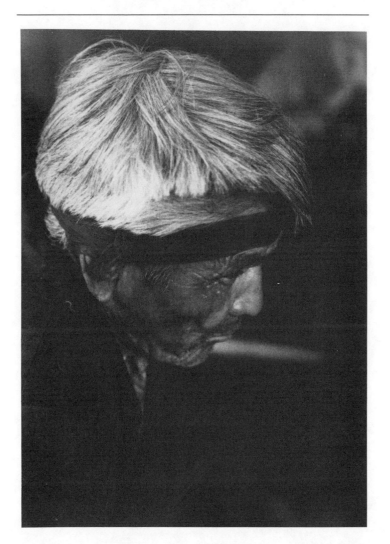

Overleaf: Charlie Yahey, 1968

9. LEARNING
ABOUT LEARNING

Individual Dunne-za have always followed the intelligence of their
dreaming in making contact with spirits of the animals that give
them life. To be human, to be Dunne-za, is to "little bit know something." There have also been people in Dunne-za communities
called Naachin, or "Dreamers." In English, the Dunne-za call these
people Prophets. Prophet River is named for Decutla the Dreamer,
who painted his dream of the Trail to Heaven on a moosehide that
Jumbie kept and showed to people on special occasions. As Charlie
Yahey, the Dreamer whose practice I knew best, explained to
me, "A person who is Prophet doesn't just dream for himself. He
dreams for everybody."

Dreamers are people who have experienced the Trail to Heaven
in person. They have known the experience of dying and going to
heaven. Unlike ordinary people, who die once and do not return
to the same body, Dreamers leave their bodies, grab hold of a song
that carries them toward heaven, and then return to earth on the
trail of that same song. When I knew him, Charlie Yahey had been
a Dreamer for many years. In 1965 he was the only Prophet remaining from the group that had dreamed ahead for the North
Peace Dunne-za since the time of the 1918 flu epidemic. The only
other Dreamer then alive was Amma (Emma Skookum), a very old
woman from Halfway who had become a Prophet only recently.
Toward the end of his life, George Chipesia also became a Dreamer.
He dreamed the song that Mary Tachie followed on the Trail to
Heaven. During the last summer of his life, he came back to life
following one of his attacks. He came back to life and then he
let it go.

The Prophet tradition, as many people described it to me, began with a Dreamer named Makenunatane, also called the Sikanni Chief. Stories about this man tell that he dreamed ahead to predict the coming of the white men. The stories say that he began his prophetic career as a leader of communal hunts just before the white men came to Dunne-za country. His ability to "dream ahead for everybody" allowed him to visualize the pattern of a perfect communal surround of an animal, during the last days in which the technique was practiced, before the introduction of firearms. He could tell people where every one of them should be, in relation both to one another and to the game. Even today in Dunne-za philosophy, the animals will give themselves to people only when people are generous in giving to one another. The Dreamer's oratory elaborates upon this fundamental metaphor. It reiterates that there must be social accord before people can be in accord with the animals that give them life. The animals will not give themselves to people unless people are equally willing to accept that human life depends on people giving to one another.

Makenunatane's name is really more like a title. It means literally "His Tracks, Earth, Trail." The name suggests that his tracks circle around the edge of the world to complete a circle. People describe Makenunatane as being like the culture hero Saya, whose trail circles the sky rim like the sun. He and all the Dreamers are also like swans, in that both swans and Dreamers can fly through to heaven without dying. The stories describe them as "swan people" in their ability to migrate between the seasons and stages that make the circle of a person's life. Makenunatane is also associated with the power represented in stories about the life of Jesus, the white man's "culture hero."

The power that Dreamers have to "dream ahead for everybody" gives them a particularly close connection to the fundamental stories of creation. One of these stories, the Dunne-za version of a nearly universal "earth diver motif," describes how the creator sent Muskrat down to the bottom of a primordial body of water to bring up a speck of dirt that became the world. Muskrat's plunge "to the bottom of things" parallels the flights that swans make to the place where the spirits of people and animals continue to exist beyond the sky. The plunge of Muskrat and the flight of swans represent two extensions of a Dreamer's power and personality. In anthropological terms, these make up the vertical axis of a shamanic cosmology. The Dreamer's journey is a shamanic flight through the appearances of ordinary reality. The Dreamer flies to a realm of meaning at the "center of the universe."

10. WORDS OF THE DREAMERS

Charlie Yahey

In the summer of 1965, Tonia and I returned to Prophet River for an entire year of fieldwork. In July, we drove with Sam and Jean and Jumbie and Granny down to Blueberry to visit the Dreamer Charlie Yahey. We had met him at the Fort St. John Stampede the previous summer and I remembered him from 1959. Beyond those casual contacts, I did not yet understand much of what it meant to be a Dreamer. On July 29, 1965, I recorded the words he spoke to the old people from Prophet River. Although I did not understand much of his oratory at the time, younger people later translated the tapes into English for me. Much of the Dreamer's oratory referred to information that he and his audience understood in common. The first thing he said was that Japasa had made it through to heaven. The people in heaven had sent down the song the old man had followed. Charlie Yahey had grabbed hold of it in his dreams. His words to us were simple and direct:

> One person die when I was a kid [probably a reference to his own initiatory experience of death and return].
> Old Chipesia got to heaven.

Charlie Yahey then sang the song that Japasa had followed on his journey along the Trail to Heaven. He sang the song that Japasa had followed, wearing Mary Tachie's new moccasins that Billy and I had placed on his feet. Charlie sang Japasa's song just as Japasa, before he died, had grabbed hold of the song that Mary Tachie followed to heaven. When Sam told me what the Dreamer was saying,

I was very happy. Charlie then went on to talk about the power
Japasa got from his vision quest with frogs:

Just like that—somebody going to play gamble in heaven.
Even somebody sing—he doesn't want to come near to it.
Who's going to win for us, I wonder?

Charlie sang another song. Jumbie, Granny, Sam, and Jean must
have been thinking about their old friend, play gambling with his
friends the frogs up in heaven. Charlie continued:

Like us. Like you.
You should sing until your head is like mine.
What's that? Something's gone. Just one left.
All those animals—even those say that.
They're singing. I'm not afraid.
Even people don't sing every afternoon.
Everybody takes the white man's way.
If everybody picks up the white man's way
they are not going to be alive any longer.
Long ways to heaven.

Charlie then spoke about the hard winter and the responsibility
of people to sing and dance to bring about the turn of the seasons:

This last winter was a hard time. I prayed and sang.
Nobody helped me. Now you people must help me,
for we must get warm weather.
In the middle of the winter
we will have a hard time with the cold weather
and we should sing that we must not get it.
It's going to be hard time.
Somebody hurrying with me.

Charlie also spoke to the people at Blueberry who were listening
to his words. He repeated his message that people should listen to
the Dreamers' songs. He reminded them that the Dreamer returns
from heaven to where his or her body is resting on earth in order
to dream ahead for everybody:

You people are poor for me. You people are poor for me.
I just take another chance to stay alive in this world.

That's why you see me
but now you don't believe what I say to you.
This song is supposed to be really kicking.
It sounds like white man's music on the record player.
White man's music isn't going to do anything for you.
It won't help you to get to heaven.
This kind of music—when you hear it, it's hard to make it.
Somebody really prays to God—it's not going to be hard.
Somebody gets stuck getting up, sing, sing.
They think there's no Prophet. Lots are going too far.

Like Japasa before him, Charlie Yahey talked about the confusion the Alaska Highway causes the ghosts of people looking for the Trail to Heaven:

Some people get lost and then die.
This highway fooled many dead people.
They thought it was the road to heaven.
They walk and walk and walk and get nowhere.
They've got lots of bills in heaven.
Something in heaven. Just you have a few bills.
If somebody hit lots of drums it would be nice.
Even if they didn't sing and just hit the drum.
If you sing—everybody will be happy in heaven.

Charlie paused in his oratory and sang one of the Dreamers' songs. Then he resumed his talking to explain that this song expresses the Dreamer's knowledge of the power that comes from Jesus. He reminded them that the tradition begun by Makenunatane derives its power both from Saya and from Jesus:

"When God's Son Came Down," that's the name of that song.
When God's son comes down—lots of good people will be
    saved
and the bad people will be left behind and they will cry a lot.
If somebody sings a song—even dancing—
there may be lots of people but don't be shy.
Somebody is like that. We'll be happy again.
If you die you're going to see your way to heaven.
By himself he will. If he dreams about heaven

he's going to tell somebody about it.
He will be happy about it. He's going to try
to go to heaven if he dreams about it.

Charlie also warned that people who do not sing the Dreamers'
songs and think of heaven "will be thrown away" to the fire:

We don't know.
One person—long ways from here is singing.
Just like they all move to heaven just by singing.
That's some of them will be thrown away.
If that person, those people are poor for you,
you must do something for them.
They're just ready to go to hell—
but I will try to help them.
I try my best to save them from hell.
I come back from the bush, I wash myself,
I pick up the drum. That's what a Prophet is like.
Maybe he's going to get through
when I pick up my drum and sing.
In my mind I'm going to do what the boss does.
One Prophet—that's his song.
It's sure really cold. Two guys both side cold.

Then the old man threw out a word of praise for a grandson who
gets up in the morning and makes a fire in his home:

Jimmy Appaw's boy—when the daylight's coming up,
when we ask him to make fire he gets up and makes fire.
They start to make fire. That's where he is just right.

Next, his thoughts turned to a description of how Dreamers actually follow the Trail to Heaven. The motion is smooth like a boat
going through water. The Dreamer's spirit moves along "just like
he dancing." Charlie continued:

Something like a boat. I just got into it
and it started to run with me—a person.
I thought that was the boss man.
Just like it stayed on the water—just like moving.
Just like going on the water. It goes straight across.

Sometimes it's just like he dancing.
I say that lots of times. It's going to get warm.
Just like really warm coming.
It's going to be warm a little longer.
This is a horse song.
That horse has a big mouth to say that.
They started to dance. Lots of horses burned.

Charlie finished his oratory with a reference to 1950, when a group of people and their horses died in a forest fire. He may also have been referring to a time when Japasa followed the song of an injured horse that prayed to heaven for relief.

Charlie Yahey and Amma

In the summer of 1966, I recorded the two remaining Dreamers as they talked to people at Halfway and also in conversation with one another. At Jumbie's suggestion, Tonia and I had driven down to Halfway with him and Granny to visit their relatives there. Louis Wolf and his wife, Liza, came too, because they wanted to visit Louis's brother Shorty and Liza's sister Jeannie. Once we were all settled in, people began telling us that Chikenizhia, Charlie Yahey's daughter who had married an Achla at Halfway, was "sure lonely to see her daddy." After a few days in which to let the idea of a visit from the Dreamer settle into people's minds, I set out with one of Chikenizhia's sons to fetch the old man and his wife, Anachuan. Anachuan means "Daughter's Child." The old woman's mother must have been called Ana. Anachuan's father was old Chief Attachie. Even as a very old woman she was very beautiful and a powerful presence.

Something strange and interesting happened on our drive back to Halfway. To relieve the monotony of a hot and dusty drive, I tuned the radio to CKNL in Fort St. John. To my great surprise, the young man who had been happily listening to the usual country and western fare on the drive over to Blueberry quietly reached over and turned the radio off. I asked him why. All he would say was "Old man don't like that kind music." I knew better than to ask further questions. I suspected that, in time, I would discover the answer during the normal course of events.

The episode reminded me of an event I had observed earlier when a local white settler dropped in to visit Jumbie and Granny in the camp they had set up near the Halfway River. Jumbie was sitting in stately repose by his fire at the center of a conical canvas-covered shelter that served as a living room for the wall tent in which he and Granny slept. The white woman wanted to take Jumbie's picture with a flash camera. A crowd of younger people filled the tent, enjoying the sense of occasion the visit provided. As soon as the white woman brought out her camera, several of them told her gently but firmly the same thing Charlie's grandson was telling me about the radio: "Old man don't like that kind." She did not understand that the young people were very serious. She proceeded to aim the camera.

Suddenly, Jumbie did something utterly remarkable. As if in a samurai movie, he leaped from his position of repose beside the fire, flew into the back of the wall tent, and disappeared beneath his bedroll. One moment he was there—the next he had vanished. The white woman could not believe her eyes. She stood there for a moment, camera still in hand. Then she turned and muttered something about "Indian superstition—how can a grown man be afraid of a little thing like a flash?" I knew she had misinterpreted the situation, even though I was not sure of the explanation myself. I was certain, though, that Jumbie's disappearing act demonstrated his power, not his weakness. I suspected that I would find clues in Indian stories.

A day or two after the old people had made their camps and visited their relatives, Charlie Yahey, Anachuan, Jumbie, and Granny gathered together in a tepee with Mrs. Skookum. Amma had become a Dreamer several years before after recovering from a serious illness and regaining partial vision following a long period of blindness. She was very old. According to the official band list, she was born on April 7, 1873, a year before Anachuan and seven years before Charlie Yahey. She and Charlie Yahey began to talk about what it means to be a Dreamer. Amma began the conversation:

I'm dreaming about people waiting at the gate to heaven.
The people in heaven are waiting
for their relatives to come to heaven.
They are crying for their relatives to come to heaven.

Everybody in heaven sings that song
waiting for their relatives.
That's the gate to heaven song.

Like Charlie Yahey in an "audience" I had with him two years later, Mrs. Skookum recognized the value of our tape recorder as an instrument for communicating with people in other communities and in other times, even though she did not particularly like using the medium:

I don't like to sing for the tape recorder but I do [she sings].
I don't like to sing for the tape recorder
but I dream that song.
It's not lying. That's true—that's right.
I dream of heaven and somebody told me,
"You people should play drums and sing
so you won't have any trouble with meat this summer.
Sing and drum and you will kill lots of moose this summer."
The guy I dream about told me to get everyone together
and sing for the moose but there's just one person here [she
    means Jumbie].

Amma then turned from the topic of dreaming ahead to help people in hunting to the more personal and emotional topic of her role as a guide for lost spirits trying to find the Trail to Heaven. She sang a song the people in heaven gave her:

I feel like crying when I sing that song.
Ruby, his song. [A young man from Halfway, Ruby Wokeley,
    froze to death the previous winter.]
That's Ruby's song.
The people in heaven sing that to put him to dance in heaven.
All his life he didn't dance when he was on the earth
so he had to dance as soon as he got to heaven.
That's the first time he dance.
That's the song he dance to.
Heaven is really nice, really pretty.

When you die, your ghost must walk in the great shadow of darkness back along the trail you made on earth. The shadow must walk at night until it gets to the place where it is light enough to rise toward heaven. The ghost is dangerous. It will try to separate a good person's shadow from his or her body and follow it up to heaven. It will startle children and try to follow them up the Trail to Heaven. When you die with unresolved conflicts and bad deeds holding your shadow down to the tracks of your past life, your ghost is particularly dangerous. While you are alive you may shorten the dark danger of your shadow trail only by dancing to the songs of the Dreamers. When you dance with your relatives on a common trail that circles the fire that rises with smoke to the highest place, your shadow trail is shortened, as are those of all the others. When your feet follow the turns of the Dreamers' songs, your tracks merge with those of your relatives as your mind begins to follow the Trail to Heaven, Yagatunne.

Amma began another song. Her voice was husky, growly, and very deep. She sang unaccompanied. Women do not play the drum. Her song came to an end and she paused for a moment. Then she sang another song. When it was over, she spoke to the kids who were crowded around listening to the old people. "Yagewut-dunne," she declaimed. "Heaven people." Then she sang a special song. She explained it to the people who were listening. She explained that it was Japasa's song:

That's the song from Old Man Chipesia's going to heaven.
When he got to heaven this is the song he sang.
He was really happy.
He went with his first wife. He was chasing girls.
I dream that when he went to heaven [she sings].
That's all I know.
I going to quit.

Amma rested for a while. Then she began another song. When the last resounding thunder of its final phrase subsided, she mused, as if talking to herself, "I can't think of what to sing." Then a song came to her mind and she delivered it. When it was finished, she finally referred to the experience through which she became a Dreamer:

That's my own song. About two years ago I just about died.
They—one of my husbands in heaven—
told me to sing that song. I got better.

That's Nachan's [John Notseta's] song.
I dreamed of him. He is worrying about his kids [he said].
"I only have one here [Julie].
There's lots of my kids on earth. What's the matter?"
He wants his kids to go with him.

Later, as Liza Wolf, Nachan's daughter, translated Amma's words she commented wryly, "If he loves us, why doesn't he stay with us?" Amma continued:

I dream lots of times about different things
but the people at Halfway don't believe me.
When I sing Ruby's song I said people should dance.
People should sing that song and dance.
But nobody sings that song.
Here I'm the only one who sings in Halfway.
The people just think that's bullshit.
When Ruby died I dreamed about him.
He was drunk when he died and he couldn't get to heaven.
"Help me," he said. And I did. I sang that song.
That's why he went to heaven.
He said, "I'm drunk. I can't see.
I can't get to heaven. Help me."
He talked to me. He told me,
"If I get to heaven I'll take you with me."
I said, "No. I can't go to heaven with you.
I'm not ready to go yet. I'm too poor."
He said, "If you help me, you'll go to heaven."
When he got to heaven he told me,
"Nobody at Halfway believe you."
I was dreaming about that.

The memory of Ruby seemed to tire the old woman. Then she turned to Shorty Wolf and spoke sharply to him, reminding us all of her seniority. It was not an angry remark. Rather, it served to bring us back to the present moment: "Why you let Bob beat up Harry Jackson the other night when they were drunk?" Shorty replied matter of factly, "We tried to get him to go to bed but he wouldn't." Amma then returned to the story of becoming a Dreamer:

First time I start dreaming was a few years ago.
It was May. It was cold and snowy and summer wasn't
   coming.
I dreamed about my two husbands
and they gave me that song to sing.
I sang it and after a week my throat was sore.
Aballi and Bob took over singing. It turned warm then.
I feel bad about Harry
because I raise him since he was a baby.

The old lady sang another song and returned to the oratory to
which she had warmed. Her message was simple and straight-
forward. People who are together with one another in singing and
dancing to the Dreamers' songs will find themselves together with
the spirits of the animals. They will be the ones who encounter the
animals in their dreams:

Whichever reserve plays the drum
they're going to win all the moose for winter.
If 232 [Prophet River] people play all the time, they'll get all
   the moose.
If Halfway people play they'll win.
But nobody plays here.
I'm not a boy. I can't play.
I'm the only one who sings.
People who don't sing can't get any moose.
I sing well early in the morning.
I already sang this morning. I can't sing good now.
I dreamed about that. It's really true. I'm not lying.

Amma then turned to Charlie Yahey, as if seeing him sitting next
to her for the first time. Her term of address once again reminded
us of her seniority, but this time the person to whom she referred
was not Shorty Wolf but the Dreamer himself. Her next words then
indicated that she had finished speaking. Charlie was at liberty to
follow her with his own words:

"Ashitle [younger brother]. I didn't see you sitting there.
If you heard me, why didn't you sing my songs along with me?
I'm hungry now. I'm going to quit.

Charlie Yahey took up the oratory she had turned over to him in response to her last remark. He reminded us all that the two of them are probably the last of the Dreamers. He reminded us that he and Amma are ending the tradition begun by Makenunatane. He spoke slowly in a strong voice and for a long time:

I can sing but I can't sing very good.
When I sing two, three songs my wind gets weak.
My head's not right. I can't sing much.
I thought that we were going to sing at Halfway—
that's why I came here, but everywhere it's just the same.
Only the old people can sing.
I'm the only one who can sing.
At Doig, Halfway, Blueberry. Everywhere it's the same.
The young fellows won't help. They think they're white men.
The young people don't believe me. They go to school
and the school teaches those bad children bad business.
The schoolteachers do that.
The young people don't believe me.
When I'm singing they don't come to help.
The only time they come to me is after they've been drinking.
One week, two weeks, and they go a little crazy.
Then they come to me and say,
"Help me. Fix me up."
I'm not going to do much about people like that.

His words reminded young and old alike that they will find the Trail to Heaven only when they reach the place where their spirit is light enough to rise on a trail of song:

There's no ladder into the sky.
The ghosts have to make it on their own.
There's a road to the sky—Yagatunne.
You've got to be good to make it.
It used to be that people who dreamed about heaven
put water and feathers on the people's heads
so they could go straight to heaven—
just the way the priests baptize.
Now people don't believe us anymore so we don't do that.

No use to talk sense to people like that.
From now on if a woman who is going to have a baby
doesn't think of God every night when she is pregnant
she is going to have a hard time when the baby is born.
If the woman and her husband too—he can help her—
think about God and pray then the baby will be born right.
It used to be
that everyone believed the ones who dreamed to heaven.
Now the young people don't believe.
No use calling them back because they won't believe.
All the people who have died already—
they are the ones who believe.
Ever since they made new houses
people think they are white men.
This money and drinking—it's a bad business.
You don't have to hate me for saying that.
Some Indians steal lots of money from each other.
That's why I say that.

Charlie's oratory then turned toward his everyday life. He referred to the fact that his son John Charlie (John Yahey) had been unable to come to Halfway with him:

My son wants to sing in Halfway
but he doesn't have any way to get here
or anyone to look after his children.
I feel sorry for these people.

Charlie reminded people that we had come to Blueberry the previous winter in order to support his efforts to make the weather turn better. As Jumbie had been trying to tell me, it was important for him and Sam to be with the Dreamer that winter so that the circle of seasons could continue. The Dreamer reminded us that unless people sing and pray, one winter will follow another directly:

They came all the way to Blueberry in the middle of winter
when it was very cold to see me.
I sang for a long time—two weeks—
but it was still cold.

Then I sang for another week
and the weather got a little bit up.
I told the people it was going to be cold like that
if they didn't sing. It's their own fault.
Nobody sang and so it was cold.
I dreamed about heaven—
how there were going to be two winters—
but I sang and sang. That's why it didn't happen.
But they will make it happen again
if you don't believe me.
Sometime they will make two winters in a row.
All the animals will have calves in spring
and they will freeze.
Nothing will grow and the white men will starve.
He won't grow vegetables if this whole world freezes up.
One person above the heaven looks down on us.
Everything people do he marks down—
the good things, the bad things.
If a person does too much bad things—
drinking, stealing, lying all the time—
that person doesn't belong in heaven.

Charlie turned again to Amma, reminding her of the husbands
who send their songs down to her here on earth:

Amma, when you were young you had too many husbands.
That's why you dream about your husbands.
Your husbands are trying to help you come up.
You are good to people, kind to people.
You give things to poor people
but you had too many boyfriends.
That's why you haven't gone to heaven yet.
Some people think nobody knows what they do,
but nothing is hidden.
God knows everything that happens on earth.
There are lots of people who have their name in heaven
but there are some people who don't have a name there.
It's too bad for them.
They should sing like me and try to go to heaven.

That's the way it goes. That's why I say that.
I'm not lying.

Finally, the old man paused in his speaking. He paused and he began to sing a song. He sang one of the songs that will help a person's shadow make it through to heaven. Then he said:

All over the world nobody hides from me,
the sender of the song.
God stays above heaven.
If people in Heaven want to see him
they look with binoculars but you can't see him good.
It's sure bright, shiny, fancy.
The people who go to heaven—
he has them stay below him.
He sits in a chair like a big king.
Lots of people who dream to heaven—they don't see God.
They just see the people who are working for God.
Not many see God.
Some people are just like a straight spruce tree—
a spruce tree that grows straight.
Some people go straight to heaven.
The gate is open and they go right through.
Some people are like a crooked spruce tree
that twists around.
When they get to heaven the gate is closed.
They won't let them through and then they cry.
Some people don't go the straight way.
They lie, steal, and do all kinds of bad things.
Even though I dream about heaven
I worry about whether I'll go to heaven.
That's why I dance even though I'm old.
I do that because I want to go to heaven.
Sometimes when people are singing I dance.
Just like we feed dogs, just like white men feed chickens,
that's how God feeds us moose.
That's why we have to keep singing and dancing
so he will give us the moose.
If we don't it will be hard to get moose.

You will miss them or they will run away
or it will be hard to see any.

The Dreamer's experience, Charlie Yahey said, is a transformation of a person's normal life on earth. A day on this earth is measured by the sun's passage from horizon to horizon. A day in heaven is measured by the sun's entire yearly circle of "chicken steps" from its most northerly point of rising and setting at the summer solstice to the most southerly point at the winter solstice. A year in heaven is referred to as one day. Each day the Dreamer is away from his body on earth his mind experiences a year in the life of the people in heaven:

In heaven one year is just like one day.
Three years is like three days.
They told me they won't shake hands with me for one day
because I drink too much.
Sometimes I drink when I sing. That's no good.
You people here don't believe me.
You're too crazy. You don't keep what I say.

Charlie paused again to sing. It was a song of the Dreamer Maketchueson, who followed Makenunatane. Charlie explained:

Maketchueson—he's boss for the north part.
He is in charge of sending out songs—dreams—to people.
People in this country don't believe the songs,
so he take charge of the north country.
He sends songs to the Dreamer at Hay Lake.
People are better there.

Heaven, according to Charlie Yahey, is like Where Happiness Dwells. It is a place where people come together and greet their relatives they have not seen for an entire year:

In heaven people live in tents and camps
just like on this world—really beautiful tents.
When somebody dies and goes to heaven
everyone comes out of their tents
to see whose relative it is—if it is their relative.
The person says where he comes from

and who his mother and father and any relatives are
and the people are really glad to see him.
It's just like when I come visiting over here
and everyone comes and asks what's been happening
and how you got there. It's just the same in heaven.
They ask, "How you go here?" They say,
"It's so hard. How is the world?"
They ask how their relatives are.
That's the way it is in heaven.
"Where's my mother? Where's my father?"
people in heaven ask. If the newcomer says,
"He died a long time ago. She died a long time ago,"
the people cry.
They know darn well they went to the other place.
Just like in this world you ask,
"Where's my brother? Where's my sister?"
and when you say, "They died," you've got to cry.
This is the people crying in heaven.

Charlie began another song. When it was over, he reminded
people that they must dance if they want to find the Trail to
Heaven. "Dancing on earth is easy," he said. "Getting to heaven is
hard." Singing and dancing are ways of clearing the path your
shadow must take when you die:

It costs you nothing to dance.
It costs you lots to go to heaven,
so you better start singing and dancing.
The world is just sticks and dirt
but heaven is really fun, really nice,
so you better start singing and dancing.
Sometimes lots of people don't sing.
Something strange is going on in the reserve
and people don't sing.
There are some people who have bad luck.
A bear eats them up, they drown in the water,
they lose their wife, they go hungry for a little while,
or they don't get many beaver.
Those are the people who don't come to dances.

That teaches them not to think about God.
A person who sings and doesn't drink too much,
doesn't get mad all the time, and prays—
that person has good luck.
They get moose.
They don't have a hard time.
Akula. That's enough.

11. AN AUDIENCE
WITH THE DREAMER

By 1968, I had recorded many hours of Charlie Yahey's Dreamers' songs and oratory. Many of the pow-wows in which he spoke took place because I was willing to drive Charlie and Anachuan from Blueberry to Doig or Halfway. We spent much of our time during the summer of 1968 at Doig River, where we felt very much at home with the easy style of joking and plays on words that seems to be the style there. I developed new friends among people my own age, particularly Tommy Attachie, Mackenzie Ben, Gerry Attachie, and Dick and Margaret Davis. Among the older people, Tonia and I and our one-year-old boy, whom Sam named Aballi, were especially befriended by Jack Acko, old man Aku's fifty-two-year-old son, and his wife, Eskama. They made us feel at home in the same way Sam and Jean had at Prophet River.

During one of Charlie's visits to Doig, I asked if he would be willing to grant a formal "audience," in which I could ask him questions about his Dreamer's knowledge. I had come to the realization that how you come to know something is as important as what you know. I wanted the Dreamer to know that I had learned by dancing in pow-wows during the past two years. I also wanted to know more about how he learned. Thus it was that on August 14, 1968, Tonia and I found ourselves asking Charlie Yahey questions that revealed to him something of what we had already learned and something of how we had made our discoveries. The questions also let him know what we were interested in learning about his own way of knowing. The audience took place in the house of Jack and Eskama at Doig River. The old man had agreed to respond to any questions I might have about his knowledge and practice. For two years I had played a part in the creation of pow-wows by providing transportation, since in the mid-1960's no one had a vehicle or driver's license. Now it was time to reveal more of myself to him by asking him to reveal what it really feels like to be a Dreamer. Charlie Yahey took the occasion of this audience to tell us that our presence among the Dunne-za had come to the attention of the people in heaven. By telling us this he meant to say that we had the same obligation to dance to the Dreamers' songs as anyone else. It was important that we dance; should we die suddenly and become dangerous ghosts we would be forced to walk back along the tracks we had left among the people.

The old Dreamer knew we would not immediately understand much of what he was saying as we listened among a crowd of people at Jack and Eskama's. He also knew that after he was gone we and the Dunne-za children, for whom the name of Charlie Yahey will be as legendary as that of Makenunatane was in his own time, will come to study and learn from what he was saying to us. He knew there would soon be children who would never meet a Dreamer. He knew that our job was to carry his words from one world to another. Charlie Yahey chose this day to speak to us, and through us, to the children he would know only in dreams. He chose to speak through the white man's medium of a Uher 4000 Report L five-inch reel-to-reel tape recorder wired into a red and white Nine Lives Hot Shot six-volt fence battery. He chose to record his words so that both we and the children might return to them as we grow in our understanding of his world. He appreciated the Uher as a medium and also as a metaphor. Tommy Attachie put his words into English for us:

> Just like this kind of tape recording
> you can hear the song.
> That is how they grab it.
> They wake up with that song.
> When they wake up with it in the morning they won't lose it.
> They just sing the song that way—how it turns
> and other people who come in there will sing with it.
> From there that is how come there are lots of songs all over.
> Some other guys will come and straighten up that song.
> They will come in and sing it after the Dreamer
> and from there make a dance.

The Dreamer, I knew, is able to leave his body on earth and fly like a swan along a trail of song that is Yagatunne, the Trail to Heaven. Even here at Doig I had seen him go into one of the old houses while people sat quietly on the grass in a circle keeping watch. For several hours we waited quietly and kept the space around where he was dreaming clear of disturbing noises of kids and dogs and people on horseback. When he came out of the house the old man began to sing and speak to the people. It might have seemed, to an outsider, that he was just an old Indian taking an afternoon nap, but to the people keeping watch, the hours he slept were actually weeks or months of travel within sight of heaven. Dreamers are people who can fly through to heaven and return to their bodies on earth. The people kept watch over him because they wanted to give him a center to which he could return.

There have been other Dreamers before Charlie Yahey and Amma. There are many Dreamers in heaven and few on earth. There are few on earth, but the songs of those who have gone before remain. Their dreams continue to resound in the buzz of quilled snares against drum heads, in the resonance of voices quivering against these same taut, fire-tuned circles of hide, and in the names that are called as the songs echo in widening circles from hot sparks and the breath of smoke that centers the dancing of many tracks along a common trail. The names are in my mind as Jumbie and Sam and Aku and Charlie Yahey have repeated them to me—Oker, Aske Kwolan, Lilly, Decutla, Nachan, Oldman, Kayan, Atsukwa, Maketchueson, and finally Makenunatane, the Sikanni Chief, who was the first Dreamer to know ahead that the white men were coming. The songs carry the names of these Dreamers because each one of them "packed" a particular song down from heaven. The songs carry their names, but they are also the prayers of the animals. Charlie told us about the songs the animals sing. He began the audience by responding to my question about the power of a game master found at the center of a moose lick. He called it "the boss for all the moose:"

The people who lived a long time ago
all knew about how the world was first made.
Under the springs there is a great big moose,

a giant moose.
That is why all the moose on this world
stay near those places.
Before Saya made everything right on this world
there were giant moose on this world too,
but he sent them down to the world beneath this one.
Where he sent them down there are now springs
coming up from that world still.
The moose like it there
because they know the giant moose are underneath.
There is just like a house under there.
Small moose stay under there too in that house.
In wintertime they will come out from the spring or lick.
Even if there is thick ice and frozen dirt
they will break through the crust, go a little ways,
shake themselves, and all the dirt will come off.
These moose are regular size
but they have just a single set of horns like a cow,
just small ones with a single point.
They shake themselves until all the dirt is gone
and they rub themselves against the trees.
The boss for all the moose
stays under the spring in the other land.
God made it like that.
God made everything good for the world
until the end of the world.

Charlie's answer to my question indicated that he wanted to tell me more about the stories of creation. He must have known that my next questions would be about the creation story itself:

Some springs are for the moose and others are no good.
God didn't make those ones—some bad ones.
Not all the springs are good ones.
Sometimes all the moose will go to one spring.
That is his spring there.
Some other places seem like good springs
but moose seldom go there.

Those ones are different springs.
Those are bad ones.
That is what the old people said. I heard that.

Charlie paused in his explanation. Then he decided to tell us about the way people used to tell stories. He was speaking to us, but he was also speaking through us. He talked about a history his audience would not know from experience. He was speaking through us to as yet unborn children who would never know him in person. The document we were creating would *be* their experience of his teaching:

You asked me to tell you the stories about the moose springs.
It used to be that all the old people would sit
together in one place—make some tea—
and one man would begin telling a story.
Then another would tell one, and another,
and so on like that.
They would keep on telling one after another
sometimes for five or ten days.
When they would tell the stories
the people would have to behave
and just hear the story really good. I listened really well.
When the old people died
the younger ones would take all their stories
and pass them on.
That is why they had to listen and get them just right.
Some people didn't behave themselves
and would forget everything.
That is what all the old-timers said.
That is how I got these stories.

Charlie turned to the subject of naming the months, the different moons. Each moon is named for something in the yearly cycle that happens during that time of the year. The moons of spring are named for the succession of animals that come back to life during their time. March is eagle-come-back time, April is geese-come-back time, and May is frog-come-back time. There are stories that celebrate each of these returns:

A long time ago there were just five months—five moons.
There used to be only five moons
but they put in two more to make seven.
All the things the old-timers said
I put them all in my pocket and I know them.
Just like I put them in here and look after them.
I used to hear lots of old-timers' stories in the
place where I came from.
Huane [his older brother, Aku] is a little older than me
and knows lots of old-timers' stories too.
He and I both know the stories.
I was way younger than him but I know all the stories.
I tell all these young boys and even the grown-ups
to behave themselves.
That is why I talk really hard.
Some old-timers would think that is none of my business.
Why should I care?
They wouldn't tell the boys about these stories.
They are going to behave themselves.
I still know the things I heard
when these old-timers were still alive.
Since then I know it.
I don't even understand how to read and write
but I just use my mind.
I talk really hard so that people will behave themselves.
But some old people do not
because they think it is not their business.
If I knew how to write and talk English
even a smart guy won't be able to beat me.
I am telling about how the moose come to the moose spring
because this man wants to know.
He wants to know how those moose come out.

Later, as I was going over the tape of my audience with Tommy
Attachie to put the Dreamer's words into English, Tommy added
his own comment about the "boss for all the moose." It was not
until the geese-come-back moon of 1982 that Tommy told me
more directly about his own vision quest at the moose lick and

about the power he and old man John Davis both obtained from that place. In 1968, he was able to tell me what he knew only indirectly, in the form of a story. He expected me to figure out what the story meant to him:

Even in cold time those moose under the ground are
    lonesome.
They don't like it there and get tired of it.
Even if it is frozen over with ice they just break through.
They just lay down and then shake themselves.
They rub themselves on trees too.
Sometimes seven or eight moose go with them.
They are white with red eyes or some of them are just blue
when they come out. Just like blue horses.
Some of them just really blue, some of them white,
and some of them pure yellow.
That's what he said. I hear him in there.
They just have two little spike horns like cow horns.

The audience continued. I asked Charlie to tell me more about how the Dreamers get songs. I had already learned bits and pieces of information about what it means to be a Dreamer, but I wanted to hear how Charlie Yahey himself would explain his dreaming. He replied:

They just go up.
They just sleep and they get those songs.
They go up there in dream.
They haul them down and come back.
Then they get up.

Charlie Yahey explained that a Dreamer's experience is like that of the animals. He said that the Dreamers' songs are also the songs that animals use in their prayers when they are having hard times. I knew that Japasa had followed the song of a horse in his dreams. Charlie Yahey explained that the Dreamer can grab hold of an animal's song and fly toward heaven:

All the animals pray to God too, when they have hard luck.
When they start to starve they have lots of songs too.
Not only us pray to God.

The Dreamer is a person who knows the Trail to Heaven. He knows it from his experience. He knows it because he has been there. He knows it as a song. He knows its turns. He knows how it is connected to the footfalls of his own heartbeat, drumming far away. He knows the earth to which he will return. He knows the place from which his relatives are calling him. Charlie explained how a Dreamer "grabs" a song and wakes up with it. His answers made me realize that how you come to know something is as important as what you know:

Just like right now when we sing
it is just like we knew that song before.
Then he starts to sing.
That is how he gets it.
They just grab it up there
and they wake up with that song.
They just start to sing it right then.
They know how it turns—
how the song turns up and down.

A Dreamer can follow the songs of any animal as it prays to heaven, but he is particularly like the swans who can fly from one season to another. Swans, like Dreamers, can "go right through the sky to heaven without dying." The Dreamer is also like Saya, the first hunter, whose power began near the beginning of time when a boy named Swan received the first gift of power from his namesake. The Dreamer follows in the tracks of Makenunatane, the chief named Swan who dreamed the hunt plan of a perfect surround and who later dreamed of Jesus. The Dreamer is a hunter who uses his power to dream ahead for everybody. He is a guide on Yagatunne, the Trail to Heaven. Charlie continued to explain the connection between Dreamers and swans:

Even swans, when they have hard luck in the fall time
and start to starve, they can just go right through the sky
to heaven without dying.
Swans are the only big animals that God made
that can go to heaven without dying.
Swans are hard to get for food.
They go right through the sky.

Charlie Yahey explained that people in heaven feel sorry for their relatives on earth. They are lonely for them. If their relatives are suffering or are having a hard time, they send down songs for them. If a person is good, if her spirit is light, it will be easy to grab hold of the song and follow its turns. It will be easy to follow Yagatunne. Sometimes it is very hard. That is when a person needs the help of a Dreamer's song. If she has danced to the songs, it will be easier for her to grab hold of it when the time comes:

Sometimes they grab the song in heaven
but it is like something covers it up.
They get up and try to sing it
but they get lost.
They take it away again.
Sometimes when a person goes to heaven
and gets really tired so he can hardly walk
they send a song down.
They send it down to that person walking
and the song hits him.
From there he sings the song really hard.
He sings it with a long voice
and after that he does not feel tired
and feels nothing going over those bad places in the road.
He just keeps going.

Swans are the only animals that fly through to heaven without dying. Dreamers are the only people who can fly in their dreams, like swans, to another world. Dreamers can leave their bodies on earth and follow Yagatunne with a long voice, a strong mind. Dreamers are people who know Swan, the boss of everything that moves with the seasons. Charlie Yahey explained the connection between swans and Dreamers:

Saya wanted big groups of swans in heaven so there would
be lots up there.
That is why there are only a few that he kept on earth.
Most of them are up in heaven—only a few down here.

There are many Dreamers in heaven and only a few down here. They are sending their songs to the people who remain. They are sending their songs to the Swan People who grab hold of them in dreams. Charlie summarized what he had been telling me:

That is how a medicine man
who is still alive here
gets that person in dream.
He takes that song in his dream.
The medicine man hears in his dream
the song that woman or man is singing.
The next morning he dreams
about how that person has started walking
and singing that song.

The Dreamers fly between heaven and earth, like the swans who fly to a land where water is flowing when winter is taking the northern lakes and streams in its teeth of ice. People on earth see the swans flying south. They know that swans must have warm weather in order to stay alive. When swans return to Dunne-za country following the northern winter, people know that a summerland exists somewhere to the south. Swans are the proof of it. When Dreamers return from their journey to heaven with songs, people know that their relatives are alive in a land where the spirit continues somewhere beyond the sky. Dreamers' songs are the proof of it. Charlie explained how swans pray to heaven:

In fall time the swans always go late.
When they have a hard time in fall
they pray to God in their own way
and go to heaven without dying.
When it starts to get warm in the spring
and all the chickens begin to lay eggs
and grow up into big ones, even if people kill lots
there will still be lots of them.
But there only a few swans.
Only when the swans have a really hard time from the cold
they go up to heaven.
When the rabbits eat the bark from the trees
until there is very little left for them to eat,
they disappear.

Then when the trees start to grow again
they begin to come back and there are lots of them.
Chickens do that too.
They go away when there is not enough food
and come back when the food returns.
They stay somewhere south.

Amma (Mrs. Skookum), 1966

From left: Aku, Charlie Yahey, and Anachuan, 1968

Anachuan and Charlie Yahey, 1968

Charlie Yahey, 1968

Charlie Yahey and the Dreamer's drum, 1966

Anachuan and Charlie Yahey, 1968

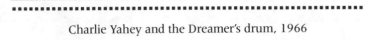

Charlie Yahey and the Dreamer's drum, 1966

Summer camp scene, Halfway River, 1966

12. CREATION

When the Dreamer came to a pause in his narrative, I asked him to tell me the story of how the world was made. I already knew the outline of a story about how Muskrat brought up the earth beneath his nails, but I wanted to hear how Charlie Yahey would tell it in his own words. He replied as if he had read my mind:

I guess you heard that story before
but you want to hear it twice to see which one is better.
He made this world and at first there were no animals.
There was just water and no land.
Then he started to make the land.
He finished all the land.
Finally this world started to move,
started to grow and kept growing.
That is what the old people said.
Just the water and no land.
There were no animals.
Where are they going to stay with no land?
Only God stayed someplace where he made it for himself.
Maybe boat or just water.
No land.

Charlie Yahey began to tell me about an essential idea of Dunne-za thought. It is an idea I already knew from being with hunters who make contact with animals following their dreams. It is an idea I knew from the stories Japasa told me about his vision quest. It is an idea that underlies everything Charlie had been saying about the Dreamer's power to dream ahead for everybody. It is an idea that has centered the thought and experience of Indian people for thousands of years. In Indian thinking, the *idea* of something is essential to its manifestation in physical time and space. The hunt must take place in dreaming before it can be realized on earth. The Dreamer must bring back the idea of a song before he can return to his body on earth. The world itself must be grown from an idea in the mind of the creator. The world is an expression of song at the very center of things.

> There was just water
> and God made a big cross that he floated up on the water.
> He floated the cross on the water.
> He floated that cross on the water
> and then he called all the animals that stay in the water.
> He sent them down to get the dirt but they just came out.
> They couldn't get it. Too far down.
> The last one was rats [Muskrat].
> He sent him down to get the dirt
> and he stayed down for how long.
> Finally he just brought up a little dirt.
> He put that little piece of dirt on the cross and told it,
> "You are going to grow."
> From there it started to grow and kept on growing
> every year like that.
> Finally it was getting bigger and pretty soon it was big.
> That is what the old people say.

The old people say the world begins with an idea. It begins with an image of the center. It begins with a cross drawn upon the water. The drawing on Charlie Yahey's drum is a model of that idea. It is a model of creation. It shows a cross at the center of a circle. It shows lines like sunbeams slanting toward heaven's arc of sky. The point of contact between hunter and game is also a model of creation. A hunter brings meat into camp only after he has dreamed a point of intersection between his trail and that of an animal. The hunt is sacramental. It is an act of creation. A hunter brings the world of animals into camp. Like Muskrat, he brings substance from the place where two trails come together. Charlie continued with the story of creation:

Then he made a dog for himself, his own dog.
He said to that dog,
"You go around to see how big that world is.
Then you come back here."
He started off—that dog—to go around the world
circling around the edge of the water
and when he came back he had a person's bone in his mouth.

The dog he created is like a wolf who knows the world's trails. It circles around to measure the growing world's sufficiency. In the Dunne-za story, God's first dog returns with a human bone in his mouth. The animal's act is a message for the creator. It tells him that the growing world is not a complete circle. It is not self-sufficient. In the finished world, a person who gives away generously is given to by the animals. In the finished world, taking an animal's life is an act of creation:

Some of the animals on the land people couldn't eat
and he just sent them down under the earth.
Those animals that people cannot live from
he sent them down.
The second time he made a wolf.
He made him out of a dog.
He made his dog first and then he threw that dog away
after it came back with a person's bone.
He didn't like that so he got rid of him and got the wolf.
You know some animals he made, they do wrong.
Even that woman he do wrong.
He stole the berries.
So animals he made that do wrong he got rid of them.
The devil took them.
Even us—we do wrong he gets rid of us.
He made us but he gets rid of us.
We go the other way.
That is what starts to happen.

My first reaction to this part of the story bordered on consternation and despair. My notion of "pure" Indian tradition did not include a reference to the woman from Genesis who "stole the berries." In time, I came to understand that an essential feature of the Prophet tradition begun by Makenunatane was to take stories that appeared to empower the white men and make them part of Dunne-za knowledge. Thus, Jesus and "the woman who stole berries" were both important to Charlie Yahey's story of creation. The Dreamer continued his story of Wolf:

That wolf started to go travelling.
Finally he was gone and he never came back.
He never showed up again.
God said,
"I love my dog but I don't know where it is. He is lost."
He really knew it—he knew his wolf—but he just pretended.
He wanted the wolf to live with his teeth,
to travel around and kill moose.
He wrote that.
He made the wolf's teeth out of steel
and even today he can grab anything just like with a knife.
His teeth cut right through.
He made this world really big and that wolf got lost.
He wanted that wolf to get lost.
That is why the wolf never came back.
The wolf is going to be on this world too.
He made everything really perfect.
And stars, everything, animals,
just like animals coming down, landing down.
Pretty soon sure lots.
Where people stayed there were some great big animals
coming around.
He made those giant animals
from the stars that he sent down to this earth.

Charlie Yahey was not bothered by the apparent anachronism of a human arm appearing in his creation story before he had explained how humans were created. He was not bothered by the wolf having teeth made of the white man's steel. Dunne-za stories are not chronological and causal in our sense. They present thoughts and images. They refer to experiences current in the lives of real people. If people know steel knives, the idea of these artifacts will have to be in the story of creation. There is no logical problem for the wolf to return with a person's arm in his mouth. In the mythic time to which his narrative refers, giant animals are the hunters and people are their game. This is this mythic time to which each Dunne-za is expected to return—the time out of time of a person's vision quest.

Charlie's narrative turned to Saya, the culture hero who was the first person to follow the trails of animals, the first person to "know something," the first hunter. Through his knowledge and power, Saya stepped over the border between mythic time and that of the ordinary world. Saya followed the animals rather than allowing himself to be followed by them. Saya changed the animals of mythic time into the ones we know today. The edge between mythic time and our own is set out by Saya's knowledge and intelligence. Saya's tracks circle the world's rim as the sun's path circles the horizon. Saya began life as a boy named Swan and later grew into a realization of the idea inherent in that name. His name suggests the idea that precedes the sun's rise. It is the idea of flying between seasons. It is the idea of experiencing the Trail to Heaven and returning to earth in the same body. Charlie said, "There was just one person on this world." Saya was the first person to "know something":

There was just one person in this world.
He wanted to put everything together.
He travelled along looking for all those bad animals,
the giant ones that killed people.
He looked for every one of them.
Everybody ran away from those giant animals that ate people
but that one person only looked after them.
He followed them instead of running away.
Everyone ran away from the camp
but this one man just went after them and killed them.
He just kept on like that.
He looked for those bad ones.
He killed Onli Nachi [something big], a great big giant
    animal,
and he cut him all into pieces.

He cut it into little pieces and scattered them all over.
He would throw one and say,
"You are going to be this or that kind of animal."
Where the piece dropped down
a weasel or some other animal would run away.
Those wolverines and everything.
He made different kinds of animals
from that one big giant one—every kind.
For a start he threw one piece of meat and made weasel.
Second he made marten
and kept on like that to make everything in the world.
The third time he threw down the Onli Nachi meat
he made wolverine.
Wolverine is boss for every fur
just like cougar is boss for the lynx.
Old people heard that.
That guy—Saya—started to work on the world
so everything would be straight for today.
Some of the animals he didn't kill.
He just chased them under that place.
That's why the ground goes high.

As I studied and thought about Charlie's narrative, I came to the astonishing realization that the very contour of the country the Dunne-za know reveals the backs of the giant animals lying beneath the surface. The land is pushed up by their presence just below the surface. In the same way that the turns of a song's melodic line carry a person's mind along the Trail to Heaven, turns of a trail on earth respond to the shapes of the giant animals lurking below. The country, and people's actions in relation to it, are merely a surface that covers over mythic time. The time of myth and vision continues to be literally an underlying force of nature. Beneath the appearance of everyday reality, the stories of Saya and the giant animals he sent beneath the earth are still being enacted. When a child goes into the bush alone, he or she enters directly back into the energy of that world and its stories. Even the mechanical world of the white men is energized, without their knowledge, by the same mythic forces. Charlie Yahey explained:

He also sent giant fish underneath
and that is why even today white men
drill a hole to them to get their fat.
The oil that they get is the fat of the giant animals.
Saya made everything straight for this world of ours.
He knew it before.
That is why they get gas from down under the ground.
They look all over for it and then find it underneath.
God made that for the white people.
That is what the person and I know.
I tell the story—true story.
He made everything straight here.

The next episode Charlie told in the story of creation surprised
me even more than the anachronisms of the woman who stole the
berries and God's dog returning with a human arm in its mouth.
This episode reinforced the identification of Saya as boss of the seasons, but it did so in an entirely irreverent way. It showed Saya the
man, a very real human character any one of us can understand
and identify with:

The ducks and all the animals that fly over the coast—
he flew with them.
The ducks and geese that flew with Saya told him,
"There's a bad people over there where you go past.
They are living there so we will go on top."
Saya thought he couldn't make it but he said,
"I'll give it a try.
Every one of you give me your feathers," he told them,
so every one of them gave him their feathers.
Finally they got to the bad people place.
They yelled to each other,
"There is a person flying with those geese."
They yelled at him and hollered at him until he fell down.
Then they grabbed him and tied him up with a rope all over
so he couldn't move.
They put him down in one place
and then everyone used him for a toilet.
Finally one old lady

came around to where they were using him for a toilet.
Saya said to her,
"Grandma—Grey Hair—toilet on me here."
So that old lady went to him.
Then he said,
"First untie me and then toilet on me."
So that old lady untied him and he killed her and ran away.
That is why all the birds—ducks and geese—
they all fly to the coast before it gets cold.
Saya made it that way.

The story then turned quickly back to the cosmic level of significance, showing Saya as the boss for seasonal changes in the growth of plants:

Around April or May
Saya over there
grabs a leaf, comes over here
and puts a leaf on the trees here.
That is why the leaves come out.
God just made the world but Saya made summer and winter.
He grabs a leaf from over at the coast
and ran away from there with a person chasing him.
They chased Saya and just nearly got him
but he was able to just throw the leaf to the tree.
He told the leaves to sit on the trees
and that is why the leaves come back.
Once the leaves start coming back
in just one day there will be leaves all over.

Saya is master of the seasons. He is like the sun in its path around the rim of the world. He is also like the sun in its yearly circle, "one chicken step" each day from the most northerly to the most southerly point of rising and setting. Like the mating spruce chickens, the sun dances in a circle of splendor to bring about a renewal of life. Saya is like the swans and like the sun, but he is also and primarily a person. He is a person who knows something.

Charlie Yahey also spoke of Jesus as a person who knows something. Jesus is someone who knows the stories that underlie the white man's world. Makenunatane dreamed of the white man coming. He told people about Jesus. Following him, the Dreamers have told stories about how Saya follows a path that circles around the rim of the world. They have also told about how Jesus showed people a trail that goes up to heaven directly. He showed a "straight cut" to heaven:

He made the world different for other people
but for Indians he made it right straight off.
Before Jesus, God made a long way around.
He went far away up here [pointing to sunup and tracing the
    sun's path] in a circle.
He had to rest up there where he started to go up.
Where God started to go up was a smooth place of rock.
He just put his hand on there
and you can see five fingers there.
Still today you can see his handprint there.
He started to travel around the road
and he put one spruce tree there.
From there, there is just one spruce tree in that place,
in the world, in here somewhere.
Someplace in there he nearly made a land himself.
He nearly made a land for himself.
There was a rock and he leveled it up
and nearly made himself a land.
Something that is really high.
He put it like this—way down. I don't know how far,
really down in the ground, pretty far,
higher than those clouds.
He made it like that [with hands shows a chasm].
Some kind of mountain sheep jump across that place.
I don't know how they do it. It's pretty far.
He was going to make a land there for himself
but he thought, That place I made, that crevasse.
Any kind of animals are going to jump across.
All those animals will follow me here
if I make a land here.
That is why he got rid of that place.

The trail went apart there too.
It was like having to jump across
from one mountain to another.
That place where he almost made a land is still here
and lots of people have seen it.
It is just around in this world someplace.
He went around the world and far away
until he started to go up.
He made a long trail.
He went around and far away
and now Jesus has changed it again.
He made a straight cut for the Indians.
One priest—a father—talked Beaver
and all kinds of languages.
He told how Indians go right on a straight cut
and I believe that.
Us, we went the far way around. No good.

13. A BOY NAMED SWAN

When I finally gave up trying to solicit stories about pictures for which Beaver people had no knowledge and experience, I began to discover the wealth of stories they did know. Johnny Chipesia, true to his name of Wuscide, proved to be one of the best storytellers. Although I knew that he was perfectly capable of making up something utterly fantastic, like his bogus demonstration of an ability to call moose ("Here moose, moose, moose!"), he was also capable of recalling and enacting powerful narratives from Dunne-za tradition. One of these stories is about a boy named Swan, Wabashu, which Johnny told me was the boy's name in Cree. From this story, I learned more about how the Dreamers' songs are related to those obtained on an individual vision quest. The story is, in fact, an account of Saya's own vision quest. It describes the very first vision quest and how that experience empowered Saya, the "culture hero," to follow the trails of animals and circle between worlds like the sun. Saya is "boss" of the seasons. He knows their changes as he knows his own life. Each day he circles the sky from one horizon to another. With each rising and setting he moves "one chicken step" around the circle of an entire year. Each spring he "grabs a leaf" and throws it to the trees, and with the ending of each year he flies through to heaven with the ducks and geese and swans. Johnny Chipesia told me the story of Wabashu, the boy named Swan:

Wabashu

This story is about a boy called Swan.
Swan lived with his mother and father.
His mother was a good woman.

She was a good woman and she loved her boy.
When Swan was still young, his mother died
and his father raised him.
Before his mother died she told Swan's father,
"I like my son.
I want you to find a good woman to look after him.
You should look for a woman
from where the sun is when it is highest in the sky.
Sunup women are no good.
Where the sun goes down is no good.
You should just find a woman
from where the sun is at dinner time.
I like my son."

The opening lines of this story establish that the boy named Swan
is unknowingly connected to the sun's circle from horizon to horizon. His mother is a "good woman." She comes from where the
sun is at dinner time. She is a woman of the zenith point. Her country is forever balanced between the inclinations of rising and setting. She wishes Swan to be there always. But that is not to be.
Swan is a boy who must grow to become a man. He must go on a
vision quest to "know something." He must follow the instructions
of a power that will become his friend. He must follow the tracks
of animals rather than being tracked by them as their game. He
must follow the sun's trail in a complete circle each day, and he
must dance like the grouse in a circle of "chicken steps" to complete the seasons. He must fly with the ducks and geese, and he
must put leaves on the trees.

Swan began to get older.
His father wanted to find a new woman to look after him.
He looked for one where the sun was at its highest
but he could not find one.
Swan's father went to look for a woman where the sun sets.
He took Swan with him and travelled toward the setting sun
until he came to the ocean.
In that country he found a nice-looking woman.
He told that woman's father,
"I need a woman for my boy.

I want to take your daughter back with me."
The woman's father said,
"I've raised lots of daughters to be good women.
I'll give you this one if you look after her well.
That's what I've raised them for."
Then Swan and his father went back to their own country.
They took that woman with them.

As a boy, Swan travelled west with his father. Then they turned to the east. Swan went with his father to find the kind of woman his mother had warned against. She warned against women of the horizons. The life and country to which Swan and his father returned with the setting sun woman was not the same as Swan's childhood world. This woman came from the world's edge, not its center. She brought some of that energy with her, back to Swan's world.

When they got back, Swan's father made a bow and arrow
for his son to use in shooting rabbits.
Swan was a good shot. He couldn't miss anything.
He got everything he shot at.
When Swan and his father got back to their country
with that woman, Swan's father went hunting.
That woman was wild.
She told Swan, "I'll go out hunting with you."
Swan said, "All right, Songe [stepmother, mother's sister]."
They went out. She told him,
"Every time you see rabbits, shoot them in the head.
You're a good shot. You can shoot anything you want."
That boy, Swan, tried to shoot a rabbit in the head.
He got it in the head.
The rabbit went down.

Swan was a good shot, but he was not yet a hunter. He shot his father's arrows. He used his father's bow. Using them, he never missed. A real hunter is not like that. His hunt begins with a dream to the east. He misses, sometimes, on the trails of a real world. He misses, but he tries again, secure in the knowledge that an animal has already given itself to him at the place where their dream trails come together. That place is essential. It is not fixed in time and space. It is a point of meeting and transformation. It is like the cross the creator drew upon the water. The hunter knows he will remember the meeting point when his trail on earth brings him to that place. He knows an animal has already given itself to the people. He remembers the cross. He remembers that Muskrat found the world beneath its center. He remembers that Saya flies through to the zenith point, the sky's center that is called *yage* ("heaven"). Even a good hunter cannot determine in advance just when and where his meeting with the animal will take place. He can only be prepared in his mind to recognize the experience when it happens to him. He can only be prepared to realize the promise of his dream. A good hunter does not get everything he shoots at. But a good hunter knows his game from their meeting at the center of a dream they share.

That woman picked up the rabbit while it was still kicking.
Any animal that you shoot in the head will kick just like that
when it dies. [A hunter should never shoot an animal
in the head if his wife is pregnant. If he does that, his wife
    will kick and thrash around when the baby is born.]
Then that woman put the rabbit Swan had shot under her
    dress.
As it died, the rabbit kicked and scratched her legs.
It spattered blood between her legs.
Still today, some women are smart like that.
Swan said, "Songe,
why did you do that? We eat that."
His stepmother told Swan,
"Well, I hold him that way with my legs
so that he will die quick."

This mother comes from where the sun goes down beneath the earth. Her land is at the opposite edge of the world from the sunrise place toward which a hunter dreams. She gives death between her legs, not life. A good hunter knows every animal he brings into camp to feed the people. He respects the meat. His dreaming is stopped by contact with the blood of menstruation—blood of a life substance that died. A menstruating woman who steps over the hunter's gun or arrow will cut off the trail of his dreaming. The sunset woman stains the earth with a trail of red.

> When Swan's father got back to camp
> he went to sleep with that woman.
> He saw that she was all scratched up
> and covered with dried blood.
> "What happened?" he asked.
> "You were not like that before."
> Then that woman lied to Swan's father.
> She told him,
> "Well, your boy did that.
> He threw me down and did that.
> He's a big boy now.
> He is stronger than me."
> Swan's father believed what she told him.
> He got mad at his own boy.
> He knew he could not kill his own son so he told Swan,
> "Let's go hunting out where the sun goes down in the
>   ocean."

Swan and his father set out on a hunt facing west. A hunt that gives life must begin toward the east. Hunters dream toward the place where their trails will meet those of the animals. They begin a hunt by sleeping with their heads to the east. That direction, the place of the reborn and rising sun, is a source of life for the people. Swan's father "got mad" at his boy. In Dunne-za usage, to "get mad" at someone is to use one's power to kill that person. The dream of a meeting between person and animal underlies its physical realization. A cross drawn on the water brings about the world. An idea of killing cuts the connection that binds two people to a common purpose. It can even sever the parent's tie to his child. An idea of healing brings people together. The Dreamer must die to one world in order to be born again to another. Even Saya must die and be reborn to the promise of his childhood name.

> He was planning to leave Swan on an island in the ocean.
> He couldn't kill him but he planned to leave him there to die.
> Swan and his father got to the ocean.

"Swan," his father said. "Let's look for country out there."
Swan looked. "Yes," he said.
"I see something black way far out."
"OK," his father said. "We go now.
We make a canoe and go out there."
Swan and his father made a canoe.
They paddled far out into the ocean
until they were almost out of sight of land.
Then they came close to the island.
Swan's father said,
"Swan, you go around one side of the island.
I'll go around the other.
We'll find out how big this ground is."

When Swan and his father reached the edge of the world they discovered a smaller, primordial world surrounded by water. Their journey took them back to an earlier stage in the story of creation. The world we know is growing from the speck of dirt Muskrat brought up from the center where two trails come together. It is growing as the creator thinks it into definition. Going west, Swan's father reversed the process of creation. Swan's father sent his son to measure this primordial world's sufficiency. He sent Swan out to diminish the world into a single speck of dirt surrounded by water. He sent Swan out in a circle, just as the creator sent out his dog to measure the speck of dirt growing from the center of the cross. The vision quest takes each child into the story of creation. It teaches each child how to become a person. It teaches that how you know is as important as what you know.

As soon as Swan was out of sight
the old man turned around and went back to the canoe.
He got into the canoe and went out into the ocean.
He waited for Swan there.
Swan went all the way around the island
but he didn't meet his father. When he got back to where
    they had left the canoe
he saw his father way out in the water.
His father shouted to Swan,
"I am leaving you here.

We have both shared the same hole.
We can't both go in the same place.
Now I am leaving you here."
Swan shouted back to his father,
"Daddy, Daddy. I never did that.
We just went hunting and when I shot a rabbit in the head
she put it under her dress."
But Swan's father didn't listen.
"Don't lie too much. I'm going back now."
Then he paddled back to the shore
and went back to his own country.

The child who is to become a person must leave family, home, and the familiar sights and smells of protective camp. There is a difference between knowing something and knowing about something. The child in camp knows about animals. He knows how they taste and he knows the uses of their skins, their antlers, their bones. It is rare for someone who is not a hunter to see them in their own country. The vision quest takes a child out of camp life and into the deeper life of the bush. The hunter's dreaming also leaps across that boundary. People must not make camp trails behind where a hunter sleeps. Women who may be menstruating must be particularly careful about where they step. The country behind a hunter's place of sleeping must be solely animal country. When Japasa left camp, he was a child. When he returned, he knew foxes. He gambled with frogs at the bottom of a lake. He knew them. He understood their way of communicating. The people in camp may be dreaming of their child when he or she is out in the bush, but knowing something comes only to a person alone. Only when he or she is alone will the friend make itself known.

Swan lay down next to the water and cried.
He didn't know what to do.
Pretty soon he cried himself to sleep.
Then he heard someone talking to him
but he saw no one there.
It must be a spirit power who was helping him.
The voice said,
"Why do you cry? Don't cry. You're going to live."

It told him,
"Do you see all those geese and ducks flying over there
going to a different place?"
It was fall time and the geese and ducks were flying south.
"You get lots of pitch. Put it on the rocks of this island
wherever the sun strikes. The ducks and geese will get
stuck there. You can live like that."
His friend told him this and Swan got up and felt better.
Swan put lots of pitch on the flat rocks of the island.
It was a hot day and the pitch melted when the sun struck it.
The next morning Swan began to make a house
on the highest part of the island.
All he had was a stone knife, but he cut a stick
and dug into the ground to make a hole for his house.
The next morning he went out to check the pitch
just the way you go out to check a trap.
When he got to the place he found forty ducks and geese
stuck in the pitch wherever the sun had made it soft.
He just hit them with a stick.
After that he was happy and thought,
"Maybe I'll live."
Swan took the feathers from the ducks and geese
and put them in the hole he had dug.
That way he made a good house lined with down.
Then he cut up the birds into fine pieces
with his stone knife and dried the meat.
He kept on doing this for a month
while the birds were flying south.
By then he had caught hundreds and hundreds
and made lots of drymeat.
He fixed his house with down and feathers inside
and he put a flat rock for the door.
He made a toilet, found a place to get water,
and began to live in his new house.
All this he did with only a stone knife.

The friend who came to Swan told him, "You can live from the
ducks and geese flying to a different land." Swan's friend reminded

him of a power he knew already. The friend reminded Swan of his
own name. The friend taught him to recognize a power that already
existed at his own center. Like the cross on the water and like the
hunter's dream contact with an animal, Swan came to know something that was already in his possession.

> Swan lived in his house
> and the cold of winter did not bother him.
> Soon it was March time but he still had lots of drymeat.
> Swan did not go back to the place
> where his father had left him.
> He didn't want to leave any tracks there
> in case his father might come back.
> Springtime came and he began to see the first bluebirds.
> He knew that summer was coming soon.
> By then he did not have very many bundles of drymeat
> but he still had some dried fat and guts.
> After the summer birds
> the geese and ducks began to come back from the south.
> Swan tried to catch them
> but this time the pitch wouldn't melt on the rocks.
> It was cold and he couldn't get anything.
> Soon he had only one bundle of drymeat left.
> He thought,
> Maybe my father will come back.

As the seasons turn, one circle comes to completion and another
begins. When people dance to the Dreamers' songs, their trails circle together around a common center. Swan did not tread upon the
old trail his father left in the world of a sunset season. He waited to
begin a fresh trail into the lengthening days of another year. He did
not want the man who had left him for dead to discover him here
and alive in a world that was still close to Muskrat's speck of dirt.
He did not want his father to know that the resources of this tiny
world are sufficient to support a person who knows something.

> One day he heard somebody singing way out in the water
> and hitting a canoe like a drum.
> It was his father,

singing as he paddled his canoe toward the island.
"Swan," he sang. "I want to see your headbone.
We shared the same woman and now I come to see your
    bones."
Swan hid himself
and watched his father take the canoe up on the shore.
He kept on singing.
"Now Swan, you're smart enough. You fooled around with
    my
woman and now I want to see how your headbone sets. Is it
in the water or in the bush? I want to see where it is."
The old man went around one side of the island.
As soon as he was gone from sight Swan jumped in the boat
and paddled away from the shore.

The hunter is careful to place an animal's bones in a place that
will not cause offense. A wolf circles the newly created world to
measure the sufficiency of its natural community. It returns with a
human bone in its mouth. A person circles the Dreamer's dance fire
to measure the sufficiency of a human community. An old man
completes the circle his son began as he turns toward the Trail to
Heaven.

The old man kept walking around the island.
Soon the sun came out and he saw fresh tracks.
Swan had been smart.
He had not left tracks where his father landed the canoe.
The man ran back when he saw the fresh tracks
but it was too late.
He shouted to his son in the canoe,
"Swan, my son! I just wanted to see how tough you were.
That's why I left you here."
But Swan shouted back to him,
"Now you are going to live the way I lived."
He paddled his canoe back to the mainland.
Swan thought to himself,
My dad is crazy so I will just leave him there ten days.
He can't die in ten days. Look how long I stayed there.

But when Swan came back in ten days he found his father
   dead
with a little bit of feathers in his mouth.
He had starved to death and tried to eat feathers.
Then Swan got mad.

When a person "gets mad" his power turns toward the taking of
life. In the spring of a new year, Swan was a person of knowledge
and power. He knew the power of summer and winter. He knew
how to "grab a leaf from over at the coast and run away from there
with a person chasing him." The old man ran back upon the tracks
of his son. One generation runs after the one that comes after. The
old man did not complete the trail that circled around the edge of
Swan's world. Swan was a different person. In the turn of a season,
the return of a dream, he can fly through to heaven and back to his
body on earth. He flies with the power of Swan, his namesake, boss
of the seasons.

"It's that bad woman who did this.
Now I'm going to kill her."
He went back to his country and saw that woman.
"Swan," she said. "Where's your dad?"
Swan didn't say anything. He got mad.
He took an arrow and shot it in the ground by her feet.
The arrow caught fire when it hit the ground.
The woman started to run away
and every time Swan shot an arrow at her feet it caught fire.
Finally she ran into the water.
Swan shot his arrow into the water after her.
The arrow was so hot the water boiled.
When the woman came out of the water she was just bones.
That is how Swan killed that bad woman.

That woman did wrong when she took the lives of animals between her legs. She took their lives, but she did not transform their
bodies into food by cooking. Swan's arrows completed the circle
she began. They did not pierce her flesh, nor did they draw her
blood. Instead, they heated water and cooked the flesh from her
bones. They cooked her so that the story of her demise would nourish the people.

After that, Swan became a man
but he stayed with a big animal, Onli Nachi,
a monster that ate people.
After he killed that bad woman, Swan met a monster, Onli
   Nachi.
The monster said to him,
"I can't make babies anymore. You stay with me."
So Swan lived with her.
After awhile, Swan told Onli Nachi his story.
She told him she lived by eating people.
"You try it too," she said.
But Swan said,
"No, I can't do that. I only eat ducks and geese
and chickens. I can't eat people like myself."
Pretty soon Onli Nachi saw tracks of game.
"Look," she said, "a bull, a cow, and two calves."
Swan didn't see any game tracks.
There were only people tracks.
Swan couldn't follow them.
Onli Nachi ran after the tracks.
"That's good game. I hope there's lots of fat," she said.
Pretty soon Onli Nachi came to a little camp in the bush.
There was a man, a woman, and two children.
Onli Nachi started to go after them.
Swan tried to stop her.
"Mommy, Mommy, don't go after them. They're my people."
"That's your people yourself," she said. "That's my game."
She started after them again.
They tried to run away but she hit the man
and he fell down flat.
Then she hit the woman and she fell down too.
Swan got mad.
"Mommy, Mommy! You leave them alone. You've killed two.
You leave the others alone."
Still, Onli Nachi kept on after the two children.
They were smart and rolled themselves fast down a hill.
Onli Nachi was too big to catch up with them.
Swan ran down the hill and put the children behind him
to hide them from the monster.

Onli Nachi came down. She said,
"My son, do you want to die too? That's my food.
If you don't let me have it I can eat you too."
Then Swan took an arrow and shot Onli Nachi in the breast.
"Swan, my son," she cried.
"I should have listened."
But Swan shot her again and killed her.
After that, Swan changed his name
and took the name of Saya.
Since that time he became just like a soldier
looking for bad things that ate people.
He cleaned up all the monsters
that used to live in the world.
If he didn't do that
maybe those things would still make trouble for people.
When Saya finished killing all the monsters
he turned to stone.
He said that he would come back
when the world comes to an end.
He will come back to fix it up.
Sometime when Jesus comes back
Saya will come back too.

Saya puts leaves on the trees with every return of his season. Saya
flies like the sun in the sky in a circle around the edge of the world.
Saya flies with the ducks and geese. Saya follows the trails of animals. Saya is the first person. Saya knows something. Even today,
kids refer to him as "Santa Claus." He is the first person, the first
Dreamer. He is a bringer of gifts. He is a person who knows
something.

14. THE NAME
OF MAKENUNATANE
WAS CALLED

According to Dunne-za tradition, a Dreamer named Makenunatane prophesied that white men with a new technology were coming to Dunne-za country. Storytellers call him the Sikanni Chief in English. Makenunatane taught people about Jesus and a "shortcut to heaven." People say that Makenunatane knew about heaven because he died and went there in his dreams. They say he brought back songs to help them follow Yagatunne, the Trail to Heaven. They say he told people not to use their powers to kill. He told them, instead, to think about heaven.

Dunne-za tradition is rich in stories about the life and times of Makenunatane. There are only a few documentary sources of information about that period in the written history of the white men. One is a twenty-seven-page fragment of an anonymous Northwest Company fur trader's journal "written in a clear and beautiful hand" (according to Marion O'Neil, who transcribed it) during the winter of 1799–1800. It reports that a chief of the Dunne-za band trading into the Northwest Company fort was called "the Cigne." His Indian name must have been Swan, and he may have been the Dreamer known as Makenunatane to the Dunne-za.

Dunne-za storytellers recognize Makenunatane as a Dreamer who understood the new ways of the white people. His name means, literally, Ma ke ("his tracks") Nun ("earth") Atunne ("trail"). A more symbolic translation of the name would be "his tracks circle around the edge of the world." This section of *Trail to Heaven* is about Makenunatane. It begins with a blending of stories from the Dunne-za tradition, with excerpts from the fur trader's journal. Taken together, the two stories document moments of first contact between two cultures that are still very different from one another. Each story speaks from within the metaphors and assumptions of its culture. The trader's journal uses abbreviations that refer to conventions of the fur trade credit system. The Dunne-za story assumes an understanding of Dreaming as a way of knowledge. By juxtaposing the two stories I hope to suggest a flavor of early fur trade reality.

The Cigne

In the fall of 1799, the small, recently established Northwest Company trading post called Rocky Mountain Fort was "the most westerly English (and French) speaking outpost on the continent of North America," in the words of Knud Fladmark, an archaeologist who surveyed the site in the 1970s (Fladmark 1985: 49).

The name of Makenunatane was called.

During the cold and lonely months that spanned the turn of the Sun King's century into that of Queen Victoria, an anonymous English-speaking trader, most likely a Scot, kept a sparse journal of the events that took place at his post.

Something is happening around here.
They all look after it.

Fri. 5th Octr. Set off from the Forks Peace River with two Canoes loaded with 18 1/2 Pieces, four women, five children and 12 Men and arrived here the 13th not without a few Accidents. Gave the Men each a Dram and mixed a keg Rum— gave all the Indians that are here each a Dram and a Ps of Tob. and they brought a little Meat to the Fort

One time Makenunatane went to sleep for a long time.
The people looked after him always.

The trader's notes brought Beaver Indian names into the record of European history for the first time. We know from his journal and from an archaeological survey of the site across the Peace River from the present town of Fort St. John that Rocky Mountain Fort consisted of a shop, living quarters for twelve men, four women, and five children, a storage cellar referred to as a "hangard," a fifty-five-foot flagpole, and a fur press.

Around noon the next day
in his dream
he went to heaven.

We know that the post was not self-sufficient. The trader and his French-speaking voyageurs seem to have subsisted largely by trading rum, tobacco, and the few precious goods of European manufacture they brought up from Montreal in freight canoes for furs, meat, and hides provided by Beaver Indian men and women.

They knew he was still living
But he was someplace—
A long ways in his dreams.

Alcohol was integral to the system. It produced a novel route to the experience of being out of one's body. It was a product of high value and low bulk, ideal for fueling the trading economy.

They just looked after him
and knew he was in heaven
because they could see in his throat
it was moving.

Sun 14th Octr. Part of the Indians came over with all their things. Recd 70 Sks Beavr [beaver skins] and 88 Do Mt Crs [credits] from the F.P. River—

They just kept watching him.
His throat was still moving—always
so they just watched him

Mon. 15th Octr. Recd 66 Sks Br and 70 Sks Mt Crs and they begun to Drink. The Men arranged their old houses to make a hangard for I have taken the Shop for my room and the Old hangard is too small

and finally about noon he came down
and he slept again.

Tues. 16th Octr. The Indians are Drinking yet—undone all the Goods and found the Gun flints wanting. I Cannot get a Single Dog from the Indians

He sat up and started singing.
He woke up and sat up and started singing.

Wed 5th December D'Allair, Mondou and three Boys arrived from four Lodges who have almost all their Crs made already and the Cigne [Swan] told the Men to ask to trade rum but refused them. Gave them each a Dram and they drank 4 Phiols— The hunter killed a Bieche and wounded another— Gave him 1 Ps of Tobacco

He sang that song and told about it.
He told people about heaven.
Everything what is wrong and bad.

The journal tells us that by 1799, at least one Dunne-za band had established a regular trading relationship with the company. It also tells us that the trader attempted to select one man in this band to be a trading chief.

That person was called Makenunatane.

The trader referred to the man he selected as "the Cigne," a misspelling of the French *cygne*, meaning "swan." The French name must have been a translation of the man's name in Beaver made by the Francophone voyageurs. From the trader's spelling of "Cigne," it seems likely that he Anglicized his pronunciation of the French word to Cig-ne.

When a person gets to be like that
he hardly eats when there are lots of people around.

Fri 7th December D'Allair and Mondou set off to go to the Lodges gave 8 Sks Crs to them and one small Ps of Tob for the Cigne who works very well— Sent the hunter for Tea with them and gave him 3 M Amn.

He has a hard time eating meat
when there are lots of people around.

This "Cigne Chief," the Swan, was respected by his own people. He did not accept the trader's view that a chief should have super-ordinate authority. The trader knew the Cigne was an important person, but he did not understand what it means to be a Dreamer.

Sometime he may choke
if someone stands up when he is eating.
That is the way it goes.
Even now you have to go look for it.

Sun 16th December Beison and Maniant are set off with the Letters for Mr. F. Fort with the Letters and took 40lb Pemecan, 10lb Dryed Mt 1 Gunflint, 1 firesteel and 8 pr Shoes— The Cigne with 9 others arrived and paid 539 Sks Br Crs. as they worked so well and they have nothing to Drink I gave them 45 Sks Crs in rum and they Drank what provisions they— The Mt weighed 480lb and the hunter with L'homme Seul's son killed 2 Biches and 1 Buffloe

He told them to eat whatever has been killed with an axe.
He told them,
"They will listen to you if they do that."

The journal records that, to the trader's considerable displeasure, the Swan refused to accept his offer of a special chief's coat and asked that it be given to L'Homme Seul, another respected member of the band.

It sure was cold for them
but some of them did not believe him.
Some of them thought that he was just saying that.

Wed 1st April— All the Indians arrived and paid 542 Sks Br Crs and begun to drink— Spoke to the Cigne and his parents to cloth the Cigne but when I offered it to him he refused and told me to give it to L'Homme Seul for that he was the most proper in the Band but when I told them that since they re-fused the Cigne that they should not have any Chief till next winter—gave them 5 Sks rum and 1 foot Tob. for nothing

Some others thought,
He is the one who said this
so let's go look for something with just an axe.

In addition to wanting the Swan to become a trading chief for his
band, the trader required Indian support for his own subsistence.
He persuaded one of the Indians, a young unmarried man, to stay
at the post during the winter of 1799–1800 as a full-time hunter
responsible for provisioning the twenty-two men, women, and
children who lived there. In order to keep him company, the trader
arranged for a little boy, the son of L'Homme Seul, to stay with him
in the fort. The Indian hunter was also given the task of recruiting
new Indians to the trade, although the journal does not record an
instance of success in this endeavor.

They just took an axe and looked for something.
They followed a fresh moose track
and from the tracks they knew it was a good moose.

Mon 17th December The Indians drank all night and traded
47 Sks Br 30 1/2 Sks Br Mt 17 1/2 Sks Br Tails. 3 Sks Grease,
9 1/2 Sks Castorum, 3 Orig. [moose] Sks, 1 Buffloe hide
Dressed and 1 Green and gave 22 Sks Crs to the hunter. The
Mt weighed 1080lb gave 3 Inches Tob. to smoak for nothing—

Some of them stood so as to form a surround
and one old man with an axe
stood one place by the tree.

Tues 18th December Gave out 210 1/2 Skins Br and 49 Sks
Mt Crs to the Indians and traded 8 Sks Br and 6 Do Mt— The
Indians complains very much of the prices of the Goods here

The old man saw the moose running toward him.
He stood well behind that tree and held the axe.

Sun 3rd February— Q. D. Comrade and Renard says that they
must go to the other Fort for the hunter of the other Fort asks
them to go there. I kept a little Boy here with the hunter in
order to encourage and keep him Compy—he kills nothing
gave him 1 Ps Tob—

Then he threw the axe at the moose—
threw that axe and it stuck in the moose.

The journal writer describes the Cigne's band as consisting of nine lodges. He says the Indians generally camped on the north side of the Peace River across from his post. His information about their camping places does not give any more detail, but the band must certainly have used the place later known as Where Happiness Dwells. The journal writer also gives us the names of other male band members. They are Jimathush, L'Homme Seul, the Gauche, Le Grand Vieux, Le Marie (*sic*) des Deux Jolie femmes, Q. D. Comrade, and the petit Renard.

Pretty soon that moose fell down.
He fell down and they all gathered around the moose—
Butchered it—and all took home lots of meat.

Save for these poignant little scraps of documentary evidence provided by the trader's journal, the life of a Northwest Company post in 1799 would be unknown to those of us immigrants who now call western North America our home.

When they got to camp he went to one tepee—one camp.
The people in that camp cooked lots of meat and fed him.

To the Dunne-za, the year documented by the Rocky Mountain Fort journal was just one winter among many in the country they have always known as their own. It was different from all the others only in that they were beginning to abandon hunting by communal surrounds under the direction of a Dreamer acting as hunt chief. They were beginning to favor a technology based on the use of steel tools and weapons. They were becoming dependent on the plugs of tobacco, the rum, and the system of credits that governed the world of these fur traders.

Then he left that camp and went to another.
He told the people there that he still wanted to eat
some more of the meat that had been killed by axe.

The year 1799 seems very far away from the oral traditions of non-native culture, but the events of that period are still very much alive in Dunne-za traditions.

They fed him lots of that new meat
everyplace he went.

As you drive north from Fort St. John on the Alaska Highway,
the first deep river valley you encounter is at Mile 147. Here, the
highway crosses the cutbank of the Sikanni Chief River and emer-
ges onto a plateau where American army engineers built the Sikanni Airstrip for lend-lease convoys of aircraft from the United
States to Russia at the beginning of World War II. Thus, the name
of the Sikanni Chief has become immortalized in the documentary
world of western cartography and local usage. Beyond that local
usage and the documents that sustain it is an Indian reality from
which it is derived.

He went into there and told them to feed him again
but they just fed him the lower part of the moose leg.

The Sikanni Chief is an important figure in Indian history.
Johnny Chipesia first told me stories about the Sikanni Chief
(which he pronounced Sig-uh-ne). Later, I heard versions and
variations from dozens of other knowledgeable Indian people. The
Dreamer's songs still resound in my dreams.

He didn't tell them he didn't want to eat that
but he just ate it.
When he went out he told them,
"Till the end of your lives it is your own fault
now because you fed me this leg
that you will always be hungry, always starving."
The people who fed him well would always have an easy
     time.

Charlie Yahey's words echo those of the Sikanni Chief. Animals
will be generous to people who are generous with one another.
The lives of people and animals move in a circle. The sun moves in
a circle each day. It also moves in a circle with the seasons. The
seasons circle around heaven and earth, like swans. The circle is a
common center.

Where there are lots of people singing
he put around lots of rope to make a pen.

The people went in there and they made a big sing.
He told them,
"I make you sit in this pen because I want all of you
to listen to me."

At first I thought the name of the fur trader's chief in English was
"Sekani Chief"; that is, a chief of the neighboring Sekani people.
Then I read the Rocky Mountain journal of 1799. The man to
whom the unnamed trader wanted to give a chief's coat was called
"the Cigne."

Makenunatane is the one who made this world good for us.
After Makenunatane made all this world good
there have been lots of prophets.
Long time ago it was not good.
Long time ago before Makenunatane
Anytime people wanted to kill each other
They would just kill each other.
It was no good—but now after him it is good.
Makenunatane told people that only good ghosts
are going to heaven.

15. FROM HUNT CHIEF TO PROPHET

In March 1966, I visited Doig River with Johnny Chipesia and spoke with Old Man Aku, whom Japasa had called Huane ("older brother"). Aku told another version of the Makenunatane story. This one told about the Prophet's death as well as his life. Aku told the story to Johnny Chipesia in Beaver and I recorded it on tape. The following is an English translation, done shortly after the recording session by Margaret Davis. Aku said that when the Dreamer first began to talk from his dreams, people did not believe him. His talk frightened them.

At first he didn't know anything.
Then, once in awhile his mind was like crazy.
Just for a little while.
Sometimes he was just crazy, singing in the wintertime.
It was just like his shadow went to a good place.
Some people thought it wasn't right. Some relations
thought he was bad to act crazy like that.
Makenunatane had a wife.
One time the people were moving on the trail.
A bunch of women were packing their things on the trail.
He took an axe.
He said, "I'm going to clean you all up with this axe."
All the women threw down their packs and started to run
away.
He chased them for a while and then he just laughed.
He started to make camp and said to them,
"You don't have enough guts. You all ran away."
For a long time he was like that.

Once in awhile he didn't know anything.
He was just like crazy.

Makenunatane frightened people when he talked about killing
something with an axe. They were afraid he might become "too
strong" and begin to kill and eat people. They were afraid he might
become Wechuge, the cannibal monster. When Makenunatane ran
after the people in his camp with an axe, they ran away from him
just as the people before Saya had run away from the giant animals
that ate people. They ran away from him as if he were Wechuge,
the cannibal monster returned to earth in human form.

Saya was the first person to follow the monsters rather than run
away from them. Makenunatane was becoming like Saya in his
dreaming. His mind flew from one world to another. It flew like
the swans who fly between worlds and seasons. He acted as if his
mind had left his body. The old people say that most of the Dreamers are up in heaven. Only a few are down here. Makenunatane
was becoming one of them. People did not believe him until they
were having a hard time. Then they turned to him. They knew that,
like the swans, he was praying to God in his own way. He was
"going through to heaven without dying." There are only a few
swans. There are only a few Dreamers. Only when the swans have
a really hard time from the cold do they go up to heaven.

One time the people were starving.
They couldn't get anything to eat.
That's when Makenunatane started. He said,
"Someday I will tell you to go kill lots of moose.
Then I'm going to eat lots."
He told them to go out hunting.
Every hunter went out
and every one came back with a fat cow moose.
They brought the meat back to camp
and every camp had lots of meat.

Every hunter goes ahead on his own dream's trail, but only
a "swan person" like Makenunatane or Charlie Yahey "dreams
ahead for everybody." The spirits of Dreamers and swans circle like

Saya between heaven and earth. Because the Dreamer's power
comes from the spirits of people and animals in heaven, the food
that is brought into camp must pass in a circle back to him.

Then, Makenunatane told his wife,
"I'm going to eat some meat."
He went around to every camp.
At the first camp he said,
"I'm hungry. Give me some food."
The men and women at that camp were good.
They gave him all the best parts.
They gave him lots of fat.
That one man was a smart man.
He gave the Prophet lots of fat. It wasn't long
before Makenunatane cleaned up everything they gave him.
As soon as he finished he went to the next camp.
He said, "I'm hungry. Feed me."
All around the camp he did the same thing.
Everywhere he went they gave him the best parts.
He finished up all they gave him.
Just one other camp he went to.
He went to that one man's camp.
"I'm hungry. Give me something to eat," he said.
But that was a bad man. His wife was lazy too.
"What happened?" she said. "You went all around the camp
and ate lots in every camp. Still you want to eat.
Here's a moose leg in the fire. You eat that.
That's all we have cooked."
That moose leg didn't have any meat on it.
It was just hide.
"No," the Prophet said. "I can't eat that."
Then he went back to his own camp.

The Dreamer says that animals give themselves to people when
people are generous and give to one another. A selfish person
breaks that circle. People who dance to the Dreamers' songs give to
one another. They think about heaven and their relatives there.

He started to sleep again. He stayed over there.
He stayed in a good place.
In the morning he started to come back.
He woke up
and he started to make Prophet talk in the morning.
He told that one man who had given him the moose leg,
"When you kill a moose it's going to be no good. No fat.
You make your own trouble for feeding me that hide.
Even if you catch one moose there will be no fat, nothing.
Everyone else who fed me,
when they get a moose it will be really nice—lots of fat.
From now on, even to your children and children's children,
that's the way it will be.
Those good people will get everything good
and that other man will get nothing but poor animals."

Makenunatane demonstrated his power as a Dreamer by saving
the people of his band from starvation. He could "dream ahead for
everybody." He dreamed to a place where the trails of all the people
come together with those of the animals. He saw that place as if it
were a cross on the water from which a world could grow. He saw
that place as a center of power, like the lick where the "boss of all
the moose" may be found. Like Dreamers who acted as hunt chiefs
for centuries before him, Makenunatane visualized a perfect communal hunt in which every person stood in relation to every other,
"so as to form a surround."

The Death of Makenunatane

That man—that man who killed Makenunatane,
he knew something too. That was his daughter's husband.
He was a good man.

The story of the Dreamer's death takes place in a different world
from that of his initial empowerment. As a hunt chief, Makenunatane was like Saya, the first person to run after animals rather than
run away from them. In the story of his death, Makenunatane was
like Jesus, the white man's culture hero.

In the wintertime he went up to the Sikanni River.
Makenunatane started to sing in the morning.
"Just like the boss came to me," he said.
"God came to me in the morning and he told me,
'You won't suffer anymore. Just like God's son
he will kill you too.'"

As hunt chief, the Dreamer visualized the place where the trails of people and animals come together. His power was like that of Saya. As a Prophet in the fur trade world, he foretold his own death like the white man's culture hero, Jesus. Hunting was different in the fur trade world. Firearms made it possible for a single hunter to bring down an animal from a distance, just as Jesus made it possible for people to find a "shortcut to heaven." Game was becoming scarce. Each hunter followed a different animal.

Makenunatane and his son-in-law started to hunt.
Makenunatane went to a different place.
He saw the fresh tracks of two elk.
He went one way and his son-in-law went another.
"Sazin, you go around the other way."
The Sikanni Chief followed the tracks
and saw them go up the mountain.
He went up after them.
He kept tracking the elk.
He put his axe handle in the tracks
to see if they were frozen.
That way he could tell how fresh they were.
He followed the tracks into a little stand of spruce.

This axe is used differently from the one in the first part of the story. The Dreamer uses it as an instrument of measurement, not to take the gift of an animal's life. Makenunatane is clearly part of the fur trade world. He dreams ahead for people as a Prophet. He brings back stories that empower the white man's technology. He wears a Hudson's Bay blanket obtained in trade for furs.

He was wearing a long coat made out of a Hudson Bay
blanket.
His son-in-law had come around below the spruce.

The son-in-law saw something move there and he shot.
He shot Makenunatane in the stomach.
He should have followed him but instead he went around.
At that time there was not much food.
Two people couldn't afford to hunt in the same place.
People had to hunt just like the lynx.
That way maybe one would be lucky and everybody would
    eat.

At the time of Makenunatane's death, people no longer hunted communally. Because game was scarce, "two people couldn't afford to hunt in the same place." Before the white men came, there had been a story for every animal, every hunting technique, every piece of equipment. Each thing of the world grew from an idea, just as the world itself grew from a speck of dirt Muskrat brought up to the place where two trails came together. Each thing of the world grows from a cross on the water's surface. Each thing of the world grows from a dream. A person knows something because he or she has experienced its story in a dream or vision alone in the bush.

At first, there were no stories for the guns and knives and snares and rum and chief's clothing brought by the fur traders. There were no stories to explain the power within these things of the new world. Makenunatane dreamed ahead for the people to discover the stories of the white men. He dreamed ahead and he came to know the story of Jesus. He knew that the story foretold his own death.

When the son-in-law shot
he heard somebody talking in the little spruce.
He cried and he started to run up there.
The Prophet sat down after he was shot.
He sat right down where he had been standing.
He told his son-in-law,
"I want to see everyone before I go."
The Prophet's son-in-law fired some shots in the air
the way people do when they have made a kill
and want everyone to come.
Pretty soon all the hunters
came to the place and made their camp.

They sent someone for the women.
All the women and children came
and moved their camp there too.
Makenunatane did not drink any water.
All the women and children came to the place
and he wanted to tell them.
He started to tell his stories.

Makenunatane started to tell his stories. He told the stories of his
knowledge just as Japasa told the stories of the powers he knew
the week before he died. He told about Jesus and the shortcut to
heaven. He told people to think about heaven. He remembered the
world. Then he let it go.

"Nobody should make any trouble," he said.
"You should be friends with that son-in-law.
I knew that this was going to happen before.
Just like God's son."
All night he told stories to the people.
In the morning he said,
"That's enough.
When I have given you all the stories, give me some water."
When they gave him the water
it came out of the hole in his stomach.
Then he went down.
After that the son-in-law wanted to suffer
for what he had done.
He cut off his fingers at the joints
and he burned his hair in the fire.
He had said,
"When you are gone I will kill myself."
But Makenunatane told him,
"If you do that you will go to the fire. That is bad."
After that, the son-in-law didn't hunt for a long time.
He just cried for father-in-law.

According to Dunne-za tradition, Makenunatane crossed over
from one world to another. At first he was a hunt chief. He
dreamed ahead to plan the hunts in which every person took part.

He dreamed of the perfect surround. Then, the white men came. He dreamed ahead to discover the stories behind their artifacts and their institutions. He dreamed of Jesus. He dreamed of the shortcut to heaven. He dreamed of Yagatunne. He told people that one winter would follow another if they were not good to one another during these hard times. He dreamed of his own death. When he had given the people all of his stories, he let go of Muskrat's world and followed the swans on Yagatunne, the Trail to Heaven.

Makenunatane was a big Prophet.
Before that time the winters were pretty bad.
Makenunatane said that for a long time
there will be good winters, not much snow.
Since I was a kid there have been two winters
when there was no snow.
Before those Prophets, lots of people and game
froze to death every year.
After them some winters have been nice—
some have been a little cold but not too bad.
Sometimes there was a little bit of snow on the hills
but those two winters there was no snow in the flat country.

The name of Makenunatane was called. His songs still carry people up on the Trail to Heaven. His name is heard when people sing and dance together. People remember him and think about heaven. There are few Dreamers on earth but many in heaven.

When people come together to dance and sing the Dreamers' songs, the dance lodge is crowded with people in circles within circles, bodies touching one another closely. The singers tune their drums, holding them close to the fire, tapping lightly as heat waves stretch them to a rising tone. They begin to strike softly—a rhythm. Then someone takes up the lead. The song may be one that was dreamed by Makenunatane. It may be a song of Maketchueson or Kayan. It may be a prayer of the animals. It may be a song of Charlie Yahey. The lead singer gathers his breath and starts out fresh upon the song's trail. Its rhythm is steady like the rise and fall of tracking feet. The melody is intricate in its turns, as the knowledge a Dreamer gains of the trail ahead is complex in its pattern of meaning.

The songs are trails you may "grab hold of" with your mind. Singers and hunters follow trails they know from dreams. They know them from the rising sun's direction. They study their dream trails closely. Dreamers follow trails others have travelled before them. There are many Dreamers in heaven but few on earth. In dreaming and singing, they become familiar with the tracks already before them. They remember the old stories.

It used to be that people who dreamed about heaven
put water and feathers on the people's heads
so they could go straight to heaven.

We dancers circle the fire, a common center. Our tracks come together on Muskrat's earth as our minds come together with those of the Dreamers in heaven. The songs are trails that take us there. Hunters and Dreamers know that the trail always returns to complete a circle. Saya knows how to return. Swans fly through to heaven and return. Dreamers come back to the bodies they leave at the place where a cross centers the world's creation. Only the wolf does not return. He does not return as a sign that the world has grown to a size in which each living thing sustains every other in a circle. God's dog measures the sufficiency of his creation.

Dreamers say the place they dream toward is beautiful like Where Happiness Dwells. It is beautiful in the way that people coming together after a long winter of isolation is beautiful. The old people already in heaven come close to the others when people come close to one another in the dance lodge. When people dance and listen to the Dreamers' songs, they know what it is like to be with their relatives before them. They know that this place is close to the Trail to Heaven.

With all the others you follow a common trail around the fire in the sun's direction, Saya's direction, leaning into it, until smoke gets in your eyes, and you hold your breath, and hold it until you are once again upwind of the searing center. It seems to take so long to move clear of the heat, because one old woman is moving serenely in the song's tracks, taking tiny little chicken steps, like the sun as it moves from one season to another. It seems to take so long because she is up there at the trail's beginning, and you are dancing in the smoke and heat that rise toward the place from which the swans return each spring. Because of her, we are all dancing close together, getting close enough to feel how the others dance, as the touch of bodies is passed around the circle.

Someone gives the fire hotly rising breath with fresh wood, and you stand, stamping feet in the dust of the many tracks, the one trail, as spirits of all the living powers circle around the center conjured here. Your mind rises with smoke. Your feet circle like the hunter's trail, your dreams incline toward the sun. Singing is the sound of people breathing together. You share breath in the songs that float toward where the old people are dancing in *ya diskwonchi*, the shimmering waves of the aurora, somewhere far above the dance lodge. You share breath with the people who dance around a fire here, in the northern country where Swan and Muskrat made a world together. In the dance circle, these minds turn together toward a time of renewal. The people press together into the night that carries them through to dawn. In the still distance of bush that encircles camp, waves of song flow over the animals until they are diminished into a throbbing heartbeat that merges with silence and subsides.

When your tracks lead you to one of the sacred spaces, the song will return to life and take you with it. If one circle is being broken now, it can only be because there is to be a new time of beginning. Look to the old woman dancing slowly on the other side of the fire. She is giving you smoke that rises, lifting your shadow toward the light. Her feet are already dancing on the Trail to Heaven.

The name of Makenunatane was called.
She follows his name.
His tracks—earth—trail.
She follows his tracks that circle the world.
She follows his tracks that circle the world.
She follows his name.
His tracks—earth—trail.
The name of Makenunatane was called.

PART THREE

A CONVERSATION WITH PETER, JUNE 1968

Overleaf: Sitama (Julie Chipesia, Peter's mother), 1966

16. TELLING SECRETS

In 1959, I thought that Dunne-za trails were the work of Italian boy scout vandals. In 1964, I turned down an offer of "Indian stories" because they were not the scientific data I thought I needed in order to complete my proposed fieldwork. I strained and struggled to get Dunne-za "subjects" to tell me stories about TAT pictures that were meaningless to them. The need for achievement these tests measured was largely my own, not theirs.

Peter Chipesia was one of the people whose protocol I did obtain. His responses to the test (see pp. 45–46) looked like those of someone who was severely withdrawn if not virtually autistic, yet I knew him as an intelligent and thoughtful young man. In 1968, Tonia and I recorded a conversation with Peter that brought together nearly everything we had learned in the previous four years. The conversation was not unlike many of the others through which the Dunne-za nourished and reinforced our understanding of their world. It was part of the ongoing circle of stories we were telling one another. It was typical of the narrative style through which Dunne-za exchange information.

During my first summer of fieldwork, the life and death of Old Man Chipesia had worked a change in my thinking. Later, Charlie Yahey further changed the way I saw the world. Most of all, I was coming to interpret both my "field" experiences and my academic thinking through Dunne-za stories and images. The Dunne-za told me their secrets in the same way they reveal secrets to one another. I had seen Jumbie hide from a flash camera and pull eggshells from his fire. I knew that Charlie Yahey could not hear guitar music. I was told that Old Man Chipesia had avoided drums. It was up to me to figure out an explanation for these peculiarities. The answers, I learned, were in the stories.

Like a Dunne-za child, I turned to the stories to explain what I was observing in the lives of the people with whom I lived from day to day. By 1968 I had listened to many stories. I had also learned how to listen to stories and how to look into them for answers to my questions. I had learned that casual conversation is often as revealing a narrative genre as formally told "myths." Thus, when Peter spent an evening talking with us in 1968, the contrast between the complex narrative I recorded and his pathetic TAT response was phenomenal. It was not that Peter had changed between the ages of eighteen and twenty-two. It was *we* who had changed. By 1968, we were capable of carrying on simple, intelligent conversations in which the way we revealed our own knowledge made it possible for people to reveal what they knew to us. This conversation with Peter was different from many others, largely because I recorded it. It is important because it documents both Peter's knowledge and his beautiful narrative style.

The Setting

The conversation with Peter took place when Tonia and I and our year-old son, Aballi, were staying in a new house built for Paul Notseta and Sally St. Pierre, who were out camping at the time. Peter was twenty-two years old then, Tonia was twenty-five, and I was twenty-eight. I recorded the conversation on one side of a 5-inch reel, using the Uher 4000 Report L at the astonishingly slow speed of 15/16 IPS. I chose the slow speed so that I could document a long conversation without interruption. This document turned out to be the most complete, spontaneous, and sustained narrative dealing with medicine power and traditional stories in the entire Dunne-za archive, now amounting to hundreds of hours of tape.

The background ambience of this tape documents a typical summer evening soundscape on the Prophet River Reserve at Mile 232 on the Alaska Highway. Paul and Sally's house was near the teacherage, the only house in the community with electricity. The low thrumming of an English Lister diesel generator is a constant keynote sound. Against its steady presence, camp dogs yelp and shout greetings to one another through the cold, clear air. Diesel trucks pass on the highway, gearing down to claw their way up the grade of the Adsett Creek crossing, a mile north of the reserve. The conversation was possible only because of mutual understandings based on experiences we shared with Peter. During the course of the relaxed and gently paced conversation, Peter told, or referred to, a large number of traditional stories. Many of these references would not have made sense if Peter had not known that we already knew and understood what he was talking about. He used our knowledge as an integral part of his narrative. Peter also added to our knowledge by telling a story about his mother's vision quest as she had related it to him and by telling us details of his grandfather's powers as he knew them.

Peter's narrative is notable because of its relaxed style and the long silences that are integral to its form. We, in turn, contribute to the narrative by respecting Peter's spaces and by asking questions only when there is a genuine pause in his speech. Our questions are important to the narrative in that they indicate a knowledge of the general references and assumptions on which it is based. Our questions reveal, for instance, that we know from personal experience about Jumbie's taboos relating to his Thunderbird power. We also reveal that we know about Charlie Yahey's taboo about stretched strings relating to his Spider power. The conversation provided an opportunity for us to verify our suppositions based on these experiences and to inform Peter of the degree to which we understood and participated in his narrative.

Because I recorded the conversation and later transcribed it, it has become a unique document of Dunne-za narrative performance. The following transcription of the narrative may suggest to the reader some answers to questions that may have arisen during the preceding pages. I have written out the text of our conversation verbatim from the tape, placing Peter's words on the page so as to give some sense of the beautiful way he speaks. Peter is a sensitive and eloquent storyteller. This section of *Trail to Heaven* is really Peter's. It is a very special contribution to the literature on oral traditions of native people. The recorded document begins in the middle of a conversation already in progress. Tonia is telling Peter what she recalls of a story about the man who married a beaver.

Peter responds by giving other episodes of the story and then taking part in a discussion of what the story means. He speaks in an eloquent "Indian English." Sometimes, for instance, he refers to his mother as "he," following the Dunne-za usage of gender-neutral pronouns. I would like to thank Lindy-Lou Flynn for transcribing the tape into its present form.

17. PETER'S STORIES

Beaver Woman, Mosquito Man

[Tonia: What's that story . . . about Beaver Woman? That story about that fellow camping by himself, and he finds this camp all made, and it turns out there's a woman making his camp, and she's Beaver? You know that story?]

Not too well.

[Tonia: You know, in that story, she says, "I'll be your wife, but every time I've got to cross the water, you have to make a dam for me to go across."]

That's just because he's Beaver Woman, that's why.

[Tonia: That's the only reason?]

Yeah. Can't touch the . . .
When he's person, you know, like us
I guess he can't touch the water.

[Tonia: Can't touch the water unless she's Beaver?]

Yeah.

[Robin: That's really a nice story.]

But I feel sorry for that guy.
You know, they had a little boy.
After he, lots of times he make bridge for his wife,
but you know when sometime, just a little wet place,
you know, like she can walk across
he figure. He never make a bridge.

Soon as his wife touched that wet ground, you know
just a little water, he turn beaver.
That place—that place where he crossed—
that man, he came back to that place
but it's all just big beaver dam.
And he put, he put—that woman put that baby up in a tree
you know, hang 'em up.
So his husband can get that baby.
That thing you're packin' around that baby with—
that's the kind of thing they carry.

[Tonia: Hmm. She hung it up in that?]

Yeah. On a tree.
And when his husband came back, he take his kid
and he beg, he beg his wife to come back,
but his wife told him,
"How many time do I have to tell you, 'Make bridge,
even—even that little wet spot?'
But you never, you never done that,
so I can't turn back," he tell 'em.
So, that man he just cry, cry,
and he took his baby—his little boy—to his old grandmother.
Grandmother raised—raised that kid.
That's part, you know, the story
I think, right there.

[Robin: And that kid was half beaver?]

Yeah. Half beaver and half man.
But he's just like us anyway.
That's why them beaver know everything now, you know.
They're half mans.
Even them, they say, them beaver
long time ago, think they one man.
I think that man was worry all the time, you know.
His wife done something to him.
That's why he turned to beaver too, I think,
living with his wife.
He love his wife too much, you know.

That's why his wife done that to him.
Something like that.
Can't remember it.

[Robin: Is that how come you're called Beaver Indian? Tsadunne?]

Maybe. Maybe that's how come.
If that guy didn't done that
there be nice-looking girls around here—
round all the Indians, like.
Say that woman was really nice looking.
Red headed.
And that guy done that—no more.   ˙
No more nice-looking girls.
Things would be a lot better.
A lot different around here now.
Nobody fool around.
Maybe that time
if that woman was still a person like us
even these woman wouldn't—
wouldn't fool around with their husbands.
Everything change.
A lot of them guys long time ago they do something wrong.
If they didn't done that
everything be good around here now.

[Robin: Anybody ever have Mosquito for a friend?]

No, I don't think so.
That guy too, that guy that making this world
everything good you know,
you know, he kill all the bad animals?

[Robin: Yeah. Usakindji.]

Yeah. This Mosquito too—he kill.
Now he eat all the people all the time, you know.
He just live on people.
He say, if he seen you in the camp he say,
"You're a animal."
He just like animal.

We're just like animal to him, you know.
Kill beaver.
When he go under the ice
he gotta kill all the beaver there is in the beaver dam, like.
That's why he caught up with him and he kill him.
Now he—he outsmart him—that's why he kill him.
He kill him you know.
He know there's a man on top the ice—
that Mosquito Man.
And he was staying under—he just was going to come out,
come out. He say, "Hey, can you catch this rope?
I gonna catch this rope."
He pulled that guy on top the ice up—on above, you know.
And that guy pulled that rope.
Pulled that rope, you know.
And he pulled that rope and he pull it
and there's about nine beaver.
And that Mosquito Man start counting them beaver.
He seen nine beaver and he say, "I got ten beaver," he say.
He say, "You haven't got ten beaver,"
that man told that Mosquito Man.
"But what about your hide?" he tell 'em.
He gotta kill 'em, see.
He don't give nobody a chance that Mosquito Man.
But that man outsmart 'em—he—
that Mosquito Man got his axe right close to that hole, you know
where the ice got a hole to that bottom.
He kick that axe in the dam and the axe went in the water.
And he tell him,
"Hey hey, your axe slide in that hole," he tell him.
He told that guy to go get it, but—
"When I go in the water I'm too cold. I might froze to death,"
he tell him.
So that Mosquito Man got no choice.
He have to go get 'em himself.
So he went down again. He say,
"When I come back up again, I gonna kill you," he tell him.
So that guy [Usakindji] look around, you know.

There's a big stump standing right close by.
Soon as that Mosquito went back in the water
he plugged that hole with that stick.
You know that stump?
Everything dark inside that water.
Mosquito Man can't see nothing where the hole is.
He don't know.
So he start calling calling—after him.
He say—he got his own axe, that man—
so he make that sound in the ice, you know.
"Up here," he tell him. "Up here," he tell.
He run him around that dam, all the way around.
Finally that Mosquito Man he can't talk no more.
He say he's dead.
He say—
I guess he got froze to death, you know.
And they know he's dead, so—
the last time he hear him he's right close to that beaver house.
So, "I think that's where he's dead," he's figure.
If he didn't chop that beaver house open
there'd be no Mosquito now.
But he chop it open—
there's that Mosquito Man
just laying down in that house.
That little mosquito fly away and he say,
"The rest of your life I gonna suck your blood," he tell him.

[Robin: That's how come mosquitoes live underneath the water all
winter?]

You know that's why whenever there's wet place
they lots of mosquitoes.
Even in them lake, you know.
There's lots of mosquito.
That's why even now them mosquito suck your blood out.
He shouldn't done that.
Everything they do wrong.
If he didn't done that they be no mosquito now.

When You're Close to Something

[Robin: If it wasn't for Usakindji, why, all those giant animals would still be around.]

Yeah. It'd be rough—rough now.

[Tonia: How come when kids go out and get an animal, they can't drink water and tea?]

When you go out, you know
when you're close to something
you're just like drunk.
You don't know nothing, you know.
Soon as you—you can't think straight, though.
Just like you're drunk.
And everything just like, when they see these animal,
just like person with you.
Even if you take the water
everything just get away from you.
You're a person again.
You won't see nothing, you know.
That's why you can't drink water.
You won't know nothing if you drink water.
That's why.

[Robin: It's like you'd be, sort of like a little kid who's still drinking milk?]

Yeah.

[Robin: Kids start to go out after they stop drinking milk?]

Yeah. After they're about the same size Joe, you know [age 10].
Just enough to think, you know.
To talk, and think. Walk.

[Tonia: That's why they put water on somebody who's getting too strong? That makes him go back to normal again?]

No.
I think that's—I don't know what's that got to do

but if you're more powerful than that guy that got strong
you can stop, you know.
After you stop him you throw water on him so he can wake up.
That's why, I think.

[Robin: Do you have to know the same animal to stop him?]

No.
Different animal.
More stronger animal.

[Robin: How do you know which one is stronger?]

Well, they know all kinds of different animal you know.
Not only one animal.
He know all different kinds.
They look—they know—they look for stronger animals,
for stronger things.

[Robin: Nobody really knows how many animals some guy
knows?]

Yeah. But only thing, only thing no good to know, is—
he just fool you all the time—is the wolverine.
When he talk to somebody he just lying, you know.
Too smart.

[Tonia: He doesn't tell the truth?]

He doesn't tell the truth.
That's why they call him *nowa*.

[Tonia: *Nowa*. What does that mean?]

Say, he lie, you know.
Smart. He's too smart.

[Tonia: So maybe he tell him to go one place, when that's not a
good place to go?]

Yeah. *Nowa*, he tell,
"When you're stuck you just call my name and I'll help you,"
he tell somebody and he just lying, you know.

[Tonia: He won't help?]

He won't help.

[Tonia: That's really bad.]

[Robin: People really get fooled by that sometime?]

Yeah.

[Robin: They think that he's going to help?]

Yeah.
Even when he's caught in a trap
that time I think one guy try it.
He say, "If you release me," you know—
"When if you need a help I'll help you," he tell.
And he just sing him a song, you know.
He figure, that guy figure,
"It gonna be my song."
He say—he sing him a little song and he go on his way
that wolverine.
And that guy was smart, you know—he hide.
Soon as he go, he go way around and he hide, you know.
Soon as that wolverine stop one place he say,
"I didn't give you no song. I just fool you,"
he tell that guy and that guy kill him right there.
For lying, he kill that wolverine.

[Robin: Just one animal like that?]

Yeah. Just one animal.
That's the only thing.
He's too smart.
Even now, you know, when you see a moose—
you know, somebody kill a moose?
He spoil it.
When wolverine—you know wolverine stay by your meat,
you can't take all the meat.
He's too smart.

You know, inside the moose, you know, he pee on the moose
   meat.

That's why it's no good that animal.

Too smart.

He don't eat the meat.

He eat little meat but he just spoil it.

You can't take.

One place we—one hunters, Dad and me we went—
he steal the meat, we just have to go back.

Can't take it.

He spoil all the meat.

You can smell it, you know—all in them meat.

Inside he eat meat, everything smell it.

[Tonia: Do some people still take wolverine for their friend all the
same?]

No.

[Tonia: Nobody wants that?]

No.

I guess some guys know it, but who knows?

Maybe sometime he tell the truth, but nobody know.

[Robin: But most kinds you can tell if there's some food that some
old guy can't eat, then that's how you know?]

Yeah.

[Tonia: If somebody knows wolverine, is he tricky too? If some
person knows wolverine, is he tricky just like wolverine?]

Maybe.

Never did see that kind of guy.

Maybe he's tricky just like wolverine, maybe.

It's hard to say.

He's too smart, that animal.

[Robin: When kids go out when they're little, do they make themselves a medicine bundle right away?]

What?

[Robin: You know, some kind of stuff they put in a little bag? Do they do that right away, or only old men had to do that?]

I think when they grow older, you know.
That animal give them their stuff, you know.

[Tonia: But they wait till they're older?]

Yeah. To get it . . . even the Old Man.

The Trail Below

Old Man he keep one—one for himself.
One time he show me that frog, you know.
He move on his hand.
It's kind of rubber thing but he move.
He jump.

[Robin: Did he have flies in that, too?]

No.

[Robin: He didn't keep that?]

He don't know that.
He didn't know that flies,
but any guys don't want that fly eggs in their meat, you know.
Even if I know something you feed me right now
and I look at the food and I know there's fly eggs in there.
Even when Grandpa was alive Mom always careful—
to feed him you know.
When we feed him, we tell him,
"Look through the meat," we tell him.
He know.

[Tonia: And if you see something in, you say, "I just don't want to eat this?"]

Yeah. I don't want to eat.
But lots of guys made a mistake, you know.
Lots of guys—that's why lots of guys get strong, you know.

Made a mistake.
I wouldn't be like that, me.
I wouldn't be like that now.
I know it helps lots, you know
to be like, to know something
but you gotta watch all the time.
People scared of you, you know.
Even down in Rose Prairie, you know
they're afraid to feed me anything.
They have to ask me first if I like to eat that, you know.
Even them beaver meat
they tell me if you eat these kind meat, they tell.
I say, "Sure. I eat 'em."
Lots of Indians afraid of any kind of man, you know.
You never know if—me if I know something,
you wouldn't know.
See, just like that.
Don't know each—any—kind of person, you know.

[Tonia: You've got to be careful.]

Yeah.

[Robin: When kids first get their friends, they can't eat that kind of meat right away?]

No.

[Tonia: Or is that later?]

Later, I think.

[Robin: So it must be really hard to tell when a kid goes out. Just his parents know?]

Yeah. Their parents know ahead of them, what.

[Robin: They dream about what's going to happen?]

Yeah.
Lots of guys, you know
sometime they're, you know, the kids they raised—
they're gone about a ten days, fifteen days.

They started worry,
and pretty soon that old man started look for them,
dream where they are—where to find 'em, you know.
This thing he talk, he stay with him about that long.
And he tell this boy this, that boy, you know,
"Your parents worrying about you,
I better take you home," he tell that boy.
He put him close to home, you know
where the people can find him.
He's go back—that thing go back.

[Tonia: So then people know that kid's got . . . ?]

Yeah.

[Tonia: Then they treat him more careful after that?]

Yeah, but it's, after they—
it's pretty hard to get 'em after that, you know.
They stay with animal that long
you can't be strange to you if you stay that long with animal, you
    know.

[Robin: And they just talk to the animal?]

Yeah.

[Robin: And they forget how to talk to people?]

Yeah.
They kind of forget about—you know they look strange.
When you see your people they start to run away.
Even Mom was like that that time.
A long time ago he tell us about that—know he was but—
he say, "I travel about sixty mile I think," she say.
I think it's that guy, them people who raised him, you know
who raise her, tell him to get—just on purpose you know—
they leave the axe that far. They told her to get that axe.
So Mom starts travelling in the wintertime, like.
They say, she say,
"There's a wolf travelling ahead of me," he say, she say.
"That wolf, I keep following that wolf—just keep following."

There's another hunters, you know—just camp out hunters.
They about that far away, you know.

"Soon as I came close to that—
I just came close to that place you know—
where the, where that camp is, maybe about a mile, you know—
there's a trail too,
the bottom trail or something came close to that place,
and that wolf walk on you know—just shadow—
and he just kind of saying things like."
It's old wolf tracks but just the shadow he see—
she see, you know.
"That thing is still gone so I just keep going.
Soon as I seen that fire, I can't go," she say,
"I can't go near it."
"But them guys spotted," she say,
"That one woman spotted me—
start toward me, and I run away," she say.
She say, "I got knocked out for two days."
I think that animal kind of make him mad you know, make her
    mad.
And that one old man he started dreaming, you know.
After two days she don't know nothing—
just knocked out, you know.
After two days that old man cover him with his jacket
and she go to sleep.
Next morning she wake up.
She woke up and the old man give 'em water and he's OK again.

[Robin: It's like an animal's shadow stays near it's tracks, by it's
tracks, for a long time?]

Yeah.
If them guys didn't camp there he would have catch up with him
and they stay together real like—real life, like.

Dance All Your Life

[Robin: Is that why, when a person dies, his shadow has to go
back—follow all his tracks back?]

No.

That's when you gotta pay for your sin if you're bad.

If you're bad, you can't make it to heaven.

Gotta follow your tracks all over the place.

You know, you have to pay for your sin.

They tell you it just like courthouse, you know.

Up there they say, them older people, you know,

they dream about that place. They say.

They say you gotta stay in this place

for so long till you pay up your sin, you know.

You can't see nothing.

You just stay—you just like staying in dark all the time.

You can't see nothing.

You travel all over where you been altogether, you know.

That's why you have to pay for your sin.

That's why you have to do that.

[Robin: And then, after you follow all those tracks back, then you can go to heaven?]

Yeah.

[Robin: When people dance, that's like walking to heaven?]

Yeah, you pay for your . . .

even one time you dance, you know, you put it up in the book.

Just like book, you know.

How many time you dance,

you stay there where them guys playing drums,

you stay there—you dance—just like you paying for your sin.

Some guys don't believe that.

Lots of guys feel sorry when they dead.

[Robin: Yeah. That's pretty tough. If people aren't dancing.]

[Tonia: Yeah. You've got to be a ghost for a long time.]

Yeah.

If you don't dance all your life till you die, you know

they gotta make you dance in the heaven.

You know, it's pretty hard.

All the guys they wearing fancy clothes.
Everything fancy, you know.
If you start a dance, you do wrong.
You feel ashamed of yourself.
Even Old Man—
Old Man before he die
he told us about that.
He say,
"They let me dance."
He say he never dance before, say,
"So they let me start a dance and I do wrong
and I," he say, "I just feel shame of myself," he say.
But I think the wife he got before—he dance—
she dance for him, I think.

[Tonia: How come he never want to dance himself?]

You know, that long time ago she—
he don't like to hear, he don't like to hear even drums.

[Tonia: Was that from the frog . . . ?]

Yeah.
You know them frog?
Even now you can hear them gamble, you know.
One frogs, bunch of frog up, up the river
and bunch down the, down the creek.
You can hear them making lots of noise.

[Tonia: Yeah. Back and forth.]

Yeah. Back and forth.
And when some night the bottom stream frogs,
they don't make no sound—that's when they lose, you know.
That top one making lots of noise, they're the winners.
And the next night they start a gamble again.
Both place.
And the next night that upstream one they don't talk
and they never make a sound.
They lose again.
They just go back and forth.

Old man told me about that.
That's why he don't like to hear drums, long time ago.

[Robin: When people play gamble, does—is it people who have lots of power who win? Does having friends help you win?]

No.
No, I try that on Old Man. He say,
"I been standing with them guys
on the bottom—bottom of the lake," he say.
He say, "You can't beat me."
I try him, you know. We just play, you know.
He say, "Let's play," he told me.
So we try, we try to play and every shot he get me.
And I couldn't get him, you know.
When it's my turn I try to get him
and I couldn't get him.

[Tonia: That's when he was with the frogs?]

Yeah.
He was with them for a while, I think.
He say bottom of the lake.

[Tonia: If you hear people gambling, is that like eating fly eggs? You can get too strong?]

No, eh.
He hear that drum in the bottom of the lake.
That's why he don't like to hear that drum
long time ago, when he was younger.
But when he's get older he get used to it.
He say, "Some day I gonna try." He say, "I gonna try drum,"
he said, but he's gone before that.
He say,
"Pretty soon I gonna make myself a drum.
Going to start playing drum," he say.
But he's gone before that.

[Tonia: I don't understand. He heard it down under the water.]

Yeah.

[Tonia: How does that mean he doesn't want to hear it up on land again?]

'Cause he heard it down there, you know.
He stay with them and they give him his power.
Them frog give him his power—their power to him.
And they hear that drum up there in the same time.
They play.
Up here on land, that's different.
You know, on the land?
That's different.
That's why he don't like it.

[Tonia: 'Cause it's not the same thing? It's not the real thing?]

Yeah.

He Just Doesn't Like It

[Robin: And that's the reason why Charlie Yahey can't listen to guitar music? Because he heard that spider?]

Yeah.

[Tonia: But if Charlie Yahey hears music up on this land, does that make him get too strong, too? Or he just doesn't like to hear that?]

He just doesn't like it.
You know whats he told me one time?
I was going to play guitar, you know.
He say,
"Leave that guitar alone."
He say,
"If I listen to that guitar," he say,
"I gonna get—I gonna get knocked out for one night
and after that I gonna go in the bush.
That's where I gonna die," you know.
He say,
"I won't come back to the house.
I just go in the bush. That's where I die," he say.

"Nobody gonna find me. That's where I gonna die," he say.
That's why I guess he's kinda 'fraid of that.
You know, even in them, that's why, I don't—
I can't understand why he go in them beer parlors.
You know, the jukebox playing all the time.
One time they done that to him, you know.
They playing—the radio was playing music, you know.
He heard that—he got knocked out for four days.
Never woked up.
This fifth morning he woke up and he told them—told them guys.
That's why he don't like to hear music.

[Robin: Yeah. One time, he was riding in the car with us, and I had
the radio on and, who was it? Jimmy Field was there, too, and he
told me to turn it off, 'cause he couldn't hear that. I didn't know
why, then.]

Yeah.
All kinda people are different, you know.
You can't—I don't think you can find very many around,
around here, but you can find them older people, like.
Them older people they're like that.

[Robin: Like Jumbie—Jumbie, you can't take flash pictures.]

Yeah. Grandpa was like that too.

[Robin: Same thing?]

Yeah.

[Tonia: You couldn't take flash pictures?]

Yeah.
One time they were gonna make a flash camera, you know.
They were drinking and this white guy want to make a flash
    camera.
He say, "Asah." I told him,
"Grandpa. They going to make a picture with that light,"
I tell him.
And I took him home.
You know he don't like that.

[Robin: Is that from *natane* ("thunderbird")?]

I think so.

[Robin: Another time somebody started to throw some eggshells into Jumbie's fire.]

[Tonia: We were down at Halfway at that time.]

[Robin: He said, "No, you can't do that."]

[Tonia: He got up and he took them out fast—out of the fire with a stick.]

[Robin: Same time down there, some . . . What was that woman's name? Westegaard. Mrs. Westegaard tried to take a flash picture, and she was so dumb, she didn't know she shouldn't. You know, people told her, "Don't do that."]

Yeah.

[Tonia: But she didn't listen.]

[Robin: She kept on, and Jumbie got up and went in the back of his tent and closed it up.]

You know that old Aku up in Rose Prairie?
That's my grandpa's brother.

[Robin: Yeah.]

He know something too that old man.

[Robin: What kind of things can't he do?]

I don't know. I never did find out about him, but—
I never see him all the time now.
And I just don't like to go to Doig River
on account of them boys, you know.
Don't like them boys.
I like them but they just act too—too crazy.
That's why I don't like.
They always want to fight.
That's why I never see that old man.
I seen him in town once.

He told me, "You got any money?"
I say I got money, he try to give me money
but I say, "No." I tell him,
"You buy something with that money."

[Robin: Yeah. He must know a lot, that old guy.]

Yeah. He still good too. Still sawing wood.
Last time I saw him
he still sawing wood, splitting wood, getting water.

[Robin: He's got that baby.]

Yeah. He got that little baby.
Boy. He's must be pretty tough.
I never did see that baby
but I hear about it.

[Tonia: We saw that baby one time.]

I wish I know all them story.
I tell 'em right.
Know them old-timer story.
I just pick up from what they told me, you know.
But maybe when I get older I remember all them now.
I'm too young yet.
I just forget.
But when I'm about forty, maybe them story come back to me
again and I know it.

Grab a Little Earth

[Robin: Do you know any of the stories about how the world got
made?]

Yeah. They tried—with Beaver and Muskrat.
First start, you know, you know that God?
He told that Beaver to go—to dive in, in the ocean, like.
There's no land.
Just water.
He dive in and bring back a little—

he say to grab a little earth, you know.
"Grab a little earth and bring it back to me," he told him.
He keep trying, keep trying.
He can't make it.
And so, finally he told the Muskrat to come back,
to try it.
Now Muskrat dive and he been gone for long time, you know.
So deep, you know.
I don't think he get to the bottom right away.
Was gone for a long time. They waiting up on top.
And finally that Muskrat came back.
He got a little dirt on his hand.
You know. The little earth on his hand.
He came back up,
up on top and he gave it to that God.
That's how it make.
He say them—even now them, some of them guys say—
that Muskrat make the world for us.
That's how it's made.

[Tonia: So, there's water underneath?]

Yeah.

[Tonia: All underneath the land?]

Yeah. Water.
There's nothing but ocean left, the ocean left
before that Muskrat made that ground.

[Robin: Is that where those moose come from?]

Yeah. He gathered all them animals around, you know.
That's when they make the earth, you know.

[Robin: You know from that moose lick? Do they come from underneath where there's still water?]

No. They—
they just like the king of the animals staying there, you know.
They know. King of the moose, and any kind, any kind you.
Even elk, deer—all kinds stuff.

That's why moose come every night to that lick, you know.
That king of them animals staying underneath that lick.
If you know that stuff boy you be real—real powerful.

[Tonia: When the moose go down in that lick—underneath is a different land?]

Yeah, I think so.
Maybe that's why they stay under so long, you know.
Just like—just like Dad, Dad kill at the Buckinghorse.
That moose they kill.
His horn didn't grow [a moose with single-pronged horns].
Except like this. Just like a cow, you know.
A cow. Was so big, you know.
Just straight out, like this.
It still got a hair on it too.
But I took the hair out and hang it up on a tree.
Maybe somebody found it.

[Tonia: But they can breathe underneath?]

Yeah. I think so.

[Robin: What happens to animals' shadows when they die? They have same kind of shadows that people do?]

No.
Go right straight to heaven.
They got no sin.
They don't swear.
Don't lie.
They don't steal.
You know, sometime I feel sorry, you know.
I look at lots of guys steal, you know.
I feel sorry for them.
When they die it's on the book in heaven.
Every day, what we doing, they write it down up there.
And that's what them old-timers tell me, you know.

[Robin: So, when you kill an animal, its shadow just goes straight up?]

Yeah.
Even horse, you know.
My dad, I mean, my grandpa,
Grandpa he lost a horse here.
It got hit, you know.
One eye.
He just got—that horse just got one eye, you know.
He got hit. My dad—my grandpa was worried about that,
that horse, you know, he been having that horse for a long time.
Got hit up here in [Mile] 245.
And one night he went to sleep
and "My horse," he say, "he walk—he walking to heaven."
"But he keep stopping keep stopping and looking back," he say.
I guess he looking back for his owner, you know.
He say, "My horse just keep stopping
and looking back all the time," he say.
Guess he made it to heaven.
They say if you got lots of sin, you know,
you do everything wrong, you do everything wrong, you know,
like robbing and killing and everything—
you kill somebody you know you got lots of sin.
Robbing—and fighting, like.
You got lots of sin.
If somebody, somebody kill you, you got no sin.
You go right straight to heaven.
That guy who kill you he take all—all the sin away from you.
The guy who kill you he got all the—
he pack all the sin with him till he die.

[Tonia: Yeah. That's tough.]

Yeah. Even —— you know, done that.
But I can't tell the story about it.

[Robin: Yeah. He must have a lot of . . .]

[Tonia: He must feel really bad.]

Yeah. He was really bad.

[Robin: I wonder what he thinks—about what's going to happen to him.]

Sometime he's . . . One time my mom and dad saw him.
He was crying—in town, you know.
He was crying but can't help it.

[Robin: Yeah.]

[Tonia: Too late.]

[Robin: I guess he wishes somebody would kill him.]

Yeah.

[Robin: It's the only way. But nobody wants to do that.]

Yeah.
Says he can't take it you know.
He packing all the sins.

[Tonia: Yeah. Must really be tough.]

Swan's Island

Yeah. I kinda like them books
you guys wrote, you know.
Lots of them white guys
they working with me last year
they tell me, tell me to bring them books along.
All of them old story.
They kinda like it.

[Tonia: Yeah. They're good stories.]

[Robin: Sometime we're going to put some of them together and make a real book. You know, the one we made, we just made a few of them.]

[Tonia: Yeah. We've got lots more stories. We've got stories from Old Man Aku . . .]

Yeah.

[Robin: Yeah. He told lots . . . and some that Jumbie told, too. Gee, there'd be enough for three or four books.]

Yeah. Put 'em all together.

[Robin: Yeah. That whole bunch about Usakindji is really good. That would make a nice book—just those ones.]

Tell the first—you know that—Wabashu [Swan].
That's the first one.
When he was little you know his father—that woman
fool him, make a fool out of him.
Hunt rabbit, put rabbit, when that boy shot the rabbit
in the head, you know, with a bow and arrow—
put it under his dress.
So his father put him on an island out in the ocean.
But he can't do nothing.
Got nothing, father, his father he's leave him.
And all the animals, like flying ducks,
sounds he call them, you know.
In the first started, he start, started worry.
Crying, you know.
In a little lake.
He was crying, and then, I think them geese
or something, talk to him
who were going, going back south,
south pretty soon they tell him.
So he start, start to tame 'em, you know.
I guess he just somebody help him, like.
Everything help him.
Started look for them spruce tree.
Spruce tree it sticks, you know.
Put 'em, all them on them rocks around the lake.
All around them rocks on the lake, you know.
And one day all the ducks got stuck on it.
They can't fly.
That's how he, he live.
He make a big hole in the ground
and them feathers in the ground—

you know them duck, duck's feathers?
He keep warm and then he make drymeat out of the ducks, you
    know.
He got all kinds of meat for in the winter.
That's how he live.
The next spring his dad said,
"I gonna look for his bones."
He came back to the shore and
boy saw and went away around.
His dad, dad saw his track one place
and he started look for him
but that boy he took off with that canoe.
You know. He stop right in the middle
to wait for his dad, you know.
To wait for his dad and soon as his dad
saw where he make the winter, he say,
"He made it, all right."
He go run back to his canoe
but his canoe's gone—he look right across the ocean.
That boy right in the middle.
His father can't do nothing.
He's begging his son to come and get him, but he say,
"You left me here. You left me here.
You stay there and do like I am," he tell him.
"You make the winter," he tell him.
He went across—
he went across to where his mother's staying,
his stepmother.
He kill his mother too.
Not his really mother, but his stepmother.
Kill 'em right there and he went different place after that time.
Next year he went back he saw his father.
Father's body.
That's when he started making the world.
Part of it I can't—I don't remember.
When they started, you know.

[Robin: Yeah. And then he stayed with that Onli Nachi?]

Yeah. I think so.
Can't remember part of it.
I know. I know it, but I can't remember it.
After that I think he stay with that big animal or something.
That's pretty dangerous them big animal.
I wouldn't steal it.
I wish I went—I was that year ago.
I wouldn't be living now.

Not Electricity Do That

[Robin: Was another animal that your grandfather knew was foxes?]

Yeah.

[Robin: Was there some kind of thing that he couldn't do because of that?]

No. He just saw a fox family, the kids.
He say, "When I was walking along," he say,
"there's kids playing."
They just like kids to him.
When he came to them he say,
"Where's your—where's your mother?" he told them—
little fox babies, you know.
They say, "Mom went hunting."
"They told me," he said.
That's how he know it.

[Robin: And that gives him power for hunting?]

Yeah.

[Robin: Just like foxes?]

No. He just—he say
one day he came to these little fox, you know,
they were playing outside their den,
outside their den, you know,
and he say when he walk up to them,

walk up to them little fox, he say,
"Where's your mother?"
and them little fox told him,
"Our mother and father went hunting."
Little fox told that grandfather.
That's how he know.
They never—they never sing or anything for him
but he just know 'em, you know.

[Robin: So, sometimes you can know an animal but you just don't get a song from him?]

Yeah.
You can ask for help, you know.
They remember you.

[Robin: So, if you don't know a song, like, then you can eat anything, or do anything?]

Maybe some . . .
You can eat anything
but maybe you're just like something that you don't like to eat.
You can't take it.

[Tonia: And then you can't use your song to make somebody well?]

You can use it.
Lots of times Grandpa done that to me.
And even that one time that Fort St. John Rodeo,
you know that old sports ground?
That time lightning just about kill me.
I was staying out, you know.
All night the lightning just shooting.
And all that thunder, you know.
Shooting close by me, you know.
And they nearly kill me.
Kill about three children in that night.
Three white kids.
Just about got me and the next morning I couldn't even . . .
I got so, my head just busting, you know.
I can't even open my eyes.

I got so terrible headache, you know, from that lightning.
And Grandpa he took me a way out where nobody can hear, you
    know,
and say,
"Can you make it to that far?"
he told me, I say,
"I can't make it."
He hold my arm and I walk with him quite a ways in the bush.
And he carry water in his cup. You know, his drinking cup.
And he give me a water first and he starts singing.
But I was still feeling worse
so he told me to go in the hospital.
I went in the hospital for twenty days.
Twenty days everybody went home.
I was worried.
Really worried.

[Robin: How old were you then?]

'Bout twelve. Twelve year old.
'Bout eleven or twelve, I think. Patrick was about this high.
Me and Patrick was with Daddy, you know.
Dad was just dead drunk. That's why we—
that's why lightning nearly got me then, you know.
Dad fall down in the mud all the time.
We were too little, you know
and Dad was too heavy for us.
We can't get him up.
We have to wait till he wake up, keep walking, again,
and finally make it to Charlie Yahey's camp.
Next morning I can't wake up.
Grandpa know right away.
He know what happen, gave me water—
he say, "You gonna be OK," but for a while . . .

[Robin: He sang song from *natane*?]

Yeah.

[Robin and Tonia discuss feeding their baby for a minute.]

[Robin: Did people used to use their songs to kill other people?
Long ago?]

No, I don't think so.

[Robin: Just to defend themselves?]

Yeah.
No, they know—they know when somebody . . .
If you got not enough power
they know when somebody going to kill you,
but the other guy got enough power,
they can't do nothing.
He gotta fight till he die, you know.
If he kill you that's the end.
You know, when, when somebody, yet now,
even now, I gotta wait till about,
gotta wait till about two o'clock in the morning.
And I go after you—where you are, you know?
You know if I go after you, you got not enough power,
I gotta kill you anyway.
You got no chance.
You gotta fight but that other guy enough power.
You gotta die.

[Robin: Do they do that just by dreaming or do they have to send
their animal out?]

Send their animal out.

[Tonia: And then maybe they feel sick?]

Yeah. Next morning they . . .

[Robin: Is that sometimes little animals good for that?]

Yeah.

[Tonia: Any kind?]

No.
Just like birds but it's different, you know.
Grandpa was saying that.

Say that time that guy want to try to kill him, you know.
He was go after him, he say,
"That guy was just coming straight ahead on the air."
You know, he can see him.
He spot him.
That's where they had a battle.
He say,
"If I want to I can kill him but I hurt him enough," he say.
He say,
"I throw him over that mountain."
He say,
"Next morning he came to our house."
He say,
"That guy must have been pretty sick," he say.
He say,
"He won't try that again next time," he say.
He say,
"If I want to kill him I'll kill him," he say.
"But I think about heaven."
Two times somebody did that to him.
He came to our house next morning.
He told us.

[Tonia: That time that lightning just about kill you, somebody send
that lightning?]

No.
There were—you know them guys that don't believe,
they're cooking with a grease.
You know, they were cooking bacon.
And that thunder nobody believe, eh?
They say it's just electric, but,
electricity, but
these guys that, some guys that know it they,
it's some kind of, some kind of a bird
but it's all red, they say.
Got a red thing on his head, you know.
That's what lightning, thunder is, they say.
Some guys don't believe it, you know.

So these guys start cooking bacon
and pretty soon it just went dark.
You know there's little clouds up in the,
up in the sky that time.
Nice sunshine.
Nice day.
Pretty soon just black clouds came in.
Lightning!
Holy man!
Talk about lightning!
That lightning strike not even about,
not even a half a mile from the camp.
Just bust the tree open.
That's the time lightning just about got me.
So close to the camp we stay, you know.
Where they cooking bacon, you know.

[Robin: How come that cooking with grease it makes the lightning
come?]

They say it kind of make him mad.
You know, them old-timers say that,
but these new guys that time.
Not too long ago
Mary, I told Mary [Mary St. Pierre—this happened several days
     before in our presence],
that thunder, you know that time that started raining?
Thunder's making?
I told Mary,
"There's a thunder outside.
You better not cook them with the grease," I told her.
But she say,
"It's just electricity yet," she told me.
I told him,
"Some day you find out," I told her.
Come lots of guys don't believe it.
One long time ago, Jumbie was telling me about that story.
How these two, three little kids, they were fishing, you know
and there's lightning all over the place

and they don't believe nothing.
You know, they were teasing that lightning.
They cooking them fish.
You know how strong them fish smell when they're cooking?
They were cooking.
That lightning strike right in the middle of the kids.
Where they cooking that fish, you know.
Them three kids dead right there.

[Tonia: How come that thunder doesn't—that bird doesn't like that meat? Is he hungry?]

No.

[Tonia: Or he just doesn't like people to . . .]

I guess he just doesn't like the smell.

[Tonia: The smell of the grease? In the fish?]

Yeah.

[Robin: Is it just the way the grease sort of explodes and jumps?]

Yeah.

[Tonia: Like lightning?]

Yeah. Guess that's why.
I hear lots of guys say that.
I don't, I believe the story, but it's,
I believe the story, but,
I'd like to try it but I don't,
I really believe.

[Robin: Too scared to try that?]

[Tonia: That's playing with fire, as they say.]

Yeah. I don't want to end up my life.
You never, you never tease something like that.
These kids teasing that.

[Robin: That's crazy, isn't it? It's like teasing a grizzly bear.]

Yeah.
They say them guys just lying—
"Let's try it," they say.
They start cooking them fish.
That lightning just strike right in the middle of them.
They all dead. Three kids. That's bad.
That's why when somebody cook something
when it's stormy like that
I don't trust it.
I gotta get out of there.
Lots of guys don't believe it. Can't believe it.
You know, it just not electricity do that.
Lot of the guys know that lightning.
And they got power with that lightning.

[Tonia: If somebody has power with the lightning, can he make it go? Flash?]

No.
If they told him to go away, he go away.
He won't stay by your place or anything.

[Tonia: But he can't tell lightning to go hit someplace?]

No.

[Robin: You can't kill somebody with it?]

He can kill somebody with it.

[Robin: So, if you know that and you've got some enemy, you can kill him with it?]

Yeah.
Just like if you're my enemy, like you tell me any kind.
You tell me something—
bad word—
and I remember that.
Whenever you go home I send,
I send that lightning up to you.
That lightning strike you dead.
That's why lots of guys, guys fight with that thing.

Even if you tell me a mean word like right now.
When I go home and go to sleep
I go after you, you know—two o'clock in the morning.
That's how lots of guys is long time ago, you know.
They just tell each other mean word and they got to get mad.
They go after you.
With their power.
That's how lots of guys,
lots of guys kill each other long time ago.
Not with their bow and arrows
but with their power
most of the time, you know.
But now it's different.
You got to use rifle.
Either rifle or a knife.
But what you gonna do when you die?
Gonna go to hell.
Burn—the rest of your life.

The Gate to Heaven

[Robin: What happens to somebody if he kills somebody else with
his power? Does that mean he can't go to heaven?]

They turn you away from the heaven, but they send you to a . . .
You got no choice.
Gotta go to that devil's gate.
They call him Dunne Metsele.
Devil.
You go to his fire. You gotta go in.
Don't like it but you gotta go.
Got no choice.
You can't come back here.
It's no good.
Either burn or go back up pay it. You got no choice.

[Tonia: Is that what's going to happen to ——?]

Yeah.

I don't know ahead of them
but you got too many sins ahead of them.

[Tonia: If a ghost try to take a little kid?]

He try to lead 'em up to heaven, you know.

[Tonia: And, then, like, say, your grandfather dream about that,
and then, how does he tell the ghost, he just tells the ghost, he
sends his friend up to tell the ghost to quit doing that?]

No. He just . . .
He can't help it.
If the ghost catch your little baby, you know,
the guys who got power,
they can fix it up.
But if the ghost catch your shadow, you know,
your wraith, your wraith and your shadow?
You can't last three days.
That morning three days.
Little kid like that maybe two.

[Robin: That's all it takes, then, because they don't have any power?
They don't have any sins?]

Yeah. They got no sin—nothing.
You know, little kid like that.
They got no sin.
And they figure they gonna lead 'em,
lead 'em to heaven, you know—on the right trail.
But they can't make it anyway.

[Tonia: Sometime, if a ghost tries to do that, can somebody with
lots of power get that shadow back?]

Yeah.

[Tonia: A baby?]

Yeah. He can fix 'em.

[Robin: Were you around that time that Jerry—some ghost tried to
steal his shadow?]

[Tonia: Down at Trutch. Trutch?]

[Robin: Yeah. Down at Trutch. Oh, it was terrible—one night . . .]

Yeah. I was there.

[Robin: Yeah. He ran out into the bush, and then he fell, I guess twice, or maybe three times, it happened . . .]

[Tonia: He fell out and . . .]

[Robin: He fell down . . .]

[Tonia: And his tongue came out of his mouth—all black.]

Yeah.
Trutch is a bad place. You know that?

[Tonia: Lots of ghosts?]

Yeah.

[Robin: 'Cause lots of old people who died still hanging around there?]

No, but all kinds.
Even my grandpa say, even in the States, you know,
bad guys die?
They gotta travel on this road [Alaska Highway].
Even them turnout roads, you know,
they travel on that
and when they get to the end
they turn back and go on this highway all the time.

[Tonia: They thinking that's the road to heaven?]

Yeah. They figure that's the road to heaven.

[Robin: So some of them end up on the other end of Trutch?]

Yeah.

[Robin: But it doesn't go anywhere.]

[Tonia: But you know, they're all just passing through?]

Yeah.
But I think that Trutch is kind of no good, you know.
Sandy nearly got crazy in there one time.
You know. Just about went out of his mind.
And Jumbie stop him.
"It's from that lake," Jumbie say.
We swim every night.
Night and day we swim in there.
Sandy nearly went out of his mind.
I think something nearly caught his shadow.

[Robin: Some kind of animal under the water?]

Yeah. I think so.
Yeah. I think animal done that.
Kind of bad stuff, bad animal.
It's not a animal but kinda maybe ghost.
You know guys really bad. Really bad.
Guess that kind of guys done that.
But Jumbie, one morning, one morning,
Sandy just talking kind of strange, you know,
stay with us all the time kind of talking strange.
And Jumbie he woke up one morning and he give him water,
water and he touch his—he rub his head with water.
And after that he's OK.

[Robin: How come people still camp down there if it's such a bad place?]

[Tonia: Maybe they think the hunting's good.]

Hunting's good.
It's not too bad now, you know,
but before, before that it's really bad.
When you walking in the nighttime up from Trutch,
you walking down that road,
you can hear somebody whistling at you.
You get scared right away.
One thing.

Never get scared.
If you get scared they go after you more.

[Tonia: And they figure they can get you?]

Yeah.

[Robin: What's the best thing to do? Can you yell at them? Tell them to go away?]

Yeah. You can yell. You scare them away.
You know. One time I went down with a bicycle.
I went down with a bicycle, and you know where that creek is?
Started climb in there and somebody scream at me.
Yell at me.
Call my name and everything.
Just keep on going till I got to that little,
got to that little top hill.
Went there and I had a firecracker, you know,
whole bunch of firecrackers.
I light one and it start shooting, boy.
That's when that really take off.
I got a accident in that bottom hill at that Trutch.
Bicycle turn over. Got scars all around my face.

[Robin: Was it nighttime?]

Yeah. Nighttime. I was coming back from Trutch.

[Robin: Boy, I'd be scared to do that. I don't think I've ever walked that road at nighttime.]

They say, you know, about couple, three years ago, I think—
they say it's pretty bad in Rose Prairie.
They say it's pretty bad Rose Prairie.
One time I went over there
and I was travelling at nighttime.
I went through there and I knock on the door.
Keep knocking on the one door, you know.
On that what you call him—Dan Wolf's place.
I knock on his door—he can't open.

I keep knocking. He can't open, you know.
Dogs barking all over the place.
I figure there's nothing wrong with these place.
Finally I look back, you know.
There's a fellow walking.
He came closer, like.
It's not a man.
So I call Dan Wolf and he open the door and I went in.
"Somebody walking behind me," I told him.
"Dog barking all the time," he say.
"It's no good," he told me. "No good to walk in nighttime."
It's when I don't want to walk in nighttime that place.

[Tonia: What do ghosts do during the daytime?]

They can't see nothing daytime.

[Tonia: They can only see at night?]

Yeah. They can only see at night. Not daytime.
'Cause they can't see nothing.
Just like stay in the dark.
Blind like.
Can't see nothing.

[Robin: Do they sleep? Do they just stay in one place?]

They gotta just keep going, you know.

[Robin: They just stumble around?]

Yeah.

[Robin: Like they're in the dark?]

Yeah. Just like drunk, you know.
Can't see nothing, you know.
That's why I wouldn't be like that the rest of my life.
When I die.

[Tonia: Yeah. What happened to ghosts before Indians knew about
heaven? When they walk and they walk and they walk and they

pay for—and they go back every place they lived and everything?
Then what do they do after they finish that?]

They gotta stay where they . . .

[Tonia: Where they ended up?]

Yeah. Either that or they go to somebody, you know.
Some woman—so they can have two chance, you know.

[Robin: They get born again?]

Yeah. Born again.
They can go to some woman born two time,
they second chance, you know.
If they're bad that time they're die they go to another woman.
Their last chance, I guess.

[Robin: Does that still happen?]

Oh, yeah.
Lots of guys got that.
You know, even that first Harry's wife?
You know, Mary Tachie.
She was like that.
Grandpa dream about that I think.

[Tonia: But she lived just like she was—for the first time?]

Yeah.

[Robin: What happened after she died?]

She gotta pay for her sins, I think.

[Robin: Has she gotten to heaven yet?]

No.

[Robin: She still has to walk back all her tracks?]

Yeah.

[Tonia: She's still walking?]

Till he's baby.

[Robin: And then she get born again?]

No.

[Tonia: She already got born again.]

When she was,
she was, when the first start she was born, till then,
she was how many year old.
She gotta go backwards till she was baby when.

[Tonia: So she's got to go back—like, if she was forty-five, take forty-five years?]

Yeah. Forty-five years till she, she end up,
she end up that forty-five years.

[Robin: So then after that she goes to heaven?]

Yeah. She gotta wait that long.
You know and one thing—I think she kill a baby or something.

[Tonia: Her own baby?]

Long time ago.
But nobody know about it.

[Tonia: Why would she do that?]

I don't know.

[Tonia: That's a funny thing to do.]

Yeah. I guess he was born dead.
She was afraid.
No doctor that time.
That's the reason.

[Robin: Wintertime must be really bad when it's dark all the time.]

What?

[Robin: Wintertime must be really bad.]

Cold.

[Robin: When it's dark all the time, too.]

I guess the only time they're have tough time is wintertime.
You know. When it's cold.
Patrick saw his, saw Mary Tachie's shadow.
That time she was burned to death here,
saw him just, there was a moonlight
and they were going to this, Jumbie was,
they had, they playing drum in Jumbie house.
They were going to there,
and they saw this girl coming, coming walk up to our place
and Patrick saw him first—you know, he was little boy—
and he told my mother,
"There's Mary Tachie coming to us," he say.
He started chasing, Patrick started chasing him
but he went around this house and he disappear.
Didn't see him no more.

[Robin: How come that they have to burn down a house after somebody dies in it?]

[Tonia: So that they don't have to live there—so the ghost doesn't have to stay there?]

No.
I guess they just kind of worried where he been you know?
Don't have to stay there.
You know, even Dad, you know.
Mary was staying with us in that [Mile] 210 cabin for a long time.
Whenever Dad see that cabin, go in that cabin,
he started just bust out crying.

[Tonia: 'Cause he think about it?]

Yeah.
That's why he burn it down.
When he burned it he say,
"I going to build this other cabin right on top of the other one."
"It's gonna stay there," he said.

[Tonia: The people take down, like they put up a tent someplace and when they leave to go someplace else, they take down all the poles—is that so that the ghost doesn't have to stay there?]

Yeah.

That's why I don't trust this highway in the nighttime.

Figure something going to meet me all the time.

They gotta travel on this road all the time.

They don't know where else to go.

He can't find the right trail.

[Tonia: That's really crazy. They should just start going up.]

Yeah.

Grandpa say he never go straight up.

Say you gotta, you know there's a just like a—

you seen them sun when they going down?

Can see the, just like a string,

can see from, from the window

just like a string going from the sun.

Say you can use hole of that—right through the gate

from the heaven.

[Tonia: There's a hole?]

Yeah. Say there's a man there, right there too, he say.

Just like night guard, you know.

Stay by the gate to heaven.

[Robin: What's the name of that place? That hole?]

[Tonia: That hole to the sky? To the heaven?]

Can't remember it.

Can't pronounce it on a English.

[Robin: No. In your language, I mean.]

Huh?

[Robin: In your language—how's it called?]

Yi at' dao de gat'.

Something like that.

[Tonia: That means something like "hole into Heaven?"]

Yeah.

[Tonia: And then on top, it's just like land again?]

Yeah.

[Tonia: Only heaven?]

Yeah, but fancy.
Even we dressed up now but it's nothing, what heaven is.
That's why Grandpa say,
"I feel ashamed of myself," he say.
He say,
"It's so fancy,
everything smell good just like perfume," he say.
Might make it up there someday.
Never know.
Maybe even next year.

[Tonia: See everybody again.]

Maybe I be strangers. Nobody know me.
Except that Johnny Andree old wife.

[Tonia: Is she dead?]

First wife.

[Tonia: Oh, yeah.]

Johnny Andree's first wife. She's Jumbie's daughter.

[Tonia: She made it up right away?]

Hey?

[Tonia: She made it up to heaven right away?]

Oh, yeah. She's up there all right.
Probably married.
They say you've ever seen a good woman!
She don't like to see,
she don't like to see anybody do something poor like.
If you're out of sugar she don't like that.
They say.
You never did saw her

but whenever, whenever, Mom he say, Mom, Mom say,
every morning she gotta bring something to eat to us.
When I was little, you know, I stay with her all the time
she told me—Mom told me.
She say. Mom told me,
"I never look after you.
Johnny Andree's first wife look after you all the time."
You know, when she die, she say to look after me pretty good.
"Don't talk to him rough or anything," she say,
and she's,
she's dead.
That's why when I get to heaven I thank her for that.

[Tonia: Your grandfather, too. You can see him, eh? Must be lots of
people you know. Some still working away at ghosts.]

Grandfather make it to his first wife anyway.

PART FOUR

OLD TIME RELIGION

Overleaf: Tommy Attachie, 1982

18. SOUNDMAN

I lost direct contact with the Dunne-za world for most of the 1970s. My time and energy went in other directions. I wrote articles and prepared courses in order to be granted tenure in my position with the University of British Columbia. I became attracted to life on the B.C. coast. I took on the massive project of commissioning and building a forty-five-foot traditional Nova Scotian fishing schooner named *Starswan* after the Dreamers who can fly from one season to another. By 1972, Tonia and I had three children but were going through the hard times of separation and divorce.

The 1970s were a time of hardship and loss for the Dunne-za families with whom I had been closest. At Prophet River, Granny Jumbie, Julie Chipesia, and my own stepfather, Sam St. Pierre, all passed away during my absence. I was also stunned by the tragic and untimely deaths of my brother and sister, Billy and Sally St. Pierre. Willy Olla, George Olla, and Patrick Chipesia also died when I was away. At Doig, many of the elders had passed away in the years since I last heard the drumming and singing of a Dunne-za pow-wow there in the summer of 1969, just before our daughter Amber was born in the Fort St. John hospital. Gone were Old Man Aku, the great singer Billy Makadahay, Nachin, and her sister Es-kama. I knew that an era had come to a close when I learned that the Dreamer Charlie Yahey and Anachuan were also gone. When she died, Anachuan was reported on the national news to have been the oldest woman in Canada. The same newscast that announced her death also described the safe landing of a robot space-craft on the surface of Mars.

My contact with the Dunne-za world resumed when Gerry Attachie became chief at Doig in 1976 and visited Vancouver to attend meetings of the Union of B.C. Indian Chiefs. He found my phone number and gave me a call. We met, and I gave him photographs of Charlie Yahey and other elders. I copied tapes of Charlie Yahey singing Dreamers' songs and speaking to people in the majestic cadence of his prophetic oratory. By then, I had begun to build a new life with Jillian Ridington, whom I had married the year before. When Gerry brought the Dunne-za world back into my life, he met Jillian and suggested that we come back to Doig for a visit. After the shock of feeling that the Dunne-za world I knew had fallen apart, Gerry's reaching out gave me a new sense of hope for renewed contact. Gerry continued to visit Vancouver from time to time, as lawyers for Doig and Blueberry began to do research on the circumstances surrounding the loss of the reserve that had been their summer gathering place. This research and planning for an eventual breach of trust suit against the government of Canada continued to build in intensity during the next ten years.

In 1978, Jillian and I met Howard Broomfield, an audio artist and documentarian, who had been an associate of the World Soundscape Project organized by composer R. Murray Schafer. Howard became our friend, mentor, brother. He moved into a basement room in our house and began to teach us how to listen. He taught us to be aware of the sounds around us as we had never been before. He also taught us how to produce radio programs through our mutual involvement with Vancouver's cooperative radio station, CFRO. We called the first piece we did together "Soundwalk to Heaven." In the program, I talked about the idea that Dreamers' songs reveal Yagatunne, the Trail to Heaven. As I spoke, Howard played the tapes of Charlie Yahey singing and talking. Doing that program and talking with Howard about his experience of soundscape recording made me realize how important it would be to begin a comprehensive archive of recorded actualities in the rapidly changing communities of the Dunne-za. I was able to obtain a small grant from UBC to begin the work.

In the summer of 1979, Jillian, Howard, and I, with two of my children, Eric (whom the Indians called Aballi) and Amber, set out in a blue Volvo station wagon from our home in Vancouver for the Doig River Indian Reserve. It was my first time back since the beautiful pow-wow at Doig in 1969. The object of my return was to renew contact with the community and begin a collection of audio recordings documenting the changing soundscape of a northern Indian community. Unlike my previous recordings, which had concentrated on music and oratory, I wanted now to document every aspect of life at Doig.

When the heavily loaded Volvo pulled into Doig, a swarm of kids clambered over the car. Howard and I pulled out a Jew's harp and took turns playing it. Thus, we arrived on Howard's distinctive keynote sound of musical improvisation. Our times at Doig with Howard were always musical and usually whimsical as well. We began to record "talking field notes" at the end of each day. We set up an umbrella tent and two pup tents on a spot behind the row of plywood houses that constituted downtown Doig. We put up a hand-painted sign that read "Monias City, pop. 5." *Monias* is the word both Cree and Dunne-za people use for white man. Howard's sense of naming the stories of his own experience corresponded to a similar way the people at Doig name one another and episodes from their own lives. Like everything else in Howard's life, our presence in Doig became a story with a name. They called Howard "Soundman," and in an intentional exercise in hyperbole they named a tiny rivulet near where Howard once camped with the Attachie family "Broomfield Creek."

We set up microphones. The first night, Howard was astonished by the eloquent silence of the place. That night reminded me of the first summer night I spent in the Peace River country in 1959. We stayed up through the dawn of a new day. We recorded hour upon hour of silences, punctuated by the calling of camp dogs and the undertone of a river running beside the cutbank at the edge of a dirt road in front of the row of houses. In the morning, we recorded the loud and insistent dawn chorus of birds. In the days that followed, we recorded a hunt, a soundwalk around the reserve escorted by quick-talking kids, message time on CKNL radio, snaring rabbits, skinning a deer, scraping a hide, and countless conversations and stories. We even recorded people at Doig playing cassettes of my old Charlie Yahey recordings as they beaded moccasins, did laundry, scraped hides, or just sat around to listen.

One night, as we gathered around our campfire talking with people who came by to visit, Sammy Acko told us he thought it might rain during the night. He was concerned that the intensity of the rain not take us by surprise. Sammy said, "It's good to listen to the rain falling on a tent roof." Then he retired to the house where he would be spending the night. We were in our tents. Before dawn, the skies opened and thunder rolled around the sky from horizon to horizon. We set up microphones under the tent awning. We listened to the sound of rain through the earphones. We set out inverted pots and pans to catch the irregular percussion of the torrent. Through the earphones, they sounded like a symphony of taut tapping tones of different timbre. We decided to call the piece thus realized "Sammy Says." It was the first in an archive of improvisational soundscape pieces we collected between 1979 and 1985.

Our lives became stories for everyone else at Doig. Howard scavenged pieces of old cars and farm equipment for a "sound sculpture." He wrote in his notebook, "We created an environment and then we played it." He carried a tape recorder and microphone wherever he went. He listened to the world through headphones. The name Soundman suited him perfectly. People at Doig came to accept that Howard was always "taking sound." In his persona as Soundman Howard recorded virtually every kind of activity that took place. The three of us worked together as a team. Sometimes Jillian and I made recordings as well, but Howard was constantly "on air," as we put it to one another. He recorded our conversations and interactions with people at Doig. He recorded Dunne-za music. He recorded Fort St. John bar bands. He recorded Doig guys jamming with fiddles and guitars on lazy summer afternoons. He recorded fierce drunks. He recorded the hiss and clatter of oil production machinery. He recorded white people talking about their experiences with Indian people. He recorded conversations in cars and trucks, and he recorded earnest discussions about the meaning of life. Howard experienced the world as music. His recordings created an environment, then played it.

Howard taught us to think of the soundscape as a comprehensive acoustic environment. We began to think of recording as a way of using audio "actualities" to document cultural information unavailable through any other medium. We began to think about recording long uninterrupted passages rather than arbitrarily selecting when something "important" was happening. Howard taught us the importance of recording silences. The people at Doig understood that Soundman was a listener and a composer. They understood that he experienced the world as music. They knew that when Howard recorded conversations he was experiencing them as parts in a composition he was hearing above and beyond their literal meanings as texts. Howard's way of recording revealed that he listened to the timbre of sounds as keynotes for the compositions he held in his mind. He listened to the rhythms that exist beyond meter. He listened for inner meanings that lie between the lines of spoken discourse. He listened for delicate harmonics and resonances that reveal personality and define situation.

Howard used material from the Dunne-za archive in the same way that other composers use scored instrumentation. His compositions reflect the many voices he heard in the world around him. They have a "sound" that is distinctively his own. Howard was always *in* the world he recorded. He recorded people and animals, winds and waters, junk collections and drunks. Howard was able to have a personal connection with all of them. His work created a kind of reflexive ethnography of the soundscape. The world Howard showed us was distinctive, yet familiar. He turned us all into listeners. Howard brought out a musical dimension that we all experience but cannot always sort out from the din of events we are conditioned to believe are real. Howard seemed to live in the world of a different reality, a musical reality. He lived in the world of a listener. He shared that world in the work we did with him.

In 1982, I was blessed with a sabbatical leave from my teaching responsibilities at UBC. Howard and I contrived to spend ten days at Doig in late March and early April in order to record the winter soundscape. During this visit, we stayed at the bachelor house, Tommy Attachie's "Mansion on the Hill." It was far too cold to recreate Monias City. Living at Tommy's, it was clear that whatever happened, we would be part of it. The trip was, for me and Howard, literally fabulous. We lived it like the story it was. We recorded as much of it as possible. We framed it with our arrival and our departure. We cherished it in our memories, and we dramatized it to an audience of astonished academic anthropologists at the Canadian Ethnology Society meetings in Vancouver within a month of our return. Shortly thereafter, I wrote down the story of what happened—from notes, from memory, from audio recordings, and from conversations with Howard. We called the "docudrama" we presented to the 1982 spring meetings of the Canadian Ethnology Society in Vancouver "Old Time Religion." I have kept that name for this written version of our presentation.

"Old Time Religion" is a close description of events that took place on the evening of April 2, 1982. Those of us who took part in the events of that evening experienced them in the context of a range of mutual understandings. None of our understandings were identical. Indeed, the evening's conflict arose out of a struggle between alternative versions of the story we were bringing into being. Although Howard's and my perceptions were probably at the greatest distance from those shared by other participants, the conflict was not between us and them but between two closely related constructions of the same Dunne-za reality. We were different from the other participants in the way that a moose is different from a hunter, different but essentially accommodating. We thought of ourselves, and were perceived by our hosts, as anthropologists acting like moose. We gave ourselves willingly to the story.

I have chosen to present "Old Time Religion" essentially as I wrote it in 1982, when the events were still fresh in my mind's eye and ear. I wrote it in the style of field notes, shaped through the context of a universe of mutual understandings. I wrote about events as I experienced and understood them at the time. Howard and I debated at length about how to interpret our experiences. The version presented here is merely one of many interpretations. A Dunne-za reader may laugh at what was going on in our minds. I may have made simple things appear more complex than necessary. Elsewhere, I may have reduced the complexity of what actually happened. I know that people gave me information in a subtle code that I may have misinterpreted. That, too, is part of the story. "Old Time Religion" weaves back and forth across the evening of April 2, 1982. The story of that evening is part of a larger ongoing story in which we all took part. In order to understand the events of that evening I have also described the memories we shared of other times and places. I have told other stories, beginning with an account of a time when Tommy and I rode in his father's wagon along the old wagon road east of Doig. Taken together, the stories reinforce one another to create a mosaic of interconnected meanings. Like the stories of our lives, the stories of that evening are layered with meaning and with ambiguity. The evening of April 2, 1982 was no more or less ordinary than any other. It is extraordinary only in that I have taken it as a point of focus to show how each story in the life of a small Indian community contains every other.

19. THE OLD WAGON ROAD

On the evening of April 2, 1982, a Friday, Howard and I drove out the old wagon road Doig people used to take from their sod-roofed winter cabins to the store at Cecil Lake. The cabins were still standing in a field on the hill behind the present village when I first came to Doig in 1965. Only a few years before that, the people still lived in them during the winter. They moved by wagon to their hunting grounds in Alberta during the summer. The Mennonites, who live up past where the old wagon road crosses the Osborn River, still keep it open with their tractors and 4 × 4s. In the 1960s they used to go to town on tractors, even in forty-below weather. When it was cold, the Dunne-za went to town on big sleighs, each the size of a small pickup truck. In the summer, they went by saddle horse and wagon.

I travelled the old road by wagon once in the summer of 1966. I rode with Tommy Attachie and his dad, Murray Attachie, in the wagon that still sits out behind where the Attachie house used to be on the Doig River Reserve, fifty miles northwest of Fort St. John. Tommy and I rode in the back of the wagon. Murray drove the team, sitting next to Tar Davis. We were going out to pick up a big bull moose Tar had shot the previous evening. I have a picture of us standing in the wagon holding up wine jugs full of water for the hot dusty day on the road. Tommy rode in the back of the wagon because he had burned his leg when he rolled into a fire coming off a drunk after the stampede at Fort St. John. He could not ride a horse or walk very far, but the wagon ride gave him something to do on the move.

As the old wagon lurched and bounced its load of meat and meat eaters down the road on our return to Doig, Tommy and I played a game of startle. He would remain quiet with the patience of a tree,

then jump toward me with a word or gesture. I replied with whatever came to mind. I remember once calling out the name of black
bear, *sas* in Beaver. It was an exchange of bonding, like arm wres-
tling. It said that Tommy and I were friends and would respect one
another for who we were. It also revealed that beneath the placid
surface of a slow day's journey were sudden edges. Through the
game, Tommy tested my sensitivity to the inner world of his dreaming. Tommy was twenty-three years old in 1966. I was twenty-six.
Tommy began to speak about the world of his dreams. His dream
life revealed and explained the edges that cut across the path of his
life as it appeared to be on the surface. His dreams explained the
fire and his burned leg.

Tommy told me he knew from dreaming that an enemy with
power in his mind had attacked him and driven his body toward
the edge of the fire when his dreaming mind was clouded by alcohol. While Tommy's body struggled to restore itself, the enemy
continued to direct his mind's power against Tommy. The recovery
did not go smoothly. There were infections that undermined his
strength. Tommy focused all his life's energy on dreams in which
he could confront the enemy. He drew upon powers that were the
secret legacy of his training in the bush as a child. I knew he was
referring to his medicine powers, but it was not appropriate for him
to reveal these to me at that time in our relationship.

Finally, he was able to identify and confront the enemy. The confrontation took place in a dream. They faced one another squarely,
mind to mind. The edge between them was the possibility of death.
Tommy knew he had the power to kill the enemy. He opened his
mind to reveal that knowledge to him. Tommy also knew he did
not wish to kill. He did not want to take that man's burden on his
own destiny. He thought of the Creator. He thought of what Charlie
Yahey said about the Trail to Heaven, Yagatunne. A person who
kills will be too heavy from the wrongs done by his enemy to follow the trail of song up to heaven. When his trail on earth comes
to an end, his shadow will have to walk back by night, along the
trail he took by day during his life. Tommy opened his mind to
the enemy as he thought of what the Dreamers said. Faced with
the combination of Tommy's power and his adherence to the
Dreamers' teaching, the enemy retreated. After the dream confron-

tation, Tommy began to recover. Soon, he was well enough to ride in his father's wagon.

As Tommy told me the story of his medicine fight and the teachings of the Dreamers, he began to sing some of their songs. These songs are sent down by the Dreamers in heaven to those who remain on earth. People who have died and are light enough of spirit may follow the turns of the song trails upward. Those who have done harm to others fall back to earth as shadows.

Sometimes, people come together to dance to the Dreamers' songs. They dance together along a common path that circles the fire. They circle the fire together like the sun that circles the sky in its daily and yearly movements. They circle like swans and geese who bring back the turn of the seasons. They circle together to dance away the bad feelings that separate them. The Dreamers say that each turn around the fire takes away from the time a person might have to walk back as a shadow along his tracks. They say that dancing together brings people closer to their relatives in heaven.

Tommy's voice rose and fell like the turns of the old wagon road. I thought of the horse trail that lay under the wagon road and of the older footpath that was still real in the memories and stories of people like Tommy's grandmother Nachin. Tommy accompanied his songs with a regular rhythm. He tapped his right hand against the left palm, held up as if it were a drum. The beats were like the fall of human feet on the trail. The Dreamers say that a good person can grab hold of a song's turns with the mind. I remembered that Tommy said he thought of heaven when he revealed the power in his mind to the enemy. Thoughts of heaven seemed to flood over us, like the beam of sunlight that reaches down to earth from between the hunched shoulders of a turbulent sky. Thoughts of the old people and their trails that lie beneath our own swirled around the hard, dry old wagon as it creaked and bounced its way through the quiet poplar forest and down toward the crossing place on the Osborn.

We were bringing food home to the people. It was a happy time. Tommy's leg was getting better. His enemy had backed off and Tommy was riding in his father's wagon singing Dreamers' songs. The wagon was heavy with the quarters, ribs, head, hide, and various other parts of a large moose that had given itself in a dream to Tar Davis, who spoke little but hunted as if he were born to it. I was with these people as a different kind of hunter. I carried a tape recorder, notebook, and camera rather than a rifle. I recorded the songs and oratory of Charlie Yahey the Dreamer; of Old Man Aku, who was already a strong hunter and family man in the first decade of the century; and of Tommy's grandmother Nachin, who knew the trails people travelled before they had horses. On that summer day in 1966, I studied the territory of Tommy's experience with my mind alone. I hunted for the inner meaning of the stories I was told.

By the spring of 1982, the old wagon road was a pickup road. On the night of April 2, the ruts and ruin of the last summer's gumbo were still frozen solidly in winter's embrace. Even a little highway car like my diesel Rabbit could make it through by riding astride the frozen furrows where Mennonite and Indian pickups had lurched and skidded their way through the muskeg patches. The car passed easily over the Osborn on a bridge of ice and snow that painted the river into the surrounding snowscape. In the world beyond the Doig River Reserve, the Falkland Islands conflict was about to become headline news. The summer's devastation of Beirut had not yet come to mind. We were more aware of the wolf, whose howls shimmered across the cold moon-streaked snow to chill and awe us every night than we were of the "real world."

The evening began with a slide show of pictures I had taken during previous visits to Doig. People of all ages crowded into the steamy, pungent warmth of the house that had belonged to Tommy's grandmother. After she died, Tommy's brother Gerry, the chief, and his wife, Bernice, took it over. With every slide that came on the screen, a chorus of voices called out the names of people and recollections of times the pictures brought to mind. The only silence came when I showed pictures of Mackenzie, Tommy's best friend and cousin who had died of exposure a year before.

Tommy did not come to the slide show. He lives alone in a house set back from the others. He likes to think of himself as an old man. His Beaver name is Mahzon, but the boys call him "Old Man Red." His house is the "Mansion on the Hill" after a song by Hank Williams. It is also known as the "Tommy Attachie Personal Care

Home," because from time to time it is the refuge of younger unmarried men and boys. Howard and I were staying at Tommy's but
spending much of our time visiting other people in the village.

Even though Tommy is three years my junior and I have known
him since his early twenties, I sometimes find myself relating to him
as I did to the old people I knew fifteen years before. Tommy is
more like the old people than he is like Gerry, the chief of a band
finding its way in the modern world. Tommy's fierce fascination
with the dark side of his nature that is released by alcohol has made
it difficult for him to live with a woman. He lives alone because in
his moments of ecstasy he turns the hunter's determination against
those closest to him. The young men who come to his Mansion on
the Hill take the place of children he never had. Tommy is a teacher
who knows the stories of his grandmother and the songs of the
Dreamers. He has a fine, loud, clear voice, and he knows the names
of the Dreamers who brought back each song down the Trail to
Heaven, Yagatunne. Young men come to him to learn and listen
and to practice their own mastery of the tradition.

Gerry's house is a different kind of social center from Tommy's.
Gerry is as sociable as Tommy is withdrawn into the solitude of a
world that continues to feature fierce struggle with dark and hostile
forces, alcohol, and sharp edges that periodically cut his life into
ragged slices. Gerry likes to drive around in vehicles. He has a
truck, a van, and a car. He likes to watch TV. He has been to meetings and conferences in Ottawa and Vancouver. He has many
friends among the white people who live in the areas important to
the Doig River band. He is careful in his role of chief to reflect
consensus rather than to issue orders. He is proud there is a town
on the Peace River named Attachie after his grandfather Old Man
Attachie, who died in the terrible flu of 1918.

Gerry was seventeen when I first met him in the spring of 1966.
He wanted to be like Elvis Presley and Cassius Clay. There is still a
bit of Elvis in Gerry's self-image, but he has also matured into a
sensitive diplomat and a responsible family man. Gerry is genuinely
concerned about the well-being of everyone in his community. He
lives according to the best of Christian values. With the death of
Murray and Alice, the parents of the eleven Attachie children,
Gerry has taken on the role of stepparent for his younger brothers

and one of his sister's children as well as beginning his own family with Bernice. Gerry and Bernice go to the Rose Prairie Christian Evangelical Church. It provides them with many important social contacts in the white community. They go to town often but do not visit the beer parlor or liquor store.

When I first met Gerry, he told me about having been very ill a few years before. In the hospital with a high fever, he experienced his shadow leaving his body. He told me that he looked down on his body from above the bed. Then the old people in heaven communicated with him. They told him to go back down and join his body. After the fever broke, Gerry came back to the world of Elvis and Doig. In 1966 he had a single long white hair growing from his eyebrow. Charlie Yahey told him not to pluck it. In 1982 Charlie Yahey was gone and so was the long white hair. Gerry is a born-again Christian but he also continues to believe in the Dreamers. He knows that the trails of the old people still exist beneath the roads he travels by car. He knows that their songs are good for his people.

After the slide show, people in Gerry's house settled down to watch "Dallas" on TV, but Gerry was restless. After watching for a short time, he suggested that we drive out the old wagon road to hunt. Although we might have chanced upon a moose on the road, Gerry really wanted just to go for a drive in the moonlight. Our expedition consisted of Gerry, me, Howard, Gerry's eighteen-year-old brother, also named Howard, and Howard's sixteen-year-old friend Glen. It was still very cold on the evening of April 2, perhaps twenty-five or thirty degrees below zero Celsius. Snow squeaked underfoot and under the tires of the little car. Sounds carried in the thick, still air as they do underwater. The Rabbit chortled loudly as it idled to warm up. We piled into the car, loaded with guns, camera, binoculars, and tape recorder. A waxing gibbous moon shone brightly enough over the snowscape to cast shadows.

Even just outside Gerry's house I felt very far away from "Dallas." At first the old wagon road was rough from frozen ruts, and we travelled slowly. It became smooth as we descended into the cut made by the Osborn River and crossed over its unseen liquid presence hidden beneath a painting of ice and snow. Above the river we broke out of the low land and its forest cover onto an open country road, cleared of its ancient, thickly standing poplars by the Mennonites when Tommy and Gerry were kids. We broke out of the forest's shadows and its old memories into a blaze of light undulating in ribbons and waves like a celestial incandescent surf on the shore of our northern horizon. This was the aurora, *ya diskwonchi*, "lights in the sky." The Dunne-za say these swooping, swarming presences are spirits who will dance and come down close to the edge of the earth if you whistle to them. We stopped the car in the midst of stubbled fields that were waiting still for the touch of sun to release the green of wheat and barley. The moon blazed her silver mirrored light onto the snow crystals that lay without number in every direction. She appeared to be swimming, shimmering in a sea of animated spirits that hovered above and around where we stood and whistled deep in the night's clear, cold air.

Howard brought out his microphone and tape recorder to take the sounds of our rapturous engagement with these changing spirit beings. I caught sight of them through the eye of my camera. The lights in the sky seemed to respond to us as we responded to them. They did not so much change form as suggest form. They were animated presences of light and movement rather than shapes with edges and centers. The whistling seemed to intensify their animation. It made us think of life as a spirit of light and motion. It made us think of the old people, who lived and moved along the trails now overlain by roads and fields. It made us think of the light and movement we experience in dreams.

On flat roads between huge fields we drove quickly and quietly, leaving fresh tracks in the light powder of fresh snow that lay on top of the road's compact snow surface. We drove for close to an hour, at one point following the fresh tracks of a lone wolf who followed the road in the course of his own hunting. The place where we stopped to turn around must have been nearly fifty miles away from Doig. It was a gentle wooded hill that rose like a piece of the past held dear in memory out of the recent transformations of the cleared fields. Gerry said the place is called Old Spruce Tree Hill. He said that Johnny Chipesia knew this place when he was a child before the flu of 1918. Johnny Chipesia knows all the old trails of this place. He knows where the people of an older time used to make their camps. Spruce trees grow up to their full height on the hill because forest fires always go around it. I remembered that Johnny's father, Old Man Japasa, had power from the wind and rain. I remembered how he had called on his power to extinguish a fire coming toward their camp.

The old spruce trees have withstood settlers as well as fires. They stand as they have always stood, a place of refuge and security. The Dreamers say the world's center is a place where one tall spruce tree stands apart from the others. The spruce tree is an old woman who "knows something." Even the culture hero turned to her for help in the story of Saya and Giant Eagle. I had a sense of being close to her on the hill that is circled by fire but remains untouched. On that April evening it was circled by the aurora's cold fire, circled by a lone wolf, circled by frozen fallow fields, circled by memories going back to before any of us were born.

We stopped the car in a clearing where an oil rig had driven its hopeful pipe deep into the earth a decade before. Now only the capped dry well marked the clearing's center. We made tracks in the snow and watched Jupiter and Saturn, caught in the rim of spruce trees that guarded the clearing, begin their final descent toward the horizon. We puffed clouds of warm breath toward the moon, stomped our feet, took turns with the binoculars, and then began our return to the distant warmth of the houses at Doig. The drive back made Gerry think of his own memories. As we passed places he knew, Gerry told us who had camped there and when. I thought of the stories he knew from his grandmother. At one place we stopped the car. Gerry pointed out the meat-drying racks and lean-to poles of an old summer camp, standing empty and bare like the cold bones of a past that has receded into the abstraction of memory. "This is the place where Eskama used to camp," he said. Eskama was Gerry's grandmother's sister. She raised Gerry's wife, Bernice. She was good to me and Tonia.

When I first came to Doig in 1966, Bernice was a little girl. We stayed with Eskama and her husband, Jack. I remember Eskama sitting among the summer's blush of fireweed, unfolding fresh moose meat with her knowledgeable knife into thin, wide sheets that she hung to dry on poles, like the ones that stood here silently beside the lonely tracks of a wolf on the move. The old camp spoke of memories Gerry and I shared. Gerry also remembered being in the old campsite more recently. During the past summer, he and Bernice came over to the old camping place by car. They did not bring tents or camping equipment. They spent the night sleeping next to Gerry's enormous 1972 Chrysler New Yorker. During the night, they woke up and saw a grizzly bear close to where they were sleeping. After that they tried to sleep in the car but could not get back to sleep. Finally, they drove back to Doig. Gerry enjoyed telling us the story of his adventures.

The drive that night out the old wagon road was bounded on one end by "Dallas" and on the other by a capped oil well on Old Spruce Tree Hill. In between these two points we felt part of the sky spirits dancing. I wrote in my journal:

> The sense of place is very strong. Gerry knows it all. We are scooting over the trails they took with wagons each summer, and earlier on pack and saddle horses and on foot. The driving is a restoration of that relationship. Gerry pointed out tent frames and drying racks where they camped when Eskama and his grandmother were alive—where they camped in more recent summers, where they saw a Grizzly bear last summer when they were sleeping on ground beside the car and had to get up and drive home in the night. It was a story-telling lesson for Glen and Howard who went with us.

When we returned to Doig, Howard and I squeaked our way up the snowy path to the "Care Home" past Tommy's black dog Sani-wich. We entered the candle-lit warmth of Tommy's mansion. We found Tommy in a benign and expansive frame of mind. The spirits of *ya diskwonchi*, the northern lights, seemed to flow into Tommy's house with the cloud of cold air that created a momentary halo of mist around us as we stood at a point of transition, framed in the doorway. Moose meat was cooking in a frying pan on top of the airtight heater. The stove's sheet metal sides resonated like a tin drum with the pop and crackle of dry pine logs bursting into flame inside it. Tommy was not alone. With him were Delmer, a young man who had spent his early years in white foster homes, and Leo, Bernice's older brother. Delmer had brought two dozen beers and a bottle of Silk Tassle whiskey back from town, but the mood was gentle. It was a time for eating and sipping, and perhaps singing, rather than for the fierce isolation of a major drunk. It was the Tommy Attachie Personal Care Home at its best.

I remembered that during our stay in the Care Home, Tommy had been gracious and learned in his attention to the Dreamers' songs. The enemies that I suspected still raged within his mind seemed to have retreated, as they had during the time when Tommy and I bounced and rattled along the old wagon road behind his father's team of horses. Younger men were now coming to him to listen and sing the songs. We joked about how Howard and I recorded Tommy telling stories from his early life as if he were an old-timer. Tommy was in a mellow and gentle mood. He seemed to be getting over two recent traumatic events—the death a year before of his close cousin Mackenzie and his break-up the previous summer with Mathilda, a woman he really loved.

I recalled how Tommy's mind had been troubled during the summer of 1981. I had seen him struggle with grief. Our conversations then resonated with the conflict between attack and defense, love and hate. I remembered how the Dreamers' songs gave Tommy strength during those hard times. I remembered a particularly intense moment of revelation from that summer. We were in the King Koin laundromat in Fort St. John. Our clothes swirled and tumbled next to one another. All around us, the ordinary world of white-people was busy with its own orderly facade. The other people in the laundromat did not see Tommy. They saw only a slightly disreputable, possibly drunk or hungover, heavy-set Indian man of indeterminate age whose missing front teeth testified to the violence and poverty of his integration into their world.

Howard, Tommy, and I had spent the previous day with Jumbie. We had taken a room in the Esta Villa Motel. Howard and I called it the Pancho Villa. Jumbie had been at Peace Lutheran Care Home in town for several years. Jumbie was very old. His mind had retreated almost entirely into a world of dreams. We took him to our motel room and Howard set up the microphone. Jumbie talked from his dream world. He cried. He called out to his relatives in heaven. Jumbie touched Tommy and told him, "You be like me." Tommy said this meant that Jumbie saw Tommy's mind's ability to dream ahead. Tommy told Jumbie he knew about Mackenzie's death before it happened. He knew about it, but he could not prevent it.

The thought of Mackenzie and of death seemed to release a flood of fierce anguish in Tommy. His eyes locked onto mine and the laundromat seemed to fade into a hazy, half-forgotten shadow world. "I can defend myself with thunder and wolf," I heard him say. The grip of his eyes reminded me of the strength in his hands. "You know, Robin, I love you guys, you and Howard. That's the power. I could kill you if I wanted to, but I love you so much I can't do it." In my own mind, I heard Tommy, talking about the love and violence bound up in his sense of self. I knew that Howard and I stood for some part of Tommy about which he felt both love and violence. Tommy let go of the eyes that bound us together. The laundromat began to creep back from around the edges of my vision. Tommy spoke the name of the first Dreamer, Makenunatane, "his tracks circle around the edge of the world." He spoke the name of his successor, Maketchueson. He spoke the name of Jesus. Then he made a solemn cross with his hand in the air and concluded with "Praise the Lord," spoken as he has heard it chanted by evangelical Christians. Tommy said, "Jumbie touched me on both ears." He touched me as Jumbie had him. He repeated, "Jumbie said, 'You be like me.'"

The clothes continued to tumble behind us like psychedelic soap operas. The whitepeople continued to move as slow motion shadows in and out of the walls. I remember thinking, "This is like something that might happen in the Dreamtime of Australia." Tommy had reminded me that he is an aborigine, a person with roots in the mythic, dreaming power places of this continent. Tommy was transforming the laundromat into a dream for me. He began to speak about Mackenzie. I remembered that Mackenzie and Tommy were raised together. Their grandmother Nachin lavished her stories on the two boys. Mackenzie's father was Alice Attachie's brother. That made Tommy and Mackenzie cross-cousins. Each one could flirt with and marry the other's sister. They could call each other klase ("brother-in-law"). Tommy was born on January 10, 1943. Mackenzie was born on April 4, 1942, the length of a pregnancy earlier. They were like light and dark halves of a single being.

Tommy's voice took me back to a time when he and Mackenzie were young. The old people used to send kids out into the bush alone. They sent them out to get power from the animals. I had known, since the time we were together on the old wagon road, that Tommy has power. Now was the time he chose to reveal more of himself to me. The old people knew that Tommy and Mackenzie were complementary halves of a whole. The old people sent them out into the bush together. The two boys were afraid. They knew the stories of the animals. They knew *about* them, but they did not yet *know* them. The animals must have been waiting for them. At the proper time, they revealed themselves. The boys may have slept on their tracks. They may have dreamed of their animals. They may have seen their animals and followed them. They may have played with their pups. Coyote was the animal that came to Mackenzie. Wolf came to Tommy.

The old people listened for Tommy and Mackenzie in their dreams. When they heard the boys crying, they knew it was time to come and get them. The boys they found in the bush were different from the ones that had left camp together. They were shy and wild like their animals. The sounds of people talking and the smell of smoke were foreign to them. The old people treated them like babies. They took them back to camp and washed them. Someone wrapped them in his coat. They sang over the boys. Then they turned them loose to grow in their own ways. They turned them loose to discover how the stories of their animals would become the stories of their lives.

Tommy's eyes fixed on mine again as he brought himself to confront the loss of his light half, the partner who could flirt with his sisters. After Mackenzie died, Tommy told me, he walked down to the bridge over the Doig River. It was early spring, not long after breakup. He took off his wide-brimmed brown felt cowboy hat. He took off his jeans jacket. He took off his riding boots. Then he climbed over the railing and jumped into the cold, high, muddy waters of the Doig River.

The old people heard the kids crying in their dreams.
They came to where they were in the bush.
They found them.

They treated them like babies.

They washed them.

They sang over them.

Now, Mackenzie was gone. Tommy wanted to throw his life away. He was half drunk when he hit the water. He went down and down into the water. He went down until he hit bottom. He went down to the river's muddy bottom. He went down like Muskrat who brought back the first dirt that became the world. The cold and shock made him gasp for breath. His lungs filled with water. The water was moving quickly after having been locked in the cold of winter. Tommy's body was rushed along by the current. It scraped and bounced along where the riverbed became rough with silt and gravel. Then, in a swirl of different energy, the river pushed him up to its surface. Tommy partly came to. He tried to breathe. He tried to swim, but in another caprice the river pulled him down again to its darkness.

The hot soapy water of the laundry continued to pull and swirl at Tommy's clothes. I could feel their wetness and the turbulence of their motion as they whirled around and around behind the sealed glass door. I could feel the turbulence of the Doig River in spring flood, pulling one half of the two boys toward the other. I could feel Tommy next to me making the words of the story with his breath. I could feel his breath, his life, close to mine and far away from the King Koin laundry. I could feel his body as it swept and circled with the dark, cold eddies of the river.

Finally, the river drew Tommy close to shore. He saw the branch of a tree reaching out from the riverbank. He stretched his arm to touch the branch. He fixed his watery eyes upon it. For a moment the river seemed to stop its noisy turbulence. For a moment Tommy's eyes cleared and focused. His vision came into focus on the drooping tree branch. There were ants on the branch. As he reached out in a time out of time, the ants extended to Tommy the power of their own teeming vitality. They tried to help him. They talked to him. Once before, when he was a child, they had talked to him. That time and this time merged into a single moment. Tommy became the swarming power of ants everywhere as he had been then and would be forever more. He knew them as they came to him. He knew them as he knew himself. He knew as well that he was very heavy—too heavy for even the ants to pull from the water.

Tommy thought about what they could do for him. He remembered he could call them by singing the song they gave him when he was a child. He knew that a person can take a dry ant and send it into someone. He can send it into their eyes, their nose, their ears. He can enter their body through any opening an ant would be able to find. Ants look small. They seem to be weak, but there are many of them. They are everywhere. They can help people as well as harm them. Tommy knew he could do that, but he thought of the creator. He thought of the Dreamers and their songs. He knew he could not use his power in that way.

Tommy thought about how he could use his power from ants to help his family and friends if they were in trouble. Then he let go of the branch. The ants had moved across to his arm. They were thick like mosquitoes. They covered his arm. They touched him where he had reached out to renew contact with them, but Tommy was still heavy with grief and loss and cold water and despair and alcohol. He went down beneath the water for a third time.

When he floated up to the surface once more he felt as if he had died and come to life again. He felt like Muskrat must have felt when he floated to the water's surface with the world under his fingernails. The ants were gone as a dream is gone upon waking. It remains real, but it has gone to a different place. The ants were real to Tommy, as his dreaming is real. They were real like the child within him, the twin child missing its complement. He felt like one of the Dreamers, returned to the body he left on earth while his spirit was flying along the Trail to Heaven. The body to which Tommy's spirit returned was bruised and waterlogged. It spit up brown water and bright red blood from the lungs. The river floated Tommy's shivering, gagging physical vessel toward a gentle shore and gently gave it the world.

As a result of his ordeal, Tommy came down with pneumonia. He was still weak and coughing when he told me the story of his brush with death in the warm soapy atmosphere of the King Koin laundry. He was hurt but healing, just as he had been when we rode the old wagon road together in 1966. The edge of his life remained the possibility of death, brought closer now by the loss of Mackenzie, his complement. This time he had come very close to the edge in his confrontation with the enemy within.

The wet, warm agitation of our clothes stopped. They began to spin like dervishes. When they finished spinning, I trundled them over to the dryer. Tommy had taken his departure. I could expect to find him later in the beer parlor of the Fort Hotel or passing a jug in the little park next to the liquor store. I retreated to the car to write down my notes on Tommy's revelations.

20. MANSION ON THE HILL

A year after his ordeal, Tommy's healing seemed complete. The party to which Howard and I returned after our drive out the old wagon road reflected a renewal of Tommy's social life. Delmer and Leo had something to learn from him. They came to him as to an old person with whom they could also drink and relax. The Care Home was the only place at Doig where young guys could come to drink and talk and also renew their knowledge of the Dreamers' songs. Howard and I joined Tommy and Delmer and Leo in moose meat sandwiches and beer. It was nearly midnight. The warmth of their company, the hot meat, and Tommy's friendly fire made us feel at home and well cared for.

Tommy recalled a story he had recorded earlier for Howard and me as the afternoon sun, reflected on snow, streamed into his house during the quiet of mid-afternoon. The story was about Simon Flynn, the white man who had taught school at Peterson's Crossing during the late 1950s after Joe Gallibois, the Indian agent, forced people to squat on Crown land beside the Beatton River. Tommy turned toward Leo and said, "This boy Leo, he can remember pretty good to when he was three years old." Leo acknowledged Tommy's reference to his memory by describing the old sod-roofed cabins. He said he could remember when everyone at Doig lived in small log cabins like the one Albert Askoty and Alice Moccasin still have at Peterson's Crossing. Leo remembered that when he was about three years old, Mr. Shepherd, the new Indian agent who replaced Gallibois, came by helicopter to Doig for the first time. Leo's uncle Jack was councillor then. When Leo's mother died, Jack and Eskama raised him and Bernice and the other children who were left behind. Jack was a good singer. He was a very gentle man. He taught Leo to sing with him.

Tommy said that Jack had been a Dreamer. He dreamed of his own death. When death came, it did not take him by surprise. He died on a summer evening. He walked around the village visiting people. Then he walked back to his own house. He had been lonely and incomplete since the death of Eskama. He sat down outside to watch the fading light. Then he died. Jack's name was Ga-ta, "Rabbit-daddy." He left behind two painted drums. I have a picture of Jack with Charlie Yahey, putting a fresh white moose calfskin head on the rim of an old drum.

Leo was becoming known as a good singer, even though there had not been a pow-wow at Doig since the one they put on to commemorate Mackenzie's death. Tommy told a story about how Leo and John Yahey, Charlie Yahey's son, liked to sing together. John Yahey is sixty years old. He is a singer and drummaker like his father. Some people say he has dreamed songs from heaven. Tommy laughed. He told a story about one time when Leo's brother Gordon was visiting John Yahey at the Blueberry Reserve. Gordon had come over to visit John Yahey because he was courting John's sister's daughter Bella. The old man thought at first that Gordon was Leo. He knew Leo is a good singer and asked Gordon to sing with him. Gordon is slightly impaired in the use of one arm. He doesn't usually play the drum. John Yahey was surprised and disappointed at his lack of ability. Finally someone told him that it was Gordon and not Leo. Tommy told the story by way of complimenting Leo on his acceptance by a recognized master of the tradition.

Tommy recalled that he and Leo sing well together, too. The previous Monday, only five days before, Howard had recorded them at a song session Gerry organized. Tommy asked Howard to put on the tape of that evening. As we sat back to listen, bathed in the warm embrace of the Tommy Attachie Personal Care Home, we began to recall the characters and events of the previous Monday evening at Tommy's. Although it had happened less than a week before, the evening had already become fabulous in our memories. The warm fire, the moose meat, the northern lights, and Howard's recorded document of the event brought Monday's singing back into our dreaming minds.

Monday evening had been Gerry's. It began after supper when

Gerry invited Howard and me to go with him and Bernice and Gordon to visit an old white farmer named Bob Murdock. Gerry likes old people. He likes to visit them and listen to their stories. Bob Murdock settled near Rose Prairie in 1929. He drove teams along the old sleigh trail to Fort Nelson. After our visit we stopped in at Peterson's Crossing to see Albert Askoty. Albert is about the same age as John Yahey. He lives in an old log cabin. He is a singer, storyteller, and drum maker. Recently, he made two new drums. Gerry stopped in to ask Albert if he wanted to bring his drums over to Doig and sing with him. Gerry had been to town for a meeting earlier in the day. Although he does not drink in town, he had brought back two half-gallon jugs of Bon White wine, one of the jug wines that Charlie Yahey used to drink. He brought them as a sign of respect for Albert. He brought them to let Albert know that even though he is chief, he is not anyone's boss.

For a few minutes, the Monday evening stillness of Albert's cabin was witness to a sacramental exchange between Gerry and Albert. The jug passed from hand to hand, mouth to mouth. Gerry knows that Albert likes to drink. He likes to get the most he can from whatever he is given to drink. Gerry gave Gordon the key to his van. He wanted to be with Albert in the back of the van. He wanted to honor Albert without dishonoring his own path of sobriety and responsibility. Gerry is becoming a real chief in the way he honors people like Albert rather than condemning them for drinking, even though he himself has chosen not to drink. This evening with Albert was Gerry's way of telling him that being chief and a non-drinking Christian does not mean that he thinks any less of Albert and his practice of the old ways.

As we listened at the Care Home to the tape of Monday evening, Tommy and I joked about Albert. Delmer and Leo joined in. We agreed that Albert could be described as fuel efficient. He gets off easily. Albert's two new drums were as high pitched as his voice. Tommy heard himself talking about them on the tape. We listened to Gerry trying to match his voice to Albert's high, almost querulous tone. We joked about Albert's pink shirt and black pants, the same outfit he had worn to the Treaty Eight pow-wow at Halfway the summer before. We sat back and listened to more of the tape.

Gerry had begun Monday evening sitting close to Albert on

Tommy's old sofa beneath the smeared picture windows that still have stickers saying "up" on them. After trying to follow Albert with little success, Gerry took the lead himself. He asked Howard to set up the microphone on its stand. The party had turned into a recording session. Gerry knelt on the floor, holding the single-headed drum in his left hand. His fingers and palm covered the cross of twisted thongs that ran out to touch the edge of the rim in four places. His thumb tightened the rawhide snare lines stretched across the inner surface of the drum's head to create a buzzing resonance. The jug of wine sat on the floor in front of him. Tommy, sitting on the sofa to Gerry's left, played the other drum. Albert knelt on the floor, facing Gerry across the jug. Leo and Delmer, who had been attracted by the news of a party, sat on kitchen chairs. Howard hunched over his tape recorder and listened through earphones. I reclined on my bedroll in one corner of the room.

Gerry spoke in a loud and exaggerated oratorical style: "This morning they call me to go to meeting." Then he added in a parody of TV Indian talk: "Me never speak forked tongue." The young guys laughed and Delmer quipped back, "Well, we got one anyway." Then Gerry said "OK" to Tommy, who echoed "OK" and took up the drum as Albert spoke to him in Beaver about the Dreamers' songs. Albert called Gerry *ashitle* ("little brother") and *aba* ("little boy"). When Gerry finished his song, he spoke again about his political activities. He said, in Beaver and then in English, "Don't think I'm your boss. Leo your boss, Leo Acko, Kelvin Davis [the previous chief], Rose Davis [the band manager's daughter], not me, me nothing." After the reference to Rose Davis everybody began to laugh. Gerry finished his declamation with a laugh of his own. Then Albert came back in Beaver, teasing Gerry that he was a bad guy, but in a way that made everybody laugh. Gerry replied, with the bravado required of the occasion, that he was only bad about carrying on with women.

Gerry returned Albert's taunt. He began to tease Albert about *his* exploits with women. Albert rose to the bait. He began to wail in a mixture of Beaver and English well homogenized by alcohol. Gerry played along. Then he upped the ante by saying with mock bravado, "This guy want to fight me right now." There was an appreciative chorus of laughter from the audience. Albert was hooked.

His wailing became more song than language. "Not me, I don't sleep with them," he said in Beaver, and then in English he wailed, "No way!" By now, Albert was well warmed to his performance, but Gerry knew better than to bait him further. He had established himself as a chief who does not place himself above the other people in his band.

Albert is known for his literal way of thinking, particularly when into the ecstasy of drink. He began to express the very allegation Gerry had just skillfully deflected. He said something about how Gerry thought he was a big boss, but Gerry refused to take him seriously, even when Albert called him a bad guy again. Gerry just laughed lightly and reminded us all (in English) of his dedication to Christianity. "Don't get excited," he said, "just because we're beating the government. If I meet God I might be shy, eh, but if I meet a judo I'm not going to get scared. If I meet God then it's different, eh."

At this point in Monday's performance, Tommy took matters into his own hands by beginning a song in his strong, practiced voice. The song rose and fell like the snow-covered hills and rivers that stretched in every direction from the center of the universe created every time a song is sung or a drum held by its centering cross of thongs. Albert forgot the cause of his distress in the dream of the song that took him back to the people of old and out toward where the animals wait for the trails of the hunters. When the song ended, Albert called for Leo to come and join Tommy. The song they began together was one of my favorites. Like all of the Dreamers' songs, it was without words. Its message was directed toward a level of understanding beyond the particularity of spoken language. This song, like the others, was intended to be experienced as one would experience a journey toward a well-known and secure destination.

When people dance to the Dreamers' songs, they always circle close around a fire in the direction the sun travels across the sky during the day. The fire is a center, like the center of the cross at the point where the drum is cradled in the hand. It is a center, like the cross the creator drew on the water when he made the world by sending Muskrat to dive down and bring up a speck of dirt. It is a circle, like the earth that grew from the dirt on the center of the cross, like the earth around which the sun flies during the day. It is a center, like the drawing of a cross and the Trail to Heaven, painted on the face of a drum that belonged to Charlie Yahey.

As Tommy and Leo began to sing Monday evening, I allowed my mind to slip back to the dances they used to have at Doig when Charlie Yahey was alive. The last one I remember happened in 1969 when Charlie Yahey dreamed that the spirit of Anno Davis had made it through to heaven. Her son Tar made a large tepee-shaped dance lodge of poles and tarps. He gathered abundant firewood. The fire was a hot and searing center. Outside, the northern lights danced and brash boys whistled. The lights were ephemeral and without articulation, the insubstantial wanderings of spirits in the sky. Perhaps Tar's mother was looking down on the hot fire from her place in the sky. I remembered how she had danced with slow chicken steps like those of the sun in its dance around the rim of the world. I remembered the hot smoke from the fire's searing center, blowing over me as she seemed to dance without moving when she was upwind of the fire from me. As I thought of her spirit at the pow-wow Tar made for her, my feet rose and fell in time to the regular rhythm of the drums. My mind seemed to rise with the song's melody.

The song Tommy and Leo sang together for Albert and Gerry took me back to the pow-wows that happened when Charlie Yahey was alive. It began with a few descending phrases and then soared quickly toward a high point of intensity. Their voices blended, like double reeds moving with one breath up and down the stations of a melodic line. Tommy's voice took up the foreground. Leo's filled in to shape the sound of the notes. Even through the subtle bending and modulation they gave each note, Tommy and Leo were together. I thought back to the pow-wow of 1969 when the lead singer had been Billy Makadahy, whose voice, like Tommy's, could be heard a long distance out into the stillness of the bush surrounding Doig. At that pow-wow, Tommy and I were about the ages of Leo and Delmer. The singing and dancing had gone on well into the hours of daylight. Tommy told me then that it is good to dance. He also told me it is good to sleep in the dance lodge. When I became tired, I found it easy to lie back against Tommy's shoulder and allow the voices of the singers to carry away my own dreaming spirit. Tommy took his turns among the singers, filling in the spaces behind Billy Makadahy's lead and the chorus of other voices in the same way Leo now sang the songs he and Tommy knew together. In order to sing the Dreamers' songs, a person must know them. The songs must be like familiar trails to known destinations. The singers must be like people travelling together on a trail that is known to each one independently. Tommy and Leo sang well together because each knew the path to a common destination. I understood after hearing them sing together why John Yahey liked to sing with Leo. Leo has a good memory. He knows where he came from and where he should be going. I could see a lot of Jack and Eskama in him. I thought of the places they used to camp and of Leo's memory. He knew the trail of his own life as he knew the trail of a song. Tommy's knowledge of himself in relation to the songs was more complex because of the inner torment that turned him against the love in his life. For Tommy, the songs were a lifeline protecting him from the edge that was ever present in the form of inner enemies. His thoughts about how he could use the power of his medicine songs to take the life of an enemy were held in check by the songs of the Dreamers. Whenever he came close to the edge he thought of the Dreamers. He often sang their songs to himself. The songs pulled him back from that edge toward the world of caring and sharing. They reminded him of the good people like Jack and Eskama and his grandmother Nachin, who died without enemies. The songs reminded Tommy that people without enemies can easily find their way on the Trail to Heaven, Yagatunne. Tommy's life has not been easy. He has fought with others as much as he has fought with himself, but he has also thought of the Dreamers and their songs. Listening to him sing with Leo and thinking back to the first time I heard him sing on the old wagon road, I knew that Tommy's life could not be too far removed from the Trail to Heaven. Although he may have turned against a part of himself in moments of depression and despair, he also always pulled back to the common path of the dancers that circles closely around the fire's center.

Listening to Tommy and Leo sing together took me back to the time I dreamed in the dance lodge leaning against Tommy. At that time I imagined I was among a group of hunting people, long before their Dreamers had begun to speak of the white men. The songs seemed to float like ripples out from the camp's center to where the animals were at home, each at the end of his trail at that precise moment in time. I dreamed, as a hunter might dream, of the place where an animal's trail could make contact with a person's trail. I dreamed of the people of old, whose lives continued to carry the language and songs I heard all around me. The sounds of the songs cut through a miasma of time. Closing my eyes, I could easily imagine myself among people of a distant past. Listening to Tommy and Leo was no different from listening to Billy Makadahy or Charlie Yahey. It was like listening to Jack or being with Nachin as she told stories to her grandchildren. Both Leo and Tommy have good memories. They can remember who they are. The songs take them into the memory of times before they were born. They take them into the time of the Dreamers. They take them into mythic times. The songs take me into the times of the old people.

As Howard played the tape of Tommy and Leo singing at the party Gerry put on to honor Albert, I remembered how I lay back on my bedroll in a corner of the room, watching Albert Askoty, dancing like a spirit released from the bottle of Bon wine, and listening to Tommy and Leo make music that could have been made a thousand years before. I remembered lying on my foam pad, dreaming my way back into the world of the Dreamers' songs.

Jumbie (left) and Howard Broomfield, 1982

Jumbie with picture of the game masters (Anachuan and Amma on his left and right), 1966

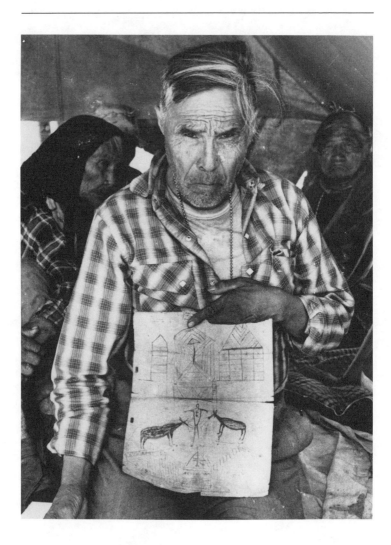

Gerry Attachie, 1981

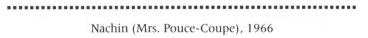

Nachin (Mrs. Pouce-Coupe), 1966

Billy Attachie (left) and Mackenzie Ben, 1968

Jack Acko and Eskama (Mrs. Jack Acko), 1966

Aku, 1966

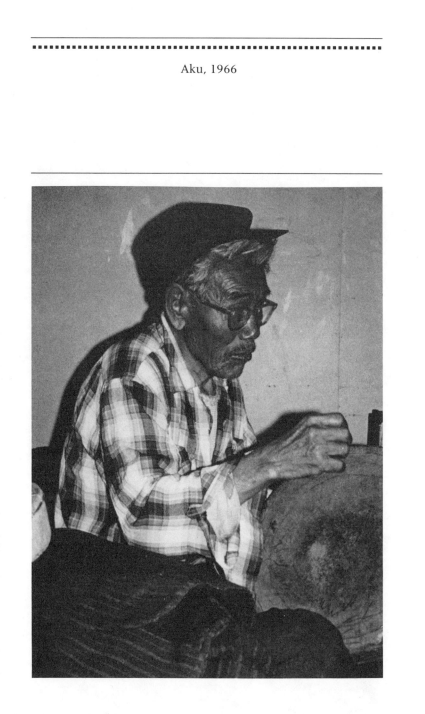

Leander Attachie and Bernice Attachie, 1981

Singers at Doig (from left), Tommy Attachie and Tar Davis, 1966

21. A BAD MIRACLE

As we listened to the tape of Monday night's session with Gerry and Albert, I felt the sense of timelessness come over me again. I knew that Tommy and Leo were also being taken back to the intensity they felt playing together. We all laughed and joked about Albert when we listened to him deliver his lament to Gerry on the tape, but when Tommy and Leo came on we became quiet and contemplative. As we were listening to them blending and bending their voices around the notes of a familiar song, there was a knock on the door. Ricky, a young man of twenty-two, came in and stood at the edge of the room near Tommy's dried and crusted kitchen sink. Ricky is Jack's sister's son, Leo's parallel cousin. Their mothers, Molly and Abu, were sisters, which means that they call one another brother. Ricky was just the age Tommy was when I first met him.

I went over to the door where Ricky stood. He was hesitant, for some reason, to join the party. I thought back to the summer before, when Ricky stayed with Tommy at the Care Home. I remembered the quiet nights in July, when Ricky and Tommy lay in their beds late at night after dark and listened to my tapes of the old people singing Dreamers' songs. Ricky told me then that he likes to study the old people. I remembered one night in early July when I came back late to the Care Home. The candle was out, but Tommy and Ricky were awake listening to my tapes of Charlie Yahey, Sam St. Pierre, and Jumbie. The music evoked a past we all shared. Ricky was a child when I recorded the songs, but he had grown up at Blueberry and knew Charlie Yahey as part of his world.

I remembered how the old Dreamers' songs had filled the dark room with memories that summer evening. Each of us had known Charlie Yahey in a different way. Together, we conjured him in the

gentle darkness that enveloped us. Ricky asked me about my own
memories of the Dreamer, and I let my mind drift back to the times
when I recorded him. I felt the fire flash and flicker against the right
side of my body as I danced among the line of people bobbing up
and down to the Dreamers' songs in the night. I recalled Charlie
Yahey leading a dance of children, the age Ricky would have been
then. He must have been among them. The Care Home was bathed
in a velvet softness that summer evening as Tommy and Ricky
gently blended their voices in the spaces between songs. I listened
to them like an animal in the dark. I felt as if their thoughts and
memories could touch mine directly under the cover of darkness.
After each song, Tommy spoke the name of the Dreamer. Ricky
listened carefully. He seemed to be studying the songs, using
Tommy as his guide. Tommy's singing took us back to his memories
of 1957, before Ricky and Leo were born. Tommy told us that
Charlie Yahey used to come around to Peterson's Crossing to make
a pow-wow several times a month during the summer. Tommy
played up his persona of Old Man Red.

Ricky seemed to have grown since the previous summer. He was
now a large, handsome young man. He was a rodeo rider. He did
not go over to where Tommy and Leo were relaxing by candlelight,
listening to the tape of their singing and drumming from Monday
evening's party. He looked ill at ease with them and ill at ease with
his own tall, rugged body. As I moved up beside Ricky, next to
Tommy's dry sink, I realized Ricky was no longer a kid. I could also
tell he had been drinking. It turned out he had just been thrown
out of a party by Rose Davis because he tried to preach about the
evils of drink with a bottle in one hand. Leo and Delmer could also
tell that Ricky was not in a happy state of mind. They did not offer
him a drink.

Ricky turned to me with an intensity that surprised me. He began
to ask me in a belligerent tone if I knew why we are placed here
on this earth. I replied that I did not know for sure. I offered him
my opinion that some things should remain a mystery. Ricky faced
me directly. He said, "I don't know what is in your mind." It felt
like a threat. Something had closed off the communication that had
flowed so easily between us the summer before. That summer, we
had spent hours talking about the meaning of life and exchanging

stories about our dreams. Ricky talked about Christ a lot then. What he said made sense to me as an honest statement of his belief. He also talked about the old people. I remembered that when Ricky and Tommy drove up to Prophet River with us that summer, Ricky told me he studied the country and thought about all the people who used to live there before the highway. He expressed a sensitivity to Jumbie's world.

This evening Ricky seemed angry and frustrated. He did not accept the music from Monday's session in the way he had accepted my old tapes of the Dreamers from when he was still a kid. Our conversation became intense. Ricky pushed me to give him an answer about why we poor humans have been placed on this earth. I knew it would be useless to examine, let alone to explain, my real feelings about the subject. Ricky obviously had his own answer to the question. The answer he proposed was couched in the language of evangelical Christianity. "Jesus is the answer," Ricky told me. "Christ is the answer."

I strained to understand his meaning. I felt the Dreamers behind me, their songs within me, the fire at the center of my world. I struggled to understand how Ricky's Christ could also be a center. Ricky spoke through a complex of emotions released by alcohol. Like Tommy when possessed of the bottle, Ricky pushed for the impossible. He pushed me away and then lashed out at me for the distance between us. He called me Dr. Ridington.

During the previous summer, Ricky was becoming known as a preacher. I had listened then with interest to the way he used the language of Christian testimony. It had seemed to be a reasonable transformation of the old-time oratorical style of the Dreamers. Then, his use of the language had seemed benign. I liked the way he used evangelical images to express his deepest emotions. He was good at preaching. The form suited him. Now, the feeling was different. Alcohol gave his language a push into the realm of rhetoric. He pushed me into the role of outsider.

Ricky was using Christian language to set himself apart from the Dreamer's dance session that was going on in the Tommy Attachie Personal Care Home. The summer before, Ricky told me that old people of long ago dreamed of Jesus before the white men came with the Bible. This was the same information I had obtained from

Charlie Yahey and Jumbie years before. The story went back to the time of Makenunatane. Ricky's own use of Christian images seemed to renew that early synthesis between the Dreamers' way of knowing and Christianity. In Ricky's lifetime, evangelical Protestants have replaced Roman Catholics. It seemed only natural that he and other young people should work their language into their underlying ideas about dreaming, just as Makenunatane had worked Jesus into Dunne-za knowledge about the Trail to Heaven. Gerry was as dedicated a Christian as Ricky but was looking for ways to integrate the two traditions. He practiced Christian values in his life, but also continued to honor masters of the old ways, like Albert Askoty.

The young man who stood, weaving slightly, at the edge of Tommy's kitchen sink seemed as much caught between two conflicting impulses of the Dunne-za world as he was between the Dreamers and Christianity. He wanted to be known as a man of power—a rodeo rider. He also knew that he would be feared and rejected if he did not give notice that his power was under control. The Dreamer's dance has always been an opportunity for people to come together in a spirit of trust and support of one another. The old people told me that for every step you take with all the others around the fire, you will be relieved of the many steps your ghost must walk at night, back along the trail of your life. When people dance together on the circle of a common path, they affirm their mutual contribution to the continuing life of the community. Ricky's preaching under the influence of alcohol seemed to set him apart from people rather than bring him together with them. His fierce evangelism seemed to go against the community instead of in support of it.

I remembered Tommy's continual struggle between his impulse to kill the enemy within and the contrary teaching of the Dreamers. I remembered Ricky talking about the same conflict the summer before. During a quiet evening at Tommy's, Howard and I had answered Ricky's questions about our own culture and beliefs, our dreams, our skills, and our ignorance. Ricky responded by telling us about the burden, the danger, and also the benefit of traditional medicine power. Howard recorded the evening's conversation. This is what Ricky said then:

Some guys get sick and they fix each other,
but maybe some people don't help each other.
Like get sick and that.
Not very good people.
Don't kill anything for a long time.
Like they're jealous of them other guys.
Another person passing by you,
like from somewhere else, like moving on,
they see you got a lot of fur.
They get mad.
They see too, up ahead how looks, gonna be.
So now this people sometime, I guess,
they sing for that, towards up, heaven, to get help.
Sometimes I guess, take quite a few days.
Those were important.
They know how to do it and that, like I don't know.
Nowadays, pretty much booze and that all mixed up with
    that.
I don't know much about medicine and doing it at somebody.
Sometimes somebody backfire, even on theirselves, like they
    don't know how much to use it.
If you don't know how to use it—
I don't think it's good anyways, the medicine,
but there's different kinds on this world I guess.
If you get sick and that and they say power,
like Jumbie, he fix somebody.
That's pretty good, but some other ones bad.
They want to do something.
Jealous, like jealous.
You got a good woman or something,
they go after you.
I don't really believe it,
but I don't want to fool around with stuff like that anyway.
I see some people and their face is pretty rough.
And it came from another Indian they said.
Those people were rodeo and some other Indians were
    jealous.
That's what they said anyways.

I see that guy too.
His face was pretty rough.
I think he used to be pretty good. His face wasn't like that.
After, that's what everybody said they seen.
I guess it's pretty true,
a miracle, I guess.
Just like a bad miracle.

I felt the energy of a bad miracle as Ricky held me with fierce intensity to his spot beside Tommy's sink. He was becoming more hostile, trying to get a reflection of his anger back from me. I sensed an undertone of jealousy beneath the babble of Ricky's attempt to preach through a cloud of alcohol. I saw hurt and jealousy in the way he carried his body and launched his words. People who are jealous can bring hurt to others with their thoughts alone. People who are down and lonely can turn against others who have things they want. Suddenly, Ricky switched from preaching to telling me he wanted to become a helicopter pilot. I knew from our conversations last summer that Ricky did not like school and had quit after grade seven. I thought that his desire was unrealistic. I knew he was not comfortable listening to his cousin-brother Leo sing the old songs so beautifully and effortlessly with Old Man Red. Ricky seemed to have caught himself in a trap. The only way he could think of to get out was to show off his Christian oratorical style. He showed off to me while at the same time calling me doctor to point out the differences in our formal education as a barrier between us.

When Ricky had talked to Howard and me the summer before, he used the old metaphors of a hunting and trapping way of life. He spoke in the language of Jumbie and Charlie Yahey. When a person is unable to kill an animal for a long time, he becomes jealous of the other successful hunters. A trapper with lots of furs may be attacked by someone whose own trapping has been unsuccessful. As he talked to us then, Ricky had switched back and forth between examples in which he was the jealous person and those in which other people were jealous of him. He also talked about an alternative to jealousy. A good person, he said, would sing to heaven to get help. A person like Jumbie would do that. A person like Jumbie would use his power to help other people when they got sick. If you were a good hunter or had a good woman, other people might be tempted to go after you. "I don't really believe it," he had said, "but I don't want to fool around with stuff like that anyway. I guess it's pretty true, a miracle, I guess. Just like a bad miracle."

A world of contradictions seemed to be swirling around in Ricky's head. He was no longer a child, but not yet an adult. He was not a hunter or trapper. He was not in a relationship with a woman. He was not a famous cowboy. He was not a helicopter pilot. He was just Ricky, and he was lonely and confused. Leo was getting all of Tommy's attention. Ricky seemed to be going after mine in compensation, but the remedy could not bring real relief. He wanted everything that was closed off to him. The situation that evening in the Care Home only reminded Ricky of the pervasive lack of direction and satisfaction in his life. He was jealous of me for my education and my possessions. He was jealous of Leo for his singing. He was even jealous of Tommy for being in a happy and expansive mood.

I remembered the stories Jumbie told me about medicine fights of long ago. I thought of the more immediate struggles that punctuate Tommy's life. Ricky seemed to be playing out the ancient interpersonal ritual of the medicine fight. In the stories and in actual events, a person who is not getting what others have becomes defensive. He believes that the people who are happy and lucky suspect him of blaming them for his misfortune. He may go to elaborate lengths to defend himself from this suspicion. He may even come to believe that they are responsible. The fortunate people often counter by suggesting that the person's misfortune is due to a violation of some taboo on his part. They say, "It's his own damn fault."

In medicine fights, people play out their differences by suggesting alternate theories to explain their misfortunes. One theory says that misfortune is caused by someone using medicine power against the victim. The other theory says that he brought it on himself by not taking proper care of meat, by disrespecting animals, or by having sex with an improper category of relative. I gradually came to understand that the two theories are specific to a person's own situation rather than alternative universal principles. Ricky was being defensive because he felt left out. He acted as if he thought Tommy and Leo and I suspected him of blaming us for his despondency. He even acted as though the Dreamers' songs themselves were acting against him.

I could speculate about what might have been in Ricky's mind, but I could not identify the enemy within him. He was closed to me and projected this closure by saying he did not know what was in my mind. I began to react to Ricky's deluge by putting up my own mental defenses. He could sense my distancing, and this strengthened his feeling of isolation. I realized that my own reaction to what Ricky was doing was to defend myself from an implicit accusation of being responsible for his distress and to think about how he brought his problems on himself. I was responding to the situation in the classic Dunne-za way, looking for some violation of taboo on Ricky's part to absolve myself of any possible blame for the contrast between my fortune and his misfortune.

As Ricky held me with the determination of a hunter, Tommy, Leo, Delmer, and Howard continued to listen to the music from Monday evening on tape. They refused to allow Ricky's resentment to spoil the good time they were having. When a song on the tape came to an end, Tommy told Howard to turn off the machine and put in a fresh tape for recording. He and Leo picked up the drums Albert had left and began to find the pace of drumming together. Tommy called out to Howard, "Me and Leo gonna sing. You got the recorder ready? He sings real good." Ricky turned his attention from me to Tommy. He spoke in a voice that carried across the room. "He sing real bullshit. He sing like this," and he pointed with his right hand to a bottle of beer. "There's only one ways and that's Jesus."

Tommy and Leo ignored his challenge and continued to build the rhythm of their drumming to the point of taking off into a song. Leo asked Howard, "Ready?" When Howard replied that he was, Leo led off and Tommy joined him a few phrases later. Because Leo was leading, Tommy sang quietly, attentive to Leo's interpretation of the song. The singers held each phrase close to a single note, modulating the sound to the rhythm of the drumbeats, as if the note were a stretched hide upon which the steady rhythm of drumming reverberated. They held the drums close to their mouths so

that the sound of their voices blended with the sound waves produced by drumsticks hitting tightly stretched hide. They picked up
the drum's rhythm and sang to it in the way they shaped each note
to an undulating pattern of vibration. The song washed over me
and took me back to the all-night pow-wows when Charlie Yahey
was alive. I remembered alternating between dancing, sleeping, and
standing out in the clear, cold night, looking at stars and the northern lights. Tommy and Leo obviously felt the same rush of memory.
Their voices were gentle and unhurried. They blended together in
delicate complementarity, as they had on the tape from Monday
night. The way they sang reminded me of Charlie Yahey's message
that when people come close together to sing and dance, animals
will come easily to hunters in their dreams.

    Without a word, I went over to my bedroll in the back corner of
the room and lay down. I closed my eyes. The songs rose up to
meet my dreams. My recent memories of moose meat and the
swooping, fleeting aurora blended in the synesthetic magic of the
dreamspace. They blended with memories of times gone by, with
the sweet hot smoke of poplar logs burning at the center of a dance
lodge, with the shadows of dancers silhouetted on a circle of canvas, with the warmth and wisdom of Jack and Eskama. Their spirits
seemed to be speaking through Leo's singing voice. They had raised
him well. The empty drymeat racks we had passed earlier in the
evening came back to my dreaming mind full of meat. I could see
Eskama slicing the last broad strips to dry. A long bone hung above
the fire, slowly bubbling with rich juice. I could hear Jack's gentle
voice singing the songs that came to me now through the voice of
Leo. Then the song came to an end and Tommy finished it off with
a flourish of loud drumbeats that brought me back to the Care
Home. He spoke in a rich and appreciative tone to compliment Leo
on his interpretation of the song. I echoed my approval by saying
in English, "Pretty good."

    I noticed, when I opened my eyes, that Ricky had moved over to
the bed across from where Tommy and Leo sat on the couch. He
was lying down next to Delmer and muttering to himself discon-
tentedly. The contrast between his tone of voice and Tommy's stood
out because of how well Tommy and Leo had blended together in
the song. He spoke coldly, like a zombie. I could make out the

words, "It's condemned, condemned, this world, this world, pretty hard condemned." Tommy called out strongly to Leo in Beaver, asking him if he knew the next song. Leo replied, "Yep" as Ricky continued his lament. "Pretty soon right there," he declaimed in a voice that was ominous in its lack of any emotional coloring. His words were a strange and twisted parody of the Dreamers' warning to people that the sun and the seasons will come to an end if people do not sing and dance together. I grabbed hold of the song in my mind as Tommy took up the next lead. I remembered Charlie Yahey saying a person must learn to hold onto the songs in his dreams. The snares on the drums buzzed like swarming insects. Tommy sang the song by himself. He sang slowly as if for a slow dance. Leo backed him up on the other drum. Tommy sang louder than he had in the duet with Leo. He shaped the notes strongly to the drum's rhythm.

Tommy did not acknowledge Ricky's doomsaying. He too grabbed hold of the song with his mind as his voice found the trail of its melodic line and the drums shook us all out of our ordinary spaces. I could hear Ricky's voice under the drums, but the strong soaring flight of Tommy's voice drowned out the words themselves. Tommy finished the song with a conventional series of high falsetto hoots and Leo said a few words in appreciation of his delivery.

Then Ricky's voice rose from across the room, snaking toward the singers with the words, "Fug off!" Tommy and Leo ignored the taunt and continued to talk about where the song had come from. Leo said he heard it was dreamed at Milligan Creek. Tommy said something about what kind of song it was and Leo replied, "Oker, yeah," meaning the song was dreamed by a Prophet named Oker who used to live with the people at Peterson's Crossing. Tommy's rich voice echoed Leo's, "Oker, yeah." Under Tommy's gentle affirmation of Leo's knowledge, I could hear Ricky trying to interrupt, like a frustrated child grasping for attention. His tone had risen from the flat, emotionless, dead sound of the way he said the word "condemned" to an insistent, intrusive vocal jab. He called out, "Hey," but no one acknowledged the call. Tommy took up the drum again and started a song. He lost his hold on it and stopped singing. He said something in Beaver to Leo and then asked Howard, "Can you shut it off for a while?"

I returned to the world of my dreams, shutting out Ricky's rising hostility and jealousy as I let my mind and spirit slip back to the old times. While I was dreaming, Tommy and Leo drank a little, collected their energies, and tuned the drums by holding them over the open top of the crackling airtight heater. Then they began another song together. Howard turned on the tape recorder again. Leo took the lead in this song, but Tommy continued to sing strongly. Their voices did not blend together as well as they had before. Leo's lead was not as clear. Tommy alternated between following slightly behind him and dropping out altogether. When the song finally ended, Leo chuckled and said in a combination of Beaver and English, "Mixed up singing." He rubbed the surface of the drum with his hand, making a high scraping noise like material being torn. "Too tight," he said in English and then repeated the same thing in Beaver with a little laugh.

Tommy hit his drum a few times, holding the snares that ran across the inside of the head loose by relaxing his hold on the loop of *babiche* around his thumb. After the last stroke, the snares continued to rattle against the head like the notes of an invisible spirit player. Then he said to Leo, "It sound pretty good, eh, that one." Leo called out, "Ready," Tommy echoed, "Yeah," and Leo began another song. This time, Tommy joined Leo clearly after the first few phrases, but he continued to let Leo lead at the beginning of each new phrase.

Leo sang with confidence. I suspected he was thinking of Jack as he sang. The song came to an end, and I imagined a circle of kids who had been bobbing up and down around the fire scurrying away like mice to the tepee's edges. Leo's eyes sparkled at the memories his singing with Tommy renewed. As the last notes resonated from the two drums, Tommy finished off the song with a strong, rich peal of laughter. I looked at Leo and said, "Pretty good" in my best oratorical style. Tommy's voice echoed my words, "Pretty good," as he continued to laugh. I followed him with, "Good show, Leo," bringing the song to a happy conclusion.

The rhythm of their dual performance reestablished itself. Tommy and Leo quickly launched into another round of song. Tommy introduced the new song by saying, "Aske Kwolan yine," the song of a Dreamer named "Young Boy, Old Man" whose name symbolized a life in which the powers of a boy's vision quest are successfully transformed into those of an old man. This time, Leo led the singing with exuberance. Halfway through the song, Tommy spoke up jokingly in Beaver and English, "I can't keep track of you. I fool myself."

I noticed that Leo's voice had taken on a different timbre. It sounded like the voice of Old Man Aku, Jack's father, whom I had recorded in 1966 when he was a very old man. People at Doig called the old man Abuta, "Abu's father." Aku's daughter Abu was Leo's mother. Ricky's mother, Molly, is another of Aku's daughters. He was Asah, "grandfather," to both Ricky and Leo. The power of Aske Kwolan's vision seemed to have given Leo his grandfather's voice. His singing took on the style and timbre of the old man. Tommy's joke acknowledged the transformation. I heard Ricky's voice jabbing toward them again, this time louder and more insistent, but I could not make out the words he was shouting above the song of Aske Kwolan. Perhaps to reinforce the impact of Leo's singing like Old Man Aku, Tommy announced the next song. He said to Leo in Beaver, "Your grandfather's song." To me and Howard he said, "This is Aku's song." Tommy ignored Ricky. He used the singular pronoun for "your," meaning he was talking specially to Leo rather than to both of Aku's grandsons. His choice of words indicated a recognition that Leo had rendered the song of Aske Kwolan with his grandfather's voice.

Aku's song brought back a flood of memories for me. I could see the old man sitting on the edge of his bed, holding the drum in his left hand and singing this same slow, stately, almost processional song in a strong but peculiarly hollow voice. I remembered the stories he told in that same voice. I knew he was one of the strong hunters before the flu brought death to so many in 1918. When Leo sang the song of Aske Kwolan and Tommy followed with Aku's song, the old times came back to me as if I had been there to experience them. The stories welled up to become real for me. As Tommy sang Old Man Aku's song, the old man's world as I knew it through his stories came back to my mind. I knew Leo and Ricky were also thinking about their grandfather and his world.

I knew they were thinking about Jack and his two sisters, their mothers. I knew they were thinking about themselves as inheritors of that world.

The song of Old Man Aku played upon a quality of sound controlled by tone of voice. Leo had gone into it as he sang the young man, old man song. Some power of his grandfather passed through him in that moment, and Tommy recognized it. Tommy knew in an instant what had happened. He knew to honor the transformation by singing the old man's song. Those among us who knew Aku conjured him in voice and song and story. Together, Leo and Tommy lent their voices to the presence of Aku. The song was paced differently from the strong round children's dances Tommy and Leo had spun around the fire before. Aku's song was a solo piece, tuned to the instrument of his voice. It descended in pitch like a river finding its path through a wrinkle of hills and valleys. The song quavered and flickered like a large winter fire in the late of night, when most people lie dreaming in their sleeping robes.

I could hear fire crackling in the airtight heater of Tommy's house, his living space. It gave me back its light in my mind's eye. The voice of Old Man Aku spoke like a twinned instrument chanted by Tommy and Leo, Leo and Tommy. The old man flowed through the two of them equally, but for Leo the ties of blood were closer than for Tommy. Ricky sat in silence. Leo's voice followed Tommy's by just enough to put them out of phase like two reeds tuned just a shade off from the same note. Tommy played the only drum. Leo sang as if in a trance. The song descended lower. Its phrasing began to take on a form that suggested words spoken by the Dreamers about heaven. Their voices became hushed at the end of the song. Leo fell silent. The drum continued to beat like a heart. Delmer spoke Leo's name. He said, "Leo Aku." Tommy's voice continued to soar on a last note that lingered like the smell of smoke from a distant campfire, like the taste of moose meat, like memories we shared of the old man, like *ya diskwonchi*, the aurora.

The pronunciation of his name seemed to bring Leo back to the present. His voice no longer sounded like his grandfather's. The sound of Leo's name seemed to complete a cycle of transformation. Almost as an echo of Leo's name, Ricky's voice broke the air. His tone was derisive and sneering. His words were, "Go to hell. Go to hell." Tommy stopped singing abruptly in the middle of his phrase. His drum fell silent. He spoke directly to Ricky in a mixture of Beaver and English. The tone was gentle but very serious. He said, "Don't you know you are in my cabin? Don't you know this is the song of our grandfather?" This time, Tommy used the plural pronoun for "our grandfather," meaning Aku had been a grandfather to all of them. He meant to impress on Ricky his connection to us all through the old people and their songs. He spoke to Ricky in Beaver using the voice of an old man.

Tommy told Ricky that what the old people say is true. He told Ricky he is connected to the other people of his generation through the old people and their songs. Ricky stood up and faced Tommy. He spit out, "Don't, liar, don't lie," overriding some of Tommy's words with the strength of his voice. For a moment the house was silent as Ricky's words sank in. Delmer stepped toward Ricky and tried to defuse the confrontation. In a friendly tone he said to Ricky, "Do you want some hooch?" Ricky ignored the offer and stood his ground in front of Tommy. Tommy spoke to Ricky again in Beaver. He asked him why he was talking this way. Ricky came back defensively, "I don't lie. I don't lie too much. Don't lie, I don't lie."

The room was silent except for the fire crackling in the airtight heater. Then Tommy picked up his drum again. He quickly put his thumb through the loop that tightens the snares. He hit the drum five times and then stopped. The sound of the crackling fire filled in the empty spaces where Tommy's drumbeats had been. He spoke in English to me and Howard. His voice stuttered slightly as it does when he is upset. "But you know ah ah I don't know why ah th-they just stop me right there." He picked up the drum again and began to beat on it with the stick. The snares buzzed in agitation. He spoke in Beaver about the power in the Dreamers' songs. Ricky replied, "I don't think so."

Then Leo turned to Howard and asked, "Hey, you gonna record me one," but Tommy began to speak again. He said he knew the Dreamers had the right way. Ricky repeated, "I don't think so." This time, Tommy's reply showed anger and impatience. He shot back, "Well OK, I'm gonna go." Underneath his words, Ricky tried to say something about, "Just we take . . . ," but Tommy drowned out the rest of his reply with a thunder of drumbeats. Tommy's and Ricky's voices rose together in a blend of Beaver and English. From the tangle of words and drumbeats I could hear Ricky's voice yelling, "Bullshit, bullshit." Leo turned again to Howard and asked, "Are you ready," but Ricky's voice rose to drown out every other as he yelled, "Bullshit" again. Leo asked Howard, "Is it on?" Then Delmer came forward to intervene. He said, "Tommy, sit down."

Tommy remained on his feet angrily facing Ricky. He held onto the drum with determination. Then he spoke quickly but decisively. "You know, I'm gonna take my drum out, OK." It was an assertion, not a question. Tommy turned and spoke to Howard, "He said he don't believe anything." Ricky's voice droned one more chorus of "Bullshit" in the background as Tommy reached for his coat and cowboy hat. "Well, OK. Hey," he said, "I'll see you guys." Howard turned off the tape recorder.

Only three and a half minutes had gone by since Ricky first cut Tommy off at the end of Aku's song. I did not fully comprehend what had happened. Suddenly, Tommy was leaving his own home. Even the chorus of Ricky's denunciation had come to me as if from a distance, through the veil of a dream. The precise details of what went on became clear to me only later, as Howard and I listened back to the tape. At first I did not understand why Tommy would choose to leave his own Mansion on the Hill rather than asking Ricky to leave. Then I remembered what Tommy had said to me in the King Koin laundry. "I love you guys, you and Howard. That's the power. I could kill you if I wanted to, but I love you so much I can't do it." Tommy loves Ricky, too. He loves Ricky like his own son. Tommy loves the teaching of the Dreamers. He loves their songs. He would rather leave his own home than get mad at Ricky. Tommy thought about Charlie Yahey. He thought about Makenunatane. He thought about the Trail to Heaven. Tommy would leave rather than direct his power against Ricky.

I did not understand that Tommy was really going until Howard came up to me and asked if he could borrow my car to drive Tommy and Leo and Delmer the fifteen miles down to Peterson's Crossing. Within a few moments of my telling Howard he could take the car if he had the energy to make the drive so late at night, I found myself alone in the Care Home. Outside in the bright, clear, cold night, Howard, Tommy, Leo, and Delmer walked across the squeaking surface of snow toward where my Rabbit was parked by Gerry's house. Ricky followed behind them like a big puppy that does not want to be left behind.

When they reached the car, Ricky tried to get in. Tommy told him there was no room and tried to get into the car himself. Suddenly Ricky's fist shot out and caught Tommy's face. It drew blood. Leo and Tommy held Ricky up against the wall of Gerry's house. Howard and Delmer got in the car. Howard started the engine. Tommy and Leo piled in. Someone shouted to Howard, "Take off. Run the bastard over." Howard saw that the way was clear in front of the car. He put the Rabbit in gear and took off, throwing a spray of snow from the spinning front wheels. Ricky faded into a shadow world. He did not return to where I was still dreaming in the Care Home.

22. RESCUE

Howard returned to the Care Home about five the next morning. We set up the tape recorder and recorded our conversation about the evening's events. We wanted to talk about what had happened while it was fresh. We wanted to understand why Ricky denounced the Dreamers and why Tommy left rather than confronting Ricky directly. Howard told me that after they made their getaway, the car was filled with angry voices. Everyone was swearing and letting out their feelings about Ricky's behavior. They agreed he had been a real asshole. The words seemed to bring some relief, and by the time they reached Peterson's Crossing Tommy was in a more reflective mood. Howard told me what Tommy had said to him:

> Tommy and I were sitting in the car kind of just talking, 'cause it was a kind of parting in a way for a while, and he was saying, um, I said, "Well, you're very strong, man. You could have killed him and you know it. You told me about the time in Pete Toy's when you had those two guys up against the wall," 'cause he had told us last year about a story in Pete Toy's where he had dumped tables over and just got a couple of guys, and he said, "Well, Ricky can throw fast punches but I would have stopped him. I could have stopped him by grabbing, by holding," and then he showed me how you would block a punch with a hold and how you would turn something fast into something slow and have power over speed.

As Howard spoke, I recognized Tommy's talk as a reference to his medicine power. I told Howard it seemed to me that his statement was a declaration of that power:

When it comes right down to it, these two theories of Christian over Dreamer's power is . . . there's a whole other level. That's one of the public level and there's the other one of personal power, which is much more serious and that's what it got down to tonight. And Tommy aced out. Tommy defended himself from Ricky's attack. Ricky made an attack. He really did. And Tommy, Tommy asserted his power by saying, "I could kill you if I had to but I won't."

Tommy's message to Howard was the same thing he said to me years before on the old wagon road. When someone makes an attack, you must have the power to kill him, but you must also have the will to refrain from using that power. This time, the person who challenged him was Ricky, the young man who was like his own son. It was Ricky with whom Tommy spent so many dreamy evenings the summer before, listening in the velvet dark to Charlie Yahey's voice from across the edge of mortality. For Ricky now the world seemed condemned, but for Tommy the Dreamers' songs were bringing it back to life. I began to understand why Tommy left his house rather than confront Ricky directly. He was more afraid of what he might be able to do to Ricky than of what Ricky could do to him. Tommy defended himself by going away, even when Ricky punched him. Tommy held back the power in his mind. Ricky, too, must have gained some form of power, but Tommy chose to avoid a confrontation. He thought of the Dreamers' songs. With the aid of Howard, Leo, and Delmer, he moved the party to a more congenial location. The fight Tommy stepped back from was of the mind. He did not allow his mind to become consumed by anger directed toward Ricky. He knew that such anger would eventually come back upon himself.

Howard and I talked quietly to one another in the cold bright hours of Saturday morning until the need for sleep overtook us. Tommy's day was different from ours. By the time we were compelled to sleep, Tommy was well into the compulsion to drink. Later in the day, he hitched a ride into Fort St. John and continued his drinking throughout the following evening. By Sunday morning, Howard and I were fully recovered from the long Friday evening that had begun with a slide show at Gerry's. We got up very early and decided to drive into town to have breakfast at the Fort Hotel. Sunday morning seemed like a safe time to be in town without becoming involved in the madness of compulsive drinking.

The morning was bright and clear but very cold. According to the local radio we listened to driving in, there had been a fire in the Condill Hotel across the street from the Fort during the night. When we arrived in town, the main street was blocked by trestle barricades. The only vehicle on the street was a red rescue truck in front of the Condill. The only living being we saw at first was a large thick-haired dog walking slowly down the street next to The Bay (the Hudson's Bay Company department store). We stopped, spoke to him, and took a picture. This moment was as magical as my conversation with Tommy in the King Koin laundry had been the summer before. Howard and I understood that it was an awesome moment in our lives.

Howard got out his tape recorder and began to walk down the empty street, kicking a can in front of him to hear its hollow scraping noise echo against the frozen buildings. I followed him with my camera, taking pictures. The dog walked from one side of the street to another in front of us. An old Indian woman from Peterson's Crossing walked toward us down the other side of the street, her face huddled in a shawl against the bitter wind. As she passed us without an exchange of greetings, I could see it was Alice Moccasin, Albert Askoty's wife. The dog seemed to own the street. He was large. He looked like a wolf. We thought he must be the spirit of some wild presence still at large upon the streets of town. He did not seem to mind the cold.

When we got to the end of the street, Tommy came around the corner by the Northern Taxi office. It seemed as natural for him to be there as it was for the dog to be freely roaming the usually busy street. Time and the ordinary world faded before the intensity of this moment. Tommy was wearing a denim jacket. Howard and I were cold even in our down parkas. Tommy was as comfortable as the dog. Howard shouted toward Tommy. He shouted into the wall of buildings that made this place a street. His words echoed against their facades. Tommy shouted back. He stood in front of the Northern Taxi office. The dog came toward him. Tommy's and Howard's voices blended as they echoed off the facades of the buildings. Tommy stooped down to be closer to the dog. For a moment they stood together, Tommy's hand resting gently on the dog's thick neck hair. I took their picture. Then Tommy rose and we shook hands.

This was the first time Howard and I had ever driven to town for breakfast. Tommy had no rational way of knowing we would be there Sunday morning. Tommy was just there in the same way that the dog was there. He was still awake from Friday evening that became Saturday morning that became a day and a night abroad in town. He was still walking around. To ask how he came to be where we were just then is the same as asking how the hunter comes to be where the animal is on the trail of the hunt. Hunters make the connection through dreams. Maybe Tommy was lucky, or maybe Fort St. John is a small town, or maybe we were lucky, or maybe the dog was a guide, or maybe the fire and the empty street attracted us to the same place. In the dream, our being together there made perfect sense.

Whatever the cause or happenstance of our meeting, Tommy took charge of the situation. As Howard continued to record and I continued to take pictures, Tommy led us toward where the large square red vehicle with RESCUE written in large white letters on the side stood puffing exhaust in a misty plume from its pipe. The truck flashed red from a beacon on its roof. It cast a regular flicker of red against the growing light of an April day in the north Peace River country. Its engine chortled gruffly to itself. A fire marshal in heavy blue clothing stood inside the charred doorway of the Condill. The taproom was blackened and soaked. Toward the entrance, water had frozen into sooty rippled sheets of ice. Tommy led us into the blackened foyer and introduced himself to the fire marshal. Then he introduced me and Howard as "broadcasters from Vancouver." The marshal seemed impressed that the Vancouver media had picked up the story so soon, but he made it clear we could obtain further information only from an authorized source at the fire station. We thanked him for his cooperation and returned to the street.

Tommy had not eaten since the night we ate moose meat together in the Care Home. Howard and I were hungry, even though we had been eating regular meals on Saturday. Now it was Sunday morning and time to bring Tommy back to the ordinary world of eating and sleeping. Tommy said he would eat with us if I paid for the meal. Then he asked to borrow ten dollars from me. I thought about writing a paper called "The Anthropologist as Moose." I took off my gloves and handed Tommy a purple piece of paper with an oil refinery pictured on one side, a white man named Sir Wilfred Laurier on the other. Then we turned our backs on the ruins of the Condill and crossed the street to the Fort.

The stained and darkened cement ramp leading up to the splintered plywood taproom door was empty. An iron bar across the door reinforced the message. After last night's bleary fight-ridden lurch and belch of closing time, this place would remain a sanctuary until Monday morning. The hotel lobby is approached by steps. Some of the glass panes in the outer set of red plywood doors have been replaced by squares of unpainted plywood. The bottoms of the doors were crushed and bruised from the blows of heavy, drunken, angry boots. Past the inner set of doors a desk clerk sat behind the lobby counter. Two rows of keys hung on the wall in back of the desk. Tommy walked to the desk. He brought out his words with difficulty but also with authority. The alcohol and lack of sleep rendered his stutter more pronounced, and he delivered his words carefully. Tommy gave his name to the clerk. He asked if he could "buy a room." The clerk replied they were filled up this morning because everyone from the Condill had moved over to the Fort after the fire. Tommy asked if he could reserve a room for later. The clerk replied that he could. Tommy added that he wanted one with a woman. Satisfied, Tommy accompanied us to the coffee shop. We took a table in the back, under the blast of a hot air fan. The contrast with the outside atmosphere was breathtaking. The waiter came to our table. We ordered ham and eggs with toast and jam. We drank coffee while we were waiting for the food to arrive. Tommy, Howard, and I felt at home in this corner of the world.

Tommy spoke for the first time about Friday night. Howard's tape recorder lay beside his chair. It was still running. Tommy said, "How you manage with them boys alone in my house?" I said, "Everybody left after you left, that night anyway." Tommy began to fill me in on his activities after he left me dreaming in the Care

Home. He also filled me in on his innermost feelings about what had happened. His voice was rough with wear and exhaustion but strong like his large, forceful hands. His missing upper front teeth and the suppressed stutter gave his words a sound of urgency. I remembered the swirl of clothes in the King Koin laundromat. I remembered the swirl of images as he had once before momentarily opened his world to mine. Tommy said:

Then I started to drink with Charlie Oker
and Henry Apsassin and, uh, Bruce Stanley.
Everybody treat me really good you know,
except uh . . . I don't know.
I treat him really good you know.
He's my boy.
The reason why, you know,
I told you.
I go out from this place.
You know, I can't fight.
I can't fight.
Sure I can fight,
can't . . .
You know, in my fist it's OK.
But not in my heart.
Really stop for that.
I can't help it.
If I do, you know, nobody going to stop me.
No way.
Just a big steel man.
I just turn around, you know.
Good-hearted.
That's why I don't get mad.

I answered Tommy, "Yeah, it's really a good thing that you hold back." Tommy replied, "I just walk away." I came back to condemn what Ricky did: "He still shouldn't have done what he did. He's a jerk." Tommy turned to look me straight in the eye with a stare nourished by his visionary journey in the streets of Fort St. John. He replied:

You know,
I don't think—but I can see it.
That's the way I think, anyway.
We're going to see each other again.
Maybe in heaven.
You know them springs, them springs.
I aim my life in there.
When I do that,
I don't know why,
for a couple of years.
Broomfield's going to be gettin' old.
I try to see Broomfield, eh.
He's gonna gettin' old.
Gonna he's whiskers.
Gonna gettin' old.
As far as I see.
But me and you.
I'm the first one,
and you be the last.
The way to heaven . . .
'Cause there's a lot of religions around.

Immediately, I knew what Tommy was talking about. I knew about the springs. In the 1968 audience, Charlie Yahey began by telling about springs where moose appear from under the ground. Tommy translated what he said for me. Tommy even gave his own commentary. His words and those of Charlie Yahey appear together as a document of the event. Charlie Yahey said:

Under the springs there is a great big moose,
a giant moose.
That is why all the moose on this world
stay near those places.
Before Saya made everything right on this world
there were giant moose on this world too
but he sent them down to the world beneath this one.
Where he sent them down there are now springs
coming up from that world still.
The moose like it there

because they know the giant moose are underneath.
There is just like a house under there.
Small moose stay under there too in that house.
In wintertime they will come out from the spring or lick.
Even if there is thick ice and frozen dirt
they will break through the crust, go a little ways,
shake themselves, and all the dirt will come off.
These moose are regular sized
but they have just a single set of horns like a cow,
just small ones with a single point.
They shake themselves until all the dirt is gone
and they rub themselves against the trees.
The boss for all the moose
stays under the spring in the other land.
God made it like that.

I remembered the explanation Tommy had added in 1968:

Even in cold time those moose under the ground are
    lonesome.
They don't like it there and get tired of it.
Even if it is frozen over with ice they just break through.
They just lay down and then shake themselves.
They rub themselves on trees too.
Sometimes seven or eight moose go with them.
They are white with red eyes, or some of them are just blue
when they come out. Just like blue horses.
Some of them just really blue, some of them white,
and some of them pure yellow.
That's what he said. I hear him in there.
They just have two little spike horns like cow horns.

As Tommy spoke of the springs and said, "I aim my life in there,"
I remembered Charlie Yahey's words. The warm air from the fan
above our heads blew across our table. The waiter came with our
ham and eggs. We began to eat. Tommy began to tell a story about
when he was young. My time of mind dissolved into a place where
animals come very close to people. I could see the salt lick, heavy
with tracks like a barnyard. Some force stronger than fences con-

centrated these tracks on a single center. The trails of many moose overlap in this place, just as the trails of many people overlap in the dance lodge. A spirit of the species centers this place. The boss for the moose may be found there. That is why all the moose on this world come around the licks. The moose like it there because they know the giant moose are underneath.

Tommy's voice took me and Howard back to when he was a boy of thirteen. He used to be a fast runner. He ran so fast, even the moose could not keep up with him. As Tommy told me this story, I knew there was another story behind it. I remembered the summer before, when Tommy shot a cow moose and calf. As he butchered the animals, Tommy told me he could hear their spirits singing, just above the treetops. The way he talked about hearing their songs made me suspect that Tommy had made contact with giant moose as a child. Now, in the Fort Hotel coffee shop he chose to give substance to my surmise. Like the old people I knew from before, he chose to reveal more of what he knew I had guessed already. How strange, I thought, to learn of Tommy's vision quests and his powers, first on the old wagon road, then in the King Koin laundry, and now in the Fort Hotel coffee shop. Then I realized Tommy had chosen perfect meeting places where his world and mine could come together. The white man's places in particular provided a perfect theater for the drama of Tommy's hierophany. From the vantage point of the Fort Hotel, moose licks were like a dream world. Howard and I accepted the gift without question.

With a start, I remembered the wolf-dog that had seemed to be Tommy's familiar only moments before in the clear, cold street outside. The dog was the first living thing Howard and I saw when we got to town. Without hesitation we had stopped the car to make contact with him. Without question we had followed him to where Tommy materialized outside the Northern Taxi stand. I realized how much I took these events for granted as they were happening. It seemed obvious and natural that the dog should lead us to Tommy. It seemed natural that they should greet one another as friends. It seemed natural for them to pose together for the instant in which I captured them as a single photographic image. Only in retrospect did these events appear strange and miraculous. I experienced neither belief nor disbelief, only a simple acceptance that what was happening was both natural and meaningful.

I could hear the high mechanical drone of the fan above our heads. From nearby tables, cups and saucers rattled the familiar percussion of civilized amenity. Behind these appearances I could imagine the reality of moose licks in the bush. I recalled the way the ground is trampled in a circle around these places. I realized that moose licks and dancing circles are similar in their concentration of many individual trails into a single space. I remembered that the Dreamers say, "Animals will come to the dreams of hunters who come together with their relatives. Animals come to the people who sing and dance together." I remembered thinking that Tommy's finding us in town was like the way a hunter comes together with his game. I wondered if Tommy had conjured us for his purposes. Whatever the mechanism, we conveniently came into his world with ten dollars, breakfast, and a ride back to Doig. Howard and I felt as if we were giving ourselves to Tommy in the way a moose gives itself to the hunter. The gift felt good because it was also an exchange. Tommy was giving us something of his deepest essence. I turned my attention away from the whine of the fan and the swirl of my own recollections and intuitions as Tommy continued his narrative:

"I aim my life in there," Tommy was saying. By the time he was thirteen, Tommy said, he was able to run down moose in the bush. Usually, he did this when no other people were around, but once his dad and old John Davis saw him running. They saw him overtaking the moose. Just as Tommy got close to the moose he sensed the presence of people. He did not want them to see him, so he circled back to the lick where the moose stayed. John Davis and Tommy's father did not follow him there, but the moose knew this place in the same way Tommy knew it. The moose circled back too. The moose came to where Tommy was resting. Their trails came together. Their tracks became superimposed on one another. They were drawn to this space by the giant moose beneath the lick. They were drawn to it because they shared a knowledge of the giant animals.

The moose like it there.
They know the giant moose is underneath.
There is just like a house under there.
Small moose stay under there too in that house.

The boss for all the moose stays under the spring
in the other land.
God made it like that.

Tommy lay down in the willows next to the moose. They both
went to sleep. They stayed together in the same house. They ate
something together. Tommy told us that what they ate was "just
like bread and jam" to him. It was both human food and the food
of moose. They spoke to him in a language he could understand.
His thoughts came together with theirs in a common understanding
of the world. The boy was nourished by his intimacy with this animal's spirit. He found he could eat the animal's food, think its
thoughts, dream its dreams, walk in its tracks. The time they spent
dreaming together belonged to a different time than that of every
day. It was a time to which Tommy can still return. Since then,
Tommy said, he knows by dreaming where the moose are staying.
He can hear their songs just above the tops of the trees.

When Tommy awoke from his visionary experience of a "time
out of time" at the center of the lick, his father and John Davis were
out of sight. He remembered the smell of smoke, the sound of his
own language, the warmth of fire. Nobody asked him where he
had been. For years, Tommy kept the experience to himself. John
Davis knew. His dad knew. Perhaps his grandmother Nachin knew
from her dreaming. That was sufficient. To have made the information public prematurely might have turned the power against
him. Instead, Tommy used his dreaming to help people by feeding
them. As we finished our breakfast, Tommy said, "You guys help
me lots." He completed the thought with a piece of hyperbole. "If
you help Tommy Attachie, you're working for the Lord." So
blessed, I paid the bill and the three of us pushed our way out of
the Fort into a day glistening with sunlight on the ice crystals that
still carpeted the main street of town.

23. A TRAIL OF SONG

The Dreamers speak of the Trail to Heaven as a song. They say a good person can grab hold of its turns with his or her mind. The good person is light and sensitive to messages coming from distant places. The animals recognize such a person and come to him in dreams. They give themselves to the person who gives to others. The Dreamers say if people are always together with one another, if they sing and dance together often, they will remain in perfect communication with the animals. The Dunne-za of old recognized Makenunatane as a Dreamer because he told them how to create a perfect surround. When each person knew his or her place in relation to every other, they were able to walk up to a moose and kill it with an axe.

In real life, communication is always less than perfect. Hunting is less than perfect. Some people have more success than others. Accidents come to some. Good fortune comes to others. The events of a person's life are as much alive as the world in which he or she lives. The power that comes to a person may be used to cause misfortune or to counter it. It may be used to bring life to the people or to take it away. When someone experiences a bad turn of events, he or she is tempted to look around to see who might be wishing to cause harm. People may become jealous of others whose lives seem easy. The Dreamers and their songs show people a trail away from jealousy and hate. They show people a Trail to Heaven.

Tommy's life has not been easy, but when accidents happen he knows how to use his dreaming to identify and confront an enemy. His powers give him strength. Tommy knows how to grab hold of the Dreamers' songs with his mind. The Dreamers' songs give him restraint and compassion. Ricky has also experienced hardship in relation to his hopes and expectations. Because he is younger than

Tommy, his frustration turned easily to jealousy. Ricky walked in on Tommy and Leo singing Dreamers' songs beautifully together. He was jealous of his brother Leo. He tried to show off his own mastery of a Christian oratorical style, but it did not work because he had been drinking. Like a child whose bid for praise has failed, he made a move for attention. He spoke against the Dreamers' songs themselves. He felt as if people were closing their minds to him. When I told Ricky I thought some things should remain a mystery, he felt as if I were withholding something from him.

At first, Howard and I interpreted Ricky's rejection of the Dreamers' songs as the symptom of a conflict between Indian and European systems of thought. Later, it seemed that Ricky was acting a role in a "medicine fight," responding to the experience of personal misfortune by dwelling upon, and even creating, a web of interpersonal hostility. We realized, finally, that the threat of a medicine fight had compelled Tommy to reveal his power in the same way that Jumbie had revealed his power when he leaped under his bedroll to avoid the consequences of being exposed to a flash camera. Tommy had responded to the threat of a fight by turning away rather than by confronting Ricky. He did not fight "his boy," as I knew he sometimes fought white men during his drinking episodes in town. I remembered what Tommy had told me in the King Koin laundromat. "You know, Robin," he had said. "I love you guys, you and Howard. That's the power. I could kill you if I wanted to, but I love you so much I can't do it." I remembered what Tommy told me and Howard over breakfast in the Fort Hotel. I remembered that he talked about the moose lick. He said, "I aim my life in there."

Tommy revealed both his power and his respect for the Dreamers' teachings in the way he responded to Ricky's challenge. Tommy walked away from his Mansion on the Hill as a consequence of the power he knew was within him. I remembered that Jumbie had told Tommy, "You be like me." Now it was coming true. Tommy really was Old Man Red. I had seen him act like Jumbie. I had seen him change into a person who could reveal his power. Tommy reminded me of what Charlie Yahey told me long ago when I began to dance to the Dreamers' songs. Charlie Yahey said that the old people in heaven began to see me when I joined in the dancing. Tommy told me, "We're going to see each other again, maybe in heaven." Tommy had seen me react to Ricky's antagonism by going into a dream. I turned my mind to the memory I held of Old Man Aku's way of singing. I turned my mind to the memory of Charlie Yahey. In my dream, their songs became the Trail to Heaven. In my dream, the old people came back to me. In my dream, I joined them in dancing. I remembered what Tommy had told me in 1968, that it is good to sleep when people are singing and dancing. I remembered falling into a dream with my head resting on Tommy's shoulder.

During the summer of 1981, Howard and I spent a few days with Tommy and Ricky in the Care Home before Jillian joined us and we recreated Monias City. In the evenings after we had blown out the candles we often talked about our dreams. One evening, Ricky talked about dreaming of Jesus. What he said made me realize that Jesus is very real for Ricky, not just an abstraction. Ricky wanted to dream toward Jesus in the way the old people dream of the Trail to Heaven. He wanted to locate himself in relation to some secure center. He wanted to locate his spirit in the way that Tommy's spirit is located at the center of the moose lick mandala. Ricky said:

I dream about Jesus too.
I see him three times.
One time I was following him back up somewhere, some hill.
A big dream.
And he was wearing Lee Rider jeans.
Three times.
Two other times I never see him that much.
Just a little bit, where he come back from up this way.
I was kind of . . .
Didn't want to ask him that question,
but I just did.
Which way he come back from?
Funny, this hill.
It's not in Blueberry.
It's not in here.
Somewhere just like this big hill, big hill.
There's top of the hill there too.
About two times I dream about that hill.

One time I saw him there.
There was a pow-wow or something like that.
A bunch of Indians there.
That pow-wow up there.
I just kind of know it's a pow-wow.
I never tell nobody about it.
That's why I don't remember much.
I don't say too many words.
When I want to do something, I do it.
I say it, and I do it.
Just know the goal.
A guy can do it.
Nobody say you can't do it.
Before, when a guy's a kid,
people will tell you something.
You believe it.
Like you can't do this and that.
You don't say nothing, but you just go with it.
You don't know how but . . .
We go as we grow up.
If something happens like that,
I like to prove it to myself.
But there's other young guys around me.
And we got to do something.
You can't fool around with old folks.
One thing I don't like much is that school.
I think it would have been better
if they'd had school in here.
I would have gone straight through.
Right from grade one all the way.
Stay around here, hunt, stuff like that.
Pretty soon I got pretty tired.
I didn't want to go in white man's way.
I didn't want anything to do with it.
Just want to go out somewhere.
I like the rodeo best, good fun anyways.
All Indians used to be cowboys around here.
I like to go in the bush a little bit.

I don't like town that much.
Money don't mean much, but a guy needs it anyway.
It doesn't cost you anything to walk around.

Ricky's dreams are like those of the old people. They follow the trail of meaningful images. They follow the Trail to Heaven. Makenunatane dreamed of Jesus and a shortcut to heaven. Ricky dreamed of Jesus on a big hill. His dream merged images of Jesus and the pow-wow. The hill was not part of the ordinary world—not the hills of Blueberry and Doig. Ricky wanted to follow Jesus. He wanted to ask him which way he came from, which way he was going. He wanted to ask Jesus why we are placed here on this earth, as he had asked me at the beginning of the evening in Tommy's house. In his dream, Ricky brought together images of Jesus and the Dreamers' dance. Jesus was near the top of a big hill, close to where the Trail to Heaven takes off. The old people were there too. They were singing. Their songs lifted up toward heaven. The dream image represented Ricky's world. In the dream, he tried to bring his image of Jesus together with an image of the Dreamers' songs rising toward heaven.

When Ricky found himself drifting and without any clear goal, the coherence of these two images began to come apart. On the evening of the party at Tommy's, they came into outright confrontation. The confrontation Ricky tried to create with Tommy was not between him and Tommy but between two parts of his own mind and spirit. Jesus and the Dreamers are not necessarily in conflict. Everyone knows that Makenunatane dreamed of Jesus, too. Jesus showed Makenunatane a shortcut to heaven, a new way. The white men showed the Dunne-za a new way. The old people explored the turns of this new trail through their dreams. Ricky's conflict was not between Jesus and the Dreamers. It was between the child part of himself and the other part that did not yet know how to be a member of the adult world. Ricky put on a brave front. As a child, people told him what to do. As a young man, he wanted to prove things to himself. Tommy understood his dilemma. He was annoyed at Ricky's behavior but not angry at Ricky himself. He was willing to leave his Mansion on the Hill rather than fight with "his boy." He was like Jumbie.

Ricky's dream of the Trail to Heaven pictured Jesus wearing Lee Rider jeans. He was ascending a hill among Indians having a pow-wow. Charlie Yahey pictured Makenunatane wearing a Hudson's Bay blanket. Like Jesus, Makenunatane foretold his own death. The Dunne-za have always turned to their dreams for an interpretation of events going on around them. Ricky's dreams of the summer were normal in their evocation of images from contemporary experience. Even his denunciation of Tommy and Leo was intelligible, as a reaction to uncertainty about his own identity. Ricky's difficulty in making the transition from child to man took him away from his relatives—those who are living, and those who have gone before. His difficulty made him turn away from the integrative power of the Dreamers' songs. His difficulty made him turn away even from the song of his own grandfather.

Ricky was jealous of Leo. He resented Leo's success, his knowledge of the Dreamers' songs, his recognition by John Yahey, and especially the closeness of his connection to Tommy. Like the hunter and trapper from whom the animal bosses withhold the game, Ricky had become suspicious and resentful of those closest to him. For Ricky that night, the Trail to Heaven did not begin at the center of a dance circle. It did not ascend lightly with the turns of the Dreamers' songs. Like a shadow who must follow his trail back from camp to camp during the hours of darkness until it reaches the last place where it was light enough of spirit to rise up on a trail of song, Ricky walked backward among his friends and relatives. The songs did not carry him easily into the world of dreams. He felt closed off from what was in our minds.

I wanted to tell Ricky about the old wagon road. I wanted him to see the aurora still glowing in the look of my eyes. That evening I felt like a mirror. I felt the old people close around me. Eskama was making drymeat nearby. Jack and Charlie Yahey put a fresh white moosehide head on the rim of an old drum. I remembered Old Man Aku, Ricky and Leo's grandfather, telling me:

One time I dreamed about a Trail to Heaven.
I went halfway up and someone met me.
The person gave me something white.
He was one of my relatives.

I knew him a long time ago.
I was worrying.
How could I sing as well as he did?
He sang this song to me in the dream.
The next morning I woke up.
I had this song.
I could sing it as well as he sang.

The Trail to Heaven begins at the place where you meet your relatives. It begins when the people you knew from long ago come down to meet you. It begins when they give you a song. It begins when your own voice and their voices become as one. Tommy and Leo took me to the beginning of the trail as they sang together. I let my mind fly away on a dream. I let it fly to where the old people remembered me. I flew toward them on a trail of song.

That evening, Ricky was worrying. He thought, "How can I sing as well as Leo?" Leo sang the song of Aske Kwolan, the Dreamer whose name suggests the integration of a child's experience with that of an old person. Leo sang the Dreamer's song in the voice of the grandfather he shares with Ricky. Then Tommy sang Aku's song. For Ricky, these songs were like a miracle, a bad miracle. He wanted to be heard in the voice of a preacher. Ricky did not hear his grandfather's song. He seemed to be walking backward along his own trail. He struck out blindly, against voices coming to him in the dark. It frightened him to hear Tommy and Leo singing in one voice. It frightened him to hear Leo's voice become that of their mutual grandfather. He refused to know what was in Tommy's and Leo's minds. He closed his mind to us all.

The evening ended when Tommy took his drum away from the house. It ended when Tommy showed his power by going away from a situation where he would have been compelled to use it against someone he loves. It ended when Tommy acted as Jumbie had acted when the well-meaning white lady tried to take a flash picture of him. The evening ended, but it remains alive in the minds and memories of those who were there. Ricky has not forgotten his grandfather's song. He will continue to dream. He will dream again about Indians having a pow-wow on a hill that reaches toward the sky. If he allows his mind to float freely within the dreamspace he may see Jesus wearing Lee Rider jeans. He may hear the song of his grandfather, Old Man Aku. In the morning, when Ricky wakes up, he may sing his grandfather's song. The Dreamers' songs can take a person out along the Trail to Heaven. From there, the people you knew over the course of a lifetime will come down to meet you. In the morning, their songs will be within you. If you close your eyes, the Dreamers' songs will take you the rest of the way there. The songs take you along Yagatunne, the Trail to Heaven.

24. IN MEMORY

The meaning of a particular event refers continually to the memories of the people who bring it into being. Sometimes an event's meaning derives from conflicting interpretations of other events from past days, weeks, and years. My own memories and interpretations are as much a part of the reality of the events I have described as are those of the other participants. Over time, past events resolve into a pattern that is understood mutually and guides ongoing interaction. The events I have described are continually being integrated into moments in lives that are ongoing. They are part of a culture that retains its identity as it changes to meet the demands of a changing environment. The events of April 2, 1982, seemed ordinary to everyone but me and Howard at the time they were happening. As time passes, they will become legendary to all concerned.

Gerry's evening with Albert Askoty was ordinary when it happened. It became legendary as we recalled it upon our return from the old wagon road a week later. I suspect that Howard, Jillian, and I have long been legendary topics of speculation and conversation among the people of Doig. Our presences in Dunne-za life have developed their own legends. I became known as one of the Tlu-kawutdunne, "people who live on the flat." Gerry sometimes calls me "Labassis," a consciously Dunne-za version of "Robin." Many things have changed since 1982. Others have remained the same. Most of the old houses at Doig have been replaced with new, modern ones. For the first time in their lives, Doig people have running water, central heating, and the other amenities of modern living. They call the main street of the new settlement "Sesame Street" because of all the kids growing up there. Behind the new street, Tommy still holds forth in his Mansion on the Hill.

I have described and interpreted the events of a particular moment in time in relation to my understanding of an overall pattern that includes the stories of Dreamers like Charlie Yahey. Although I may have missed some clues or pieces of information that would show the events in a different light, the ideas of personal power and of a Trail to Heaven set out the pattern through which events have taken on meaning for untold generations. Charlie Yahey said that the animals come to people when people are generous with one another. He said that people should use their powers for the good of all. He said we should all dance in a common trail that follows the sun's direction. I have tried to follow the spirit of his teachings in writing *Trail to Heaven*. I trust that readers, both Indian and non-Indian, will receive my words in that same spirit. Since the night of April 2, 1982, Ricky has grown in his understanding, both of Dreamers' ways and of Christian teaching. When we visited Doig in the summer of 1985, Ricky had become a powerful preacher. He led services at a tent meeting and gave testimony about the trials he has experienced. "Old Time Religion" is the witness Howard and I have given to one of those moments in Ricky's life. Howard also recorded Ricky's charismatic preaching and praying. The events described above must have contributed to Ricky's learning as they did to Howard's and mine.

April 1982 will always be a magical time in my memory. It would not have been possible without Howard. Being with Howard was different from being with anyone else I have ever known. Our times together were legendary as we lived them. Howard and I knew that our stay in Old Man Red's Mansion on the Hill was extraordinary and never to be repeated. Perhaps that is why we documented every nuance in such detail. Every moment I spent with Howard was, in fact, extraordinary. Every moment was music. Every moment was a romance. Now, those moments live only in memory.

Like Tommy, Howard had always struggled with an internal enemy, an enemy that drove him to the dark edges of existence. Unlike Tommy, he did not grow up with a Dreamer to guide him back to the world's center. His own elders had not sent him on a vision quest. The spirits he knew could not bring him back from the world's dizzy edge. On July 5, 1986, Howard stepped into the darkness with which he had always flirted. He died by his own hand. I was three thousand miles away when Howard left the world. Jillian and I were in New Jersey with my daughters, Amber and Juniper. On an impulse we had detoured off the New Jersey Turnpike to visit Littlegrange, my mother's family home. At the moment Howard died I was crying at my grandmother's grave, which I had not visited since 1952 when she, too, suddenly went out of my life.

The phone call about Howard's death came the next day at my parents' cottage in the woods of Sussex County, New Jersey. Jillian, Amber, Juniper, and I were about to drive out through the old stone fences, past where Mrs. Tinsley used to live, to the general store at Middleville. When the phone rang, Jillian and I rushed to it with a terrible prescient sense that our world would be lesser from that moment. After the call, we walked slowly from the cottage to speak the terrible words to the girls. A large blacksnake lazily stretched itself across the path between the house and the car. In all my years at the cottage I have never seen a blacksnake that close to the house. Howard always wanted to be black. He sought out snake forms—tubes, hoses—and made them instruments of his music. I thought about the foxes that came to Old Man Chipesia. I thought about the moose that came within sight of camp. I thought about Howard's spirit. That night, Jillian and I drifted out to the middle of the lake in the family's canoe. We listened to bullfrogs creaking and croaking their greetings in shimmering waves of sound above the water's surface. Our tears came down as we pulled some sour solace from a bottle of bourbon in Howard's memory. I thought about the Trail to Heaven. I thought about a trail of song. I knew that Howard's dreaming, like that of Makenunatane and Charlie Yahey, will always be musical. His spirit will follow a trail of song. Jillian and I sent our words to be read at Howard's memorial service. I chose these words from *Trail to Heaven*:

A moment in Indian Time includes every other moment shared in the individual and collective memories of individuals, community, and culture. A single moment is meaningful in relation to every other moment that is part of shared experience. Every moment is meaningful in relation to all the other moments that have gone before. Every event makes sense in relation to shared knowledge and experience. Communications within a particular moment refer back to the unstated understandings that connect people's lives together.

In April of 1982, Howard and I found ourselves connected to the lives of the Beaver Indian People. We described some of our experiences in a piece we called "Old Time Religion." This is an excerpt from the written version of that piece. It is called *Trail to Heaven*:

At first the old wagon road was rough from frozen ruts, and we travelled slowly. It became smooth as we descended into the cut made by the Osborn River and crossed over its unseen liquid presence hidden beneath a painting of ice and snow. Above the river we broke out of the low land and its forest cover into an open country, cleared of its ancient, thickly standing poplars. We broke out of the forest's shadows and its old memories into a blaze of light undulating in ribbons and waves like a celestial incandescent surf on the shore of our northern horizon. This was the aurora, *ya diskwonchi*, "lights in the sky." The Dunne-za say these swooping, swarming presences are spirits who will dance and come down close to the edge of earth if you whistle to them. We stopped the car in the midst of stubbled fields that were waiting still for the touch of sun to release their greening. The moon blazed her silver mirrored light onto the snow crystals that lay without number in every direction. She appeared to be swimming, shimmering in a sea of animated spirits that hovered above and around where we stood and whistled, deep in the night's clear, cold air.

Howard brought out his microphone and tape recorder to take the sounds of our rapturous engagement with these changing spirit beings. The lights in the sky seemed to respond to us as we responded to them. They did not so much change form as suggest form. They were animated presences of light and movement rather than shapes with edges and centers. The whistling seemed to intensify their animation. It made us think of life as a spirit of light and motion. It made us think of the old people, who lived and moved along the trails now overlain by roads and fields. It made us think of the light and movement we experience in dreams. I remembered how Old Man Aku, whom Howard knew only through his songs, talked about the Trail to Heaven:

One time I dreamed about a Trail to Heaven.
I went halfway up and someone met me.
The person gave me something white.
He was one of my relatives.
I knew him a long time ago.
I was worrying.
How could I sing as well as he did?
He sang this song to me in the dream.
The next morning I woke up.
I had this song.
I could sing it the way he did.

The Trail to Heaven begins at the place where you meet your relatives. It begins when the people you knew from long ago come down to meet you. It begins when they give you a song. It begins when your own voice and the voices of your relatives become as one.

The circle of song will be completed
when you see the tracks before you
as your own.
When you turn with the circle
you will rise on the Trail to Heaven
and leave them all behind you.
In the cold of a northern night
you will dance with *ya diskwonchi*—
all our relations.

REFERENCES RELATING TO KNOWLEDGE AND POWER IN NORTHERN NATIVE CULTURES

Black, Mary
    1977   Ojibwa Power Belief Systems. In Ray Fogelson and Richard Adams, eds., *The Anthropology of Power*, pp. 141–152. New York: Academic Press.

Brody, Hugh
    1982   *Maps and Dreams*. Vancouver: Douglas and McIntyre.

Christian, Jane, and Peter M. Gardner
    1977   *The Individual in Northern Dene Thought and Communication: A Study in Sharing and Diversity*. National Museum of Man Mercury Series, no. 35. Ottawa: National Museums of Canada.

Clifford, James, and George Marcus
    1986   *Writing Culture: The Poetics and Politics of Ethnography*. Berkeley: University of California Press.

Fladmark, Knud
    1985   Early Fur-trade Forts of the Peace River Area of British Columbia. *B.C. Studies* 65: 48–65.

Gardner, Peter
    1966   Symmetric Respect and Memorate Knowledge: The Structure and Ecology of Individualistic Culture. *Southwestern Journal of Anthropology* 22: 389–415.

Goddard, Pliny Earl
    1918   The Beaver Indians. *Anthropological Papers of the American Museum of Natural History* 10(4): 204–292.

Hallowell, A. Irving
    1955   *Culture and Experience*. Philadelphia: University of Pennsylvania Press.
    1960   Ojibwa Ontology, Behavior, and World View. In Stanley Diamond, ed., *Culture and History*. New York: Columbia University Press.

Helm, June
    1981   Subarctic. In June Helm, ed., *Handbook of North American Indians*, vol. 6, pp. 718–738. Washington, D.C.: Smithsonian Institution.

Helm, June, et al.

1975   The Contact History of the Subarctic Athapaskans: An Overview. In A. McFadyen Clark, ed., *Proceedings: Northern Athapaskan Conference, 1979, Vol. 1, Service Paper No. 27*. Ottawa: National Museums of Canada.

Krech, Shepard, III

1980   Northern Athapaskan Ethnology in the 1970s. *Annual Reviews in Anthropology* 9: 83–100. Palo Alto, Calif.: Annual Reviews.

Marano, Lou

1982   Windigo Psychosis: The Anatomy of an Emic-Etic Confusion. *Current Anthropology* 23(4): 385–412.

Marcus, George, and Michael Fischer

1986   *Anthropology as Cultural Critique: An Experimental Movement in the Social Sciences*. Chicago: University of Chicago Press.

Murdock, George Peter

1965   *Ethnographic Bibliography of North America*. New Haven, Conn.: HRAF Press.

Preston, Richard J.

1975   *Cree Narrative: Expressing the Personal Meaning of Events*. National Museum of Man Mercury Series, no. 30. Ottawa: National Museums of Canada.

Richardson, Miles

1975   Anthropologist—Myth Teller. *American Ethnologist* 2: 517–533.

Riches, David

1982   *Northern Nomadic Hunter-Gatherers: A Humanistic Approach*. London: Academic Press.

Ridington, Robin

1968   The Medicine Fight: An Instrument of Political Process among the Beaver Indians. *American Anthropologist* 70(6): 1152–1160.

1969   Kin Categories versus Kin Groups: A Two Section System without Sections. *Ethnology* 8(4): 460–467.

1971   Beaver Indian Dreaming and Singing. In Pat and Jim Lotz, eds., *Pilot not Commander: Essays in Memory of Diamond Jenness. Anthropologica* Special Issue 13(1–2): 115–128.

1976a   Wechuge and Windigo: A Comparison of Cannibal Belief among Boreal Forest Athapaskans and Algonkians. *Anthropologica* 18(2): 107–129.

1976b   Eye on the Wheel. *Io* 22: 68–81.

1978a   *Swan People: A Study of the Dunne-za Prophet Dance*. Canadian Ethnology Service Mercury Series, no. 38. Ottawa: National Museums of Canada.

1978b   Metaphor and Meaning: Healing in Dunne-za Music and Dance. *Western Canadian Journal of Anthropology* 8(2–4): 9–17.

1979a   Sequence and Hierarchy in Cultural Experience. *Anthropology and Humanism Quarterly* 4(4): 2–10.

1979b   Changes of Mind: Dunne-za Resistance to Empire. *B.C. Studies* 43: 65–80.

1980a   Monsters and the Anthropologist's Reality. In M. Halpin and M. Ames, eds., *Manlike Monsters on Trial: Early Records and Modern Evidence*, pp. 172–186. Vancouver: University of British Columbia Press.

1980b   Trails of Meaning. In Don Abbott, ed., *The World Is as Sharp as a Knife: An Anthology in Honour of Wilson Duff*, pp. 265–268. Victoria: British Columbia Provincial Museum.

1980c   A True Story. *Anthropology and Humanism Quarterly* 5(4): 11–14.

1981   Beaver Indians. In June Helm, ed., *Handbook of North American Indians*, vol. 6, pp. 350–360. Washington, D.C.: Smithsonian Institution.

1982a   When Poison Gas Come Down like a Fog: A Native Community's Response to Cultural Disaster. *Human Organization* 41(1): 36–42.

1982b   Technology, World View and Adaptive Strategy in a Northern Hunting Society. *Canadian Review of Sociology and Anthropology* 19(4): 469–481.

1982c   Telling Secrets: Stories of the Vision Quest. *Canadian Journal of Native Studies* 2: 213–219.

1983a   From Artifice to Artifact: Stages in the Industrialization of a Northern Native Community. *Journal of Canadian Studies* 18(3): 55–66.

1983b   Stories of the Vision Quest among Dunne-za Women. *Atlantis* 9(1): 68–78.

1983c   In Doig People's Ears: Portrait of a Native Community in Sound. *Anthropologica* 25(1): 9–21.

1985   The Old Wagon Road: Talking Fieldnotes from Ethnographic Fieldwork. *Canadian Journal of Native Studies* 5(2): 201–216.

1986   Keynotes of a Northern Hunting People: An Interpretive Study Guide to the Video, "In Doig People's Ears." In Philip Spaulding, ed., *Anthropology in Praxis*, pp. 44–74. Calgary: Department of Anthropology, University of Calgary.

1987a   Fox and Chicadee. In Calvin Martin, ed., *The American Indians and the Problem of History*, pp. 128–135. New York: Oxford.

1987b   From Hunt Chief to Prophet: Beaver Indian Dreamers and Christianity. *Arctic Anthropology* 24(1): 8–18.

1988   Knowledge, Power, and the Individual in Subarctic Hunting So-
        cieties. *American Anthropologist* 90: 98–110.

Ridington, Robin, and Jillian Ridington
1978   *People of the Trail: How the Northern Forest Indians Lived.* Vancou-
        ver: Douglas and McIntyre.

Ridington, Robin, and Tonia Ridington
1970   The Inner Eye of Shamanism and Totemism. *History of Religions*
        10(1): 49–61.

Ridington, Robin, and Tonia Ridington
1970   The Inner Eye of Shamanism and Totemism. *History of Religions*
        10(1): 49–61.

Rogers, Edward S.
1981   History of Ethnological Research in the Subarctic Shield and
        Mackenzie Borderlands. In June Helm, ed., *Handbook of North Ameri-
        can Indians*, vol. 6, pp. 19–29. Washington, D.C.: Smithsonian
        Institution.

Savishinsky, Joel S.
1974   *On the Trail of the Hare.* New York: Gordon and Breach.

Scollon, Ronald, and Suzanne B. K. Scollon
1979   *Linguistic Convergence: An Ethnography of Speaking at Fort Chipe-
        wyan, Alberta.* London: Academic Press.

Smith, David
1973   *Inkonze: Magico-religious Beliefs of Contact-traditional Chipewan Trad-
        ing at Fort Resolution, NWT, Canada.* National Museum of Man Mercury
        Series, no. 6. Ottawa: National Museums of Canada.

Speck, Frank
1935   *Naskapi: The Savage Hunters of the Labrador Peninsula.* Norman:
        University of Oklahoma Press.

Spier, Leslie
1935   *The Prophet Dance of the Northwest and Its Derivatives.* American
        Anthropologist General Series, no. 1.

Tanner, Adrian
1979   *Bringing Home Animals: Religious Ideology and Mode of Production of
        the Mistassini Cree Hunters.* Social and Economic Studies, no. 23. St.
        John's, Canada: Memorial University Institute of Social and Economic
        Research.

VanStone, James W.
1963   *The Snowdrift Chipewyan.* Ottawa: Northern Coordination and Re-
        search Centre, Department of Northern Affairs and National
        Resources.

Webster, Steve
1983   Ethnography as Storytelling. *Dialectical Anthropology* 8: 185–205.

Audio Documentaries

1. Soundwalk to Heaven (50 min.). Howard Broomfield and Robin Ridington. CFRO Vancouver, 1979.
2. Trails of the Dunne-za: A Suite of Four Radio Pieces (four 5-min. pieces). Howard Broomfield, Jillian Ridington, Robin Ridington. CBC Radio, Our Native Land, 1980.
3. Suffering Me Slowly (60 min.). Howard Broomfield, Jillian Ridington; Robin Ridington, consultant. CBC, The Hornby Collection, 1981.
4. Nextdoor Neighbors (30 min.). Howard Broomfield, Robin Ridington. CFRO Vancouver, 1981.
5. Old Time Religion (60 min.). Howard Broomfield, Robin Ridington. 1982. Presented as a slide-tape docudrama at the 1982 Canadian Ethnology Society meetings.
6. In Doig People's Ears (42 min.). Howard Broomfield, Robin Ridington, consultant. 1983. Composed for a conference on The Sociology of Music: An Exploration of Issues. Trent University, August 1983.

Video Documentary

1. In Doig People's Ears: Portrait of a Changing Native Community (30 min.). Howard Broomfield, Myrna Cobb, Robin Ridington. 1984.

Catalogs of Original Audio Tapes and Photographs in the Dunne-za Archive

1. Directory of Audio Tapes in the Dunne-za Archive (32 pp.). Compiled by Myrna Cobb and Robin Ridington. 1984.
2. Catalog of Beaver Indian Slides (30 pp.). Compiled by Myrna Cobb and Robin Ridington. 1984.
3. Catalog of Beaver Indian Negatives. Compiled by Myrna Cobb and Robin Ridington. 1984.

INDEX OF
DUNNE-ZA NAMES